A
HISTORY
OF THE
WORLD
IN TEN
DINNERS

A HISTORY
OF THE
WORLD
IN TEN
DINNERS

2,000 YEARS ■ 100 RECIPES

VICTORIA
FLEXNER

JAY
REIFEL

FOREWORD BY JESSICA B. HARRIS

RIZZOLI
NEW YORK

New York · Paris · London · Milan

CONT

ENTS

Foreword

A HISTORY OF THE WORLD IN TEN DINNERS by Victoria Flexner and Jay Reifel is an innovative work of food history. The culinary tour de force that you have in your hands will take you on a time machine journey that H. G. Wells could only have dreamed of—one that covers time and space at the dinner table, beginning with a splendid feast from Ancient Rome, complete with a recipe for garum, the *nuoc cham* of the time, passing through the feasts of Tudor England, Renaissance Italy, and Louis XIV's Versailles.

Lest you think that the world referred to in the title is centered in Europe, you will also sit down to meals with Harun al-Rashid, the caliph of Baghdad, of *One Thousand and One Nights* fame, and sup with Empress Taytu of Ethiopia. A chapter entitled "The Great Circulation" reinvents Crosby's Columbian Exchange as a world in movement and motion and deftly switches its Eurocentric mindset to one that is more universal in approach. And the aforementioned dinner with Empress Taytu of Ethiopia leads into a discussion of the food of the African continent.

The book's beautiful photographs by Lucy Schaeffer are visual evocations of the time periods and the cultures discussed. The Roman chapter opener recalls the Roman soiled floor mosaics of Tunisia's Bardo Museum, while the Tudor opener plays with the aristocratic predilection for creating strange cobbled together culinary beasts. The Moorish-Spanish empire of al-Andalus as well as the glories of the Silk Road are all present. From chapter openers to recipe illustrations, they add another dimension to the work and bear visual witness to the diversity of culinary riches discussed.

The recipes, with informative and helpful headnotes, offer something for every level of cook, from the casual to the seriously committed. (I can never imagine myself trying to attempt a cockenthrice—a Tudor ancestor of the Southern Louisiana turducken—but know that somewhere out there is an intrepid cook who will be gathering up the suckling pig, turkey, and other parts and setting to work.) From the simple to the head-spinningly complex, all of the recipes beckon the reader to examine and explore, try and taste.

Finally, the sidebars dazzle and present a compendium of deeply researched culinary information of the sort that we have come to expect from Victoria Flexner and Jay Reifel, the duo known as Edible History.

A History of the World in Ten Dinners more than ably fulfills Edible History's goal of "bringing people into the conversation of history through a universally accessible medium: food." The work is sure to incite many a dinner table discussion and to fill and satisfy hearts, minds, and stomachs.

—JESSICA B. HARRIS

Introduction

AT EACH EDIBLE HISTORY DINNER there is an exciting moment when the first dish emerges from the kitchen and is placed before guests. As they look down at their plates, examining the contents, cross-consulting with the menu, and exchanging curious glances with fellow diners, I begin to tell our evening's crowd about the dish placed before them, its history, and how it relates to the time period of the night. The show begins.

Each course functions as a window into the wider historical narrative. Black chicken and peaches from Emperor Domitian's rule are a taste of the madness that plagued the emperor who once served guests a meal dyed entirely black; perhaps the fall of Rome could have been prophesied from the dinner table. Spiced raw beef with a buttery dipping sauce from the Ethiopian Empire gives us a taste of Empress Taytu's fondness for high-quality and expensive ingredients. Cockenthrice, made in King Henry VIII's time by sewing the front end of a pig to the back end of a capon, demonstrates the elaborate theater and trompe l'oeil style of Tudor banquet food.

The food served and the stories told at an Edible History dinner allow guests to inhabit for a moment a shared metaphysical space with someone who died hundreds of years ago—to experience the same flavors and smells that Domitian, Taytu, and Henry did. This is food history. A unique kind of history, that provides deep insight into the actuality of past existence, and in turn breaks down preconceived notions and debunks popular myths.

For example, you might imagine that the Medici ate pasta with tomato sauce, or that the peasants working the lands of the Holy Roman Empire subsisted on a meager diet of potatoes. But they didn't—because potatoes *and* tomatoes come from the Americas and were not introduced to Europe until after 1492. Similarly, Indian curry, Sichuanese soups, and Isaan larb did not contain a single chili pepper until the Portuguese introduced the plant to the Asian continent in the sixteenth century. The study of food can dramatically alter the way we perceive our own culinary heritages.

The study of food also shows us that we have been living in a globalized world for a very long time. International commerce and trade are not by-products of our modern global world. Spices, textiles, precious stones, animals, and even people have been making their way along the Silk Road for millennia. By the thirteenth century, knights in England were sprinkling Indian pepper on their roast meat and spicing their wine with cloves from Indonesia.

And so food history reveals to us truths that exist outside traditional historiography. Your morning pastry and hot beverage of choice tell impossibly grand stories. Food speaks of whole lives lived, entire civilizations and cultures. To eat what was eaten before is, perhaps, the closest we can come to recovering the stories of those who have been largely forgotten by traditional history.

It is no secret that the history we learn today has, for the most part, been written from a Western point of view and largely by white men. The European colonization and subjugation of most of the known world starting in the fifteenth century produced a "world history" that begins with the Age of Exploration and moves through time linearly from the perspective of the conquerors. The result is a history that is not truly reflective of the actual experiences of most people who lived on this planet for the last five hundred years.

We have missed out on so many perspectives. How do we recover these lives, these voices? How do we learn about people who left nothing behind? We write history based on what remains; but what about what does not remain? What about the smell of the early morning air as Ibn Batuta set sail from Africa for the East, the conversations had at the marketplace in medieval Cusco, a meal consumed by the women who fought in the French Revolution?

Scent and taste are incredibly powerful instruments of memory. We remember vividly those dishes made for us by loved ones: what the kitchen smelled like as it was prepared, where we sat at the table, how we felt when we consumed it. We cannot know exactly how a young immigrant coming to New York in the nineteenth century felt or what she thought as she disembarked from a ship and took in this new metropolis. But we can eat what she ate.

This book provides readers and home cooks the ability to recreate the past in their own homes, to experience history in a way they never have before—through smell, touch, and taste. The following pages are divided into ten chapters, spanning a couple thousand years, multiple continents, and a multitude of cultures, peoples, and places.

We begin in ancient Rome, not because we believe this is any kind of "start" to the historical narrative writ large (or because we believe the Gregorian calendar is the only accurate measurement of time), but because we made a commitment to present meals with historical accuracy: for us to write about it, there has to be significant primary source material on the food, the cuisine, and the culinary culture of that time and place.

The earliest fully fleshed-out historical cookbook is *Apicius*, written by a Roman in the first century CE. Cuneiform tablets with recipes for bread and beer exist from as far back as ancient Sumeria, but they do not provide enough information or material for us to paint a full picture. Keeping these self-imposed restrictions in mind (you will find that we are somewhat gluttons for punishment) the ten chapters that follow do not claim to be a complete or total "history of the world" but rather one form of it. The chapters flow thematically from one to the next. You will explore the trade routes of medieval Asia in the Silk Road chapter, learning about the valuable spices that passed from east to west. The subsequent chapter about Renaissance Italy will follow these spices to Europe. The developing European obsession with spices from the East in the Middle Ages will lead to voyages to find the origin of these spices, culminating in Christopher Columbus setting sail for India in 1492, an action that will bring the Americas into contact with Europe, Asia, and Africa and change the course of history.

It is our hope that with these stories and these recipes, we can invite readers into the conversation of history, as they set out in their own kitchens to embark on a new kind of culinary journey.

—Victoria Flexner

Chef's Preface

YOU ARRIVE AT AN EDIBLE HISTORY DINNER. I am in the kitchen as Victoria unfolds the history to the guests and the dishes are sent out. I will soon emerge and introduce a Roman stew or a Jewish casserole from Islamic Spain. But I may be truly closest to my diners not when cooking for them or serving them, but when I sit down, alone, and first read a recipe. At that moment, all I have are questions: What was it meant to be? What did the Tudor or Baghdadi or Mongol that it was meant for expect and enjoy? Above all: How can I make this recipe into a culinary time machine, a vivid window into the past?

After that, it gets tricky.

Recipes in this book basically have three sources—actual cookbooks from the period, traditional recipes, often orally transmitted and later recorded, and scholarly research into food history. All of these overlap to some degree. "Cookbooks," however, is a very broad term, ranging from crude lists of ingredients with instructions to "cook it well and serve it forth," to remarkable works of precision and literature (I'm looking at you, medieval Baghdad) that contain weights, measures, directions, and poetry. Other recipes occasionally have odd specifics such as, "put back in the oven for four Our Fathers," or for, "the time it takes a man to walk around a field." But in this process of research and testing, I have always tried to seek out recipes that appeal to a modern (if adventurous) palate in their original form. What am I looking for in these recipes? The easy answer is a place, a time, and a story. Within that, however, is something I would call just a little bit impossible: a sense-memory of a place we have never actually been.

This book will present even the experienced cook with a shocking variety of unfamiliar ingredients. Often they are simply herbs that were particular to a region and a time and that have fallen out of favor over the centuries. There is also significant debate among food historians about what the modern variants are of spices and other foods whose names are no longer commonly known. There are some technical challenges here as well—techniques that have fallen out of fashion, like larding a hare with strips of fat, or that are unfamiliar, like the clever butchery that transforms a leg of lamb into something like a hanging meat chandelier. And there is pastry—yeast risen, poured, creped, layered, and even translucently stretched into a predecessor of puff pastry. It cannot be overstated: take your time and enjoy the process. Half the time you will be doing something that hasn't been attempted for centuries.

Many recipes reflect a particular truth about the nature of investigating the past through its food: we are limited to what we know from original sources that have come down through the ages. Just a glance at some of the titles, such as Soup for the Khan or Annals of the Caliph's Kitchen, reveals an obvious truth: these were recipes for people for whom money, and often the huge amount of labor involved in making these dishes, was not an issue. In fact, the extreme expense of spices, rare beasts, and even occasional gilding in silver or gold offered an opportunity to show off wealth and power. The common foods of past eras are not represented in these sources and were often monotonous.

Throughout much of history, the world was divided between rich and poor, with occasional vibrant and cosmopolitan explosions of a middle class. But for much of the world's population, through much of history, food staples consisted of gruels and pottages of grains and starches, with no salt and no spice and little meat protein. These dishes may be easily reproducible, but they rarely have the transportative quality of a window into history that a more complex dish possesses. It is my hope that if you come across spices and herbs you have never heard of or used, or if you shy away from caul fat and frogs' legs or ruinously expensive quantities of truffles (optional, of course), you will consider these as an opportunity as much as a challenge, and try to remember that the pepper and sugar that you take for granted were once equally extravagant and precious.

There is, in reality, no way to be fully true to moments that are separated from us by centuries or even millennia. I have certainly restructured the recipes in this book to use modern techniques and modern equipment —blenders, food processors, and mixers all have their place. The accurate period piece of "equipment" often was a slave, child, or servant. In one moment, the acme of kitchen gadgetry was a trained dog on a treadmill that turned a spit, replacing the young boy who previously performed this sweltering and miserable task. Should that young boy have someday worked himself up to head of the kitchen of his noble employer, I hope he would have approved of my versions of the dishes prepared here. Perfect accuracy is impossible—and not necessarily desirable—but I have always tried to be true to the spirit of the times and the deliciousness of the cuisines.

Seriously, go ahead—make yourself a cockenthrice.

—JAY REIFEL

A
HISTORY
OF THE
WORLD
IN TEN
DINNERS

ANCIENT ROME

1st century

R ome is a city. The Roman Empire was an entire world. But Rome is also a mythology. For thousands of years, different societies, cultures, and empires have attached themselves to the legacy of Rome, utilizing its past glory as a foundational myth for whatever their own contemporary power game might be.

THE ROMAN EMPIRE
IN THE
FIRST CENTURY C.E.

0   MILES   400
0 KILOMETERS 400

Somehow, we have become the inheritors of Rome. And the Romans have become our ancestors. But the family tree does not descend directly from them to us. The ancestral tree moves sideways, across oceans; it zigzags across continents, ingesting new identities along the way, reappearing in the origin myths of some new distant shore.

Benito Mussolini used the Latin language, excavated ancient Roman ruins, and styled himself as a twentieth-century Caesar incarnate. Before him, Napoleon Bonaparte modeled himself as a Caesar, declaring, "I am a true Roman Emperor; I am of the best race of the Caesars—those who are founders." The American Founding Fathers, in their writing of the Declaration of Independence, drew heavily from the work of Cicero and Cato. The power of Rome is confirmed even in those who loathe it. The Libyan dictator Muammar Gaddafi was apparently so threatened by the ancient statue of the Roman emperor Septimius Severus in Tripoli's Martyrs' Square that he had it toppled.

Rome has given us many things. Corinthian columns. Plumbing. Pandemics (more on that later). But perhaps most poignantly, it showed us what a massive empire looks like—with global interconnected trade, imperial conquests, slavery, wars, a large standing army, and a melting-pot urban metropolis with both fabulous wealth and desperate poverty.

In 509 BCE a "democracy" was established in Rome, called the Republic. The Roman Republic was ruled by a senate, filled with senators elected by the citizens of Rome. But before you wax poetic about how progressive this ancient society was, it's important to note that only men qualified for citizenship. At the top of the senate sat the consuls, two men who held a whole lot of power (though, significantly, had the ability to veto each other). But then around 27 BCE, things took a more authoritarian turn. Civil war, constitutional reforms, political assassinations, and the rise of the dictator-like Caesar created the new position of emperor and morphed the Roman Republic into the Roman Empire. We will focus on this period, the couple of centuries following the collapse of the Republic and the rise of the empire, when Rome reached the height of its power.

While political chaos ensued in the capitol, a less well-known event occurred during the first century CE: the writing of a cookbook.

The world's oldest surviving cookbook, known as *Apicius*, is a first-century collection of recipes believed to have been written by Marcus Gavius Apicius. He was known as the ultimate gourmand, famous for enjoying delicacies such as camel feet, flamingo brains, and heads of parrots. This cookbook's origins are not fully known, and there is a chance *Apicius* is a collection of Roman recipes compiled at a later date, named for him because of his notoriety as an epicurean. Regardless, this text, along with anecdotes from plays and books of the period, gives us insight into the diet of the ancient Roman. This chapter's recipes are all sourced from *Apicius*.

But before tucking into the feet of some exotic animals or cracking open a skull to savor the delicate mouthfeel of brains, *Apicius* recommended starting one's meal with an aperitif: Fine Spiced Wine, Pearled.

Fine Spiced Wine, Pearled

CONDITUM PARADOXUM

MAKES ABOUT 4 CUPS *The Apicius cookbook appropriately starts with this recipe for spiced wine, which would typically have begun a meal by arousing the senses and hinting at the dishes to come. Sweetened and spiced wine is a drink that will recur through many of the ages and cultures presented in this book, even though, throughout virtually all of history, it was available only to the richest and most powerful. Enjoy.*

1 (750-ml) bottle (about 3¼ cups) red wine (something light in body such as a Montepulciano)

⅔ cup honey

2 teaspoons whole black peppercorns

½ teaspoon whole allspice berries

6 dried bay leaves

1 teaspoon juniper berries

Large pinch of saffron

6 dates

½ cup Pearl Vinegar (recipe follows)

IN a small saucepan, combine ¼ cup of the wine with the honey, peppercorns, allspice berries, bay leaves, juniper berries, saffron, and dates. Bring just to a boil over medium-low heat, and then cover tightly with plastic wrap and allow to cool completely to room temperature, at least 1 hour. Mix with the remainder of the wine in a glass bottle or plastic container with a tight-fitting lid, cover, and refrigerate for 8 hours. Strain through a fine-mesh sieve into a bowl. Add the pearl vinegar, stir, and return to the original bottle or container. Because of the honey and spices, this will keep for a few weeks.

Pearl Vinegar

MAKES ½ CUP *Cleopatra, the Egyptian queen, had two famous Roman lovers, Julius Caesar and Marc Antony. In Pliny the Elder's history, he tells of a wager between Cleopatra and Marc Antony over who could throw a more expensive feast. After Marc Antony's lavish feast, she staged an equally over-the-top one, and then capped it off by drinking a crushed pearl dissolved in vinegar. If you are feeling particularly extravagant, you can do the same.*

1 pearl

½ cup red wine vinegar

PLACE the pearl in a small bowl and add the vinegar. Let the pearl dissolve at room temperature, which should take about 48 hours.

Croquettes of Lobster or Scallops with Cumin Sauce

ISICIA DE SCILIS VEL

MAKES 8 TO 12 CROQUETTES, SERVING 4 TO 6 *The goal of a lobster dish, especially a croquette, is to bring out the sweetness of the flesh and underline it with other flavors. These croquettes do that perfectly, with a certain rich pungency from the herbs and asafoetida. I have prepared this recipe using lobster, scallops, squid, and oysters, among other seafood, and they're all delicious. I would suggest making both the lobster and the scallop versions at the same time, in which case the other ingredients should be doubled and divided. Lovage has a flavor that is a cross between celery and parsley, with a suggestion of anise, and is a lovely addition to your spice cabinet.*

1 pound uncooked lobster meat (from about 3 lobsters), or 1 pound bay scallops, roughly chopped

2 teaspoons dried lovage

½ teaspoon freshly ground black pepper

¼ teaspoon ground cumin

¼ teaspoon asafoetida

¼ teaspoon kosher salt, plus more for finishing

About 2 cups oil for frying

2 cups Cumin Sauce for Shellfish (recipe follows)

FOR lobster croquettes: Roughly chop and set aside all the claw meat. Roughly chop the lobster tail meat and put it in the bowl of a food processor fitted with the metal blade. Add the lovage, pepper, cumin, asafoetida, and salt. Process until an almost completely smooth paste forms, 1 to 2 minutes, scraping down the sides a couple of times. Transfer to a bowl, and fold in the claw meat.

FOR scallop croquettes: Place the chopped scallops in the bowl of a food processor fitted with the metal blade. Add the lovage, pepper, cumin, asafoetida, and salt and process until an almost completely smooth paste forms, 1 to 2 minutes, scraping down the sides a couple of times.

FORM the lobster or scallop mixture into 1- to 2-ounce balls with a scoop, dipping the scoop in water between croquettes to prevent sticking. Set aside on a plate lined with parchment paper.

TO fry the croquettes, heat oil in a deep pot to 325°F. Very carefully add the croquettes and fry until just golden, 3 to 4 minutes. (If you prefer to poach them, bring a large pot of salted water to a simmer and cook the croquettes until firm and opaque, 4 to 6 minutes.) Remove with a slotted spoon or skimmer.

SPRINKLE the croquettes with a bit more salt and serve immediately with cumin sauce.

Cumin Sauce for Shellfish

CUMINATUM IN OSTREA ET CONCHYLIA

MAKES ABOUT 2 CUPS *This remarkable sauce combines brightness with deep earthy flavors and is a lovely complement to fresh, briny oysters or croquettes.*

3 tablespoons cumin seeds

¾ cup plus 1 tablespoon red wine vinegar

1 tablespoon plus 1 teaspoon freshly ground black pepper

3 tablespoons dried lovage

¼ cup dried parsley

2 tablespoons dried mint

3 tablespoons plus 1 teaspoon honey

½ teaspoon kosher salt

1 teaspoon garum or fish sauce

HEAT a small, dry skillet on high heat, add the seeds, and gently swirl them in the pan until fragrant, 1 to 2 minutes. Transfer to a spice grinder and process to a fine powder.

ADD all of the ingredients to a blender with ¼ cup plus 2 tablespoons cold water and slowly increase the speed from low to high;

blend until smooth. Transfer the pitcher to the refrigerator and chill for at least 30 minutes and ideally 8 hours. Blend again, increasing the speed from low to high; blend on high for 2 minutes. This type of sauce will always retain a bit of the texture of the vast amount of spices.

FISHPONDS

ELITE ROMANS, no matter how far they were from the sea, ate a lot of seafood. And in an age where transport was slow and there was no refrigeration, they managed to provide themselves with a steady supply of fish through the construction of large saltwater ponds (usually at their country estates). Some of these were truly spectacular, and their owners' obsession

with them was legendary. A powerful politician of the late Roman Republic, Lucullus, had the most infamous fishponds of the age. To keep them supplied with saltwater he had tunnels driven through mountains and out to the sea, and hydraulic structures were even installed to regulate the cooling effect of the tides.

For Cicero, this fish craze was evidence of the decline of the Republic itself. He mourned the integrity of the Republic because his colleagues tended to precious ponds with the devoted attention that he believed should instead be paid to the deteriorating political situation.

Lucanian Sausage

LUCANICÆ

MAKES ABOUT 2 POUNDS SAUSAGE *Lucania was an area in what is today southern Italy, near the ankle of the boot. If you are going to use the sausage to make Trimalchio's Pig (page 24), you can leave the sausage long and intestinal. On its own, this amount will serve 4 to 6 people as a main course. If you are curious to try the flavor but don't want to stuff casings, you can also make this mixture, form it into patties, sear them over medium-high heat for 3 to 4 minutes per side, then finish them in a 350°F oven for 10 minutes. This sausage is also delicious smoked.*

2 sausage casings

2 pounds boneless, skinless pork shoulder or ground pork

1 tablespoon cumin seeds, toasted and freshly ground

2 teaspoons juniper berries, roughly ground

1 teaspoon freshly ground black pepper

2 teaspoons rue (see Note)

1 tablespoon plus 1 teaspoon dried savory

2 teaspoons dried parsley

2 tablespoons garum or fish sauce

2 tablespoons low-sodium chicken stock

2 teaspoons kosher salt

1 tablespoon whole black peppercorns

½ cup pine nuts

RINSE the sausage casings in warm water and soak them in cold water for 30 minutes. Next, check to make sure they don't have any rips or tears. If you want to be old-school about it, you can blow them up like balloons to make sure.

CUT the pork into ½-inch cubes. Grind the cubes of meat in a sausage grinder with the coarse grinding plate, a stand mixer fitted with a sausage attachment, or a food processor fitted with the metal blade. Skip this step if using ground pork.

COMBINE the remaining ingredients (except the casings) with the pork. If you used a sausage grinder, stand mixer, or food processor, simply add the ingredients and process to combine. If you started with ground pork, mix everything by hand. Stuff the casings

with the mixture (see Tip). Refrigerate overnight to allow the flavors to develop.

WHEN you are ready to cook the sausages, preheat the oven to 350°F. Prick the sausages with a sharp knife tip or toothpick to keep them from bursting as they cook. Roast until the interior reaches at least 160°F on an instant-read thermometer, 12 to 15 minutes. (Alternatively, boil the sausages in salted water until firm and cooked through, 12 to 15 minutes.)

NOTE: Rue is a bitter herb that was very popular in Roman cuisine. And when I say bitter, I mean that it can range from mildly to reasonably to face-meltingly bitter. Always taste the rue first! If it is overpowering, reduce the quantity called for in the recipe.

TIP: TO STUFF THE SAUSAGES, rinse and soak your casings to loosen them and allow them to expand more easily. Tie off one end of the casing. If you have a sausage stuffer, use it, of course. If you don't, I have found with a bit of practice a piping bag works well. In either case, you want to preload the casing onto the stuffer or piping bag so that you are first filling the farther, already tied end, which will push away through your hand as you go. Once filled, tie off the casing at appropriate intervals with butcher's twine.

A NOTE ON A LOST HERB

LASER, also known as *silphium*. Also known as one of the greatest culinary mysteries of the ancient world. A number of the original recipes in this chapter call for the herb, and it encapsulates the wonderful but diabolical challenges of historical cooking—what to do when an important ingredient no longer exists. There are scholars who have dedicated significant energies to divining just what it was and, like economists looking at supply and demand curves, fail entirely to agree with one another. The dried sap was used as a spice in ancient Rome and was reputed to be worth its weight in gold. It was even believed to have magical healing properties. It was so important to the economy of Cyrene, in modern Libya, that it appeared on its coins. Then, rapidly, possibly due to drought and overharvesting, it disappeared. Scholars believe that it was related to the plant producing asafoetida, a spice now common in Indian cooking, and, as the laser plant grew scarcer and more expensive, Roman chefs believed asafoetida to be a reasonable substitute. We accept their wisdom.

ROME, THE CITY

AT DAWN, ROME CAME TO LIFE. Sounds of children rushing to school echoed through the streets as shopkeepers opened their *tabernae* (shops), heavy wooden shutters creaking open to the morning light, large amphorae jugs neatly arranged, sandaled feet flicking clouds of dust behind them as they made their way to the forum.

The early rising city was home to about one million people in the first century, as well as an additional seventy-five million living within its empire's borders. It was not, as we may imagine, a city filled with old white men dressed in togas lounging around eating grapes, pointing their fingers toward the sky as they reached the conclusion of some grandiose philosophical argument. Infant mortality was high and life expectancy was low. Rome was a young city.

While the fourteen neighborhoods of Rome were not segregated, some were more desirable than others. The Palatine Hill can be thought of as ancient Rome's Beverly Hills. But there were no sprawling slums; rather, the poor were present in nearly every neighborhood. One might walk along a street with perilously perched and overcrowded *insulae* (apartment buildings) only to turn a corner and find a row of magnificent villas.

The center of the city was the forum, a central public square around which were situated the basilica (the city's civic and administrative building), a temple (or two), libraries, baths, and the marketplace. The marketplace of imperial Rome constructed under the rule of Emperor Trajan in 112 CE was unlike any other that came before it. Though every city or municipality throughout the empire had a forum, they existed in varying degrees of scale and luxury depending on whether it was a large city or a peripheral backwater.

The remains of Trajan's marketplace reveal what an impressive commercial center it must have been. A colossal semicircular brick building snaked around the outskirts of the forum proper, a multilevel masterpiece rivaling the Mall of America or the Dubai Mall, with its grand central hall, its vaulted ceilings, the numerous floors of covered walkways looking out onto the forum, shops neatly nestled underneath each arch.

A Roman working on the construction of the new Basilica Julia nearby would approach this magnificent marketplace on his lunch break in search of something to eat. At eye level he was met with the flower and fruit stalls that occupied the shallow ground-floor rooms set underneath symmetrical archways. Floral scents filled the air as he strolled past the colorful bouquets of marigolds, hyacinths, and violets, followed by the aromatic rosemary and thyme, laid out in heaping piles for customers to sift through in the next stalls.

As he climbed the staircase to his left, he entered the shade of a colonnaded walkway, the sunny forum visible through the open arches to his right, another long row of shops running along his left. Here in deep, dark rooms, large amphorae containing wine and oil huddled close to each other in the cool, dim light. Up another set of stairs he arrived at Via Biberatica, a small winding street atop the first floors of the marketplace, home to the city's spice merchants and their precious wares from the East and beyond. Prized jars of pepper from India, ginger from China, asafoetida, cumin, caraway, and saffron lined the shop walls. He meandered down the fragrant street, the enormity of the vast forum complex unfurling itself on his left. He stopped to look out and took in the temple, the library, the buildings where senators and emperors debated and determined the fates of citizens.

Off the Via Biberatica, he climbed one final set of stairs that led up to the ground floor of the Great Hall. Soaring ceilings, more colonnaded walkways, bustling corridors filled with all the humanity that occupies any marketplace today. People exchanged gossip with their neighbors. Merchants and customers haggled. Coquettish glances were exchanged between secret lovers. Children chased each other along hallways and up stairs, shrieking in delight. Our builder stopped at his favorite small eatery, next to the *stationes arcariorum Caesarianorum* (the offices of Public Assistance), ready for a bowl of lentil stew.

DESCRIPTIONS OF ROME'S APARTMENT BUILDINGS will seem familiar to any city dweller. *Insulae* ran as high as six stories (all walk-ups, of course). Residents were crammed into small rooms with thin walls, and conditions got worse the higher up you went in the building. Sometimes the ground floor would be occupied by a middle-class family, sometimes a few *tabernae*. But lack of plumbing and running water, and the frequency with which the *insulae* either burned down or simply collapsed made them less desirable housing stock. The complaints from residents echo our own: noise from the streets made it impossible to sleep, dodgy landlords were always cheating tenants, and soaring rents kept most people barely bobbing above the surface, living paycheck to paycheck. In Juvenal's Third Satire, written around 110 CE, he wrote, "There's no joy in Rome for honest ability, and no reward any more for hard work. My means today are less than yesterday, and tomorrow will wear away a bit more." While a formerly enslaved person's tomb read, "I'm no longer worried that I shall die of hunger / I'm rid of aching legs and getting a deposit for my rent / I'm enjoying free board and lodging for eternity."

The baths were one luxury every person in Rome could enjoy. Some cost money; others were free. Because Romans started their day so early, by mid-afternoon the workday was generally over and people would retreat to the baths. The bathhouses were like neighborhood recreation centers. They were lined with porticoes with shops interspersed. There were gyms and even libraries at the bathhouses. Romans would go to get clean, catch up with friends and the neighborhood gossip, maybe read in the library or pick up something to-go for dinner.

Breakfast at dawn was not much more than a glass of water, and lunch for Romans was also a rather small meal. If you left the home for work or school, you certainly didn't come home for lunch. Luckily for Romans, their city was filled with bars, inns, and food stalls. These ranged in style and form for every budget, from street-side countertops with a few stools to more luxurious spots with private dining rooms.

The most typical type of eatery, a *thermopolium*, was open to the street, contained an L-shaped stone bar, and had a few pots built into the countertop. In each pot was a dish, such as a porridge or risotto or some kind of stew made from beans, peas, or lentils. This was everyday man's food. Other dishes included roasted meats, sausages, fishballs, meatballs, omelets, and light snacks, such as cheese or marinated vegetables. Diners might eat right at the counter, or at one of the low tables on a small stool. These eateries share a good deal in common with outdoor marketplaces all over the world today, where the proprietor only serves one or two dishes but is a master of its preparation. The menu might not change, but the quality is always excellent.

The biggest meal of the day is what we would now call dinner or *cenae*, though it was eaten earlier than ours—in the late afternoon or early evening depending on the time of the year and when the sun set. A wealthy Roman with a large retinue of enslaved people could expect to come home to a prepared dinner ready and waiting. Those lower on the social scale, who resided in *insulae*, usually did not have cooking apparatuses in their homes and therefore would rely on the city's food stalls for their evening meal.

On his way home, our Roman worker, weary from his long hours of backbreaking work, would pick up bread and a few sausages to share with his family for dinner. As he wandered home through the streets of his city, the sun began to creep behind its apartment blocks. The greasy, irresistible umami of the pork sausages and his grumbling stomach quickened his pace past shops closing up, the last crumbs of the day's diners swept out onto the street, a chamber pot emptied, just missing him and his precious cargo, as he arrived at his front door, slowly climbing four flights of stairs, legs aching, mouth salivating, opening the door to his wife and children, who arranged themselves on low stools, biting into casings that snapped open in their mouths, relishing the juicy bites of warm meat, as the sun set on Rome.

WHILE THE ROMAN REPUBLIC WAS A DEMOCRACY and the Roman Empire was a dictatorship, perhaps the real power behind the scenes of both eras resided with the aristocracy. They held senatorial seats, birthed lineages of consuls and emperors, and maintained the hierarchical structure of Roman society through their very existence.

And it wasn't just those from Rome proper who made up this ancient aristocracy. Elites from all over the empire were part of it. Tax collection, Rome's vital source of revenue, was a responsibility bestowed upon the elites of every civic center from Spain to Syria. This geographic diaspora of elites formed the backbone of power that kept the whole machine running.

In the city of Rome, the social structure was built around patron-client relationships. Every Roman male of lower, middle, and even upper classes had a patron, upon whom they would call daily. Every morning the free men of Rome would visit their patron (or even multiple patrons) and receive everything from food and money to favors great and small depending on the client's ambitions and status. This paternalistic relationship is how many free Romans made their living. For the very poor, there might not have been patrons, but there was government assistance. About one third to one half of imperial Rome was fed on the government dole. Everyone else had a patron; even the patrons with clients had someone farther up the social ladder upon whom they called upon. Perhaps the only man without a patron was the emperor of Rome himself.

Slavery existed on an unparalleled scale in ancient Rome. It wasn't just the rich who held people in slavery (often up to a thousand); the middle classes and even humbler families might inherit slaves or go to one of the markets that sold humans as property. Prisoners of Rome's many wars and campaigns across Europe, the Middle East, and North Africa supplied a steady stream of humans to be exploited. These people performed miserable, backbreaking work in fields and mines and worked in households cleaning and cooking, but they were also teachers, physicians, accountants, bakers, potters, and gladiators.

The Roman economy was built on slavery. The sheer number of jobs occupied by enslaved people made the patron-client relationship crucial to the support of free men, because most of the jobs that could have been performed in exchange for a salary were instead done by slaves.

Women who were born free possessed very few, if any, legal rights. At birth a girl belonged to her father and upon marriage she belonged to her husband. Women could not vote or hold legal office. Wealthy women were not really a part of public life—their job was to procreate and stay quiet in their lives of domestic servitude. Women of the working class were a part of public life because they had to work. They made crafts, farmed, and worked at markets and in brothels.

As a result, women occupy very little of recorded Roman history. Their lives and experiences, their thoughts and beliefs, are largely unknown to us. What we do know of them is entirely in relation to the men in their lives: who their father was, who they married, who they gave birth to. And if they're not in the history books because of one of those relationships, likely we only know about them because their behavior challenged the cultural norms and was therefore worthy of salacious and defamatory condemnations by the great men with pens.

The very existence of "Women's History" shows us that females are not a part of the historical narrative writ large, but rather a separate contingent, a section to be added into the story after the important bits have been explained.

One woman who is integral to Roman history is Agrippina the Younger, who wielded extraordinary power by the standards of any day. She was born to Emperor Germanicus, was the sister of Emperor Caligula, married Emperor Claudius, and gave birth to the emperor Nero. She was privy to the wheeling and dealing of power at the highest levels—and likely played an active role in it. However, little attention is given in history books to her own insights, despite the fact she was highly educated and even wrote a memoir. Instead she has largely been portrayed as a "power-hungry" woman, who murdered her husband and birthed a psychopath. Yet the opinions and thoughts of countless men with far less experience in the halls of power (and far less education) have come down to us through the centuries, and live with us still in ink and stone and collective memory.

If the thoughts, emotions, and beliefs of women remain largely unknown to us—at least we can attempt to access their interior worlds through the foods that they ate. For a moment we can taste the brininess of the scallop, the delicate crunch of the croquette shell, and the herbaceous acidity of an accompanying cumin sauce that a woman like Agrippina would have enjoyed.

ALL ROADS LEAD TO ROME, or so the saying goes. From Hadrian's Wall in northern England to Jerusalem, the empire of Rome covered almost two million square miles by the year 117 CE. While impressive in its size, Rome is not the largest empire to ever exist; in fact, far from it. The Abbasid caliphate, Mongol Empire, and Inca Empire all dwarfed Rome. What was perhaps most impressive about the size of this empire was how well connected it was.

Roads spanning thousands of miles kept cities, towns, and far-flung municipalities tied to one another. And while each city had its unique culture, especially given the geographic range, there was a uniformity to them. The distinctive architectural style, the amenities and public buildings that existed in every municipality, including baths, temples, amphitheaters, and forums, meant that each major city, from Alexandria to Thessaloniki to Lyon to Antioch, were clearly all part of the Roman world.

Along these roads, commodities of all kinds were traded; spices, silks, animals, people. It is how Scottish and Ethiopian warriors came to fight each other in the gladiator pits. How pepper from India found its way into European markets. How silk from China came to be worn by the Roman aristocracy. These roads, which we now attribute to progress and communication and generally all things good, were also a new way for germs to spread far and wide. Malaria, typhoid, smallpox, leprosy, tuberculosis, and the plague were all able to move more rapidly through human populations thanks to the Roman world's interconnectedness, creating devastating side effects, like the world's first recorded pandemic: the Antonine Plague that began in Rome in 166 CE.

The arteries that linked every corner of the empire together created an incredibly diverse population. The notion that Rome is the arbiter of white Western culture is about as true as the notion that the white marble statues of the classical world were white. Hint: Those statues were originally painted. They were colorful. They were not snowy alabaster bodies. Nor were the Romans.

Just look at a map of the Roman Empire and the racial diversity that would have existed becomes clear. The emperors of Rome are depicted in Hollywood films and television shows as white. But the emperor Septemius Severus was Libyan. He married the noble Syrian woman Julia Domna, and their mixed-race son, Carcalla, succeeded his father as emperor. Carcalla's successor, Macrinus, was from Algeria. Some of the rulers of Rome were white, but they were also Black and Brown, as were the aristocratic and noble families from which they came.

AS THE EMPIRE GREW, the madness of the emperors was turned up to full volume. In 192 CE, the emperor Commodus began to get involved in the action during gladiator fights. At one such game he killed an ostrich and then cut off its head. Holding the decapitated ostrich head in one hand, Commodus marched up to where a group of senators were sitting in the stands. He began waving the ostrich head at them, smiling maniacally, indicating with the sword in his other hand, that if they did not play their cards right, this too would be their fate.

Shocking scenes were not new to the gladiatorial pits—but imagine *your* boss waving a decapitated ostrich head at you. One of the senators present at this feathery slaughter recalled later that he began eating laurel leaves from the garland he was wearing to stifle his nervous laughter. The other senators followed suit, shoving fistfuls of those symbolically Roman leaves into their mouths, praying the unpleasant green snack would temper unwanted laughter and help them avoid certain death.

While Commodus's performance was surreal, around 90 CE the emperor Domitian, who had a reputation for knocking off anyone who displeased him, put on his own unique display of insanity. He invited a group of senators over for dinner. Guests found themselves in a dining room painted entirely black. Funereal lights lit the room. At each place setting was a tombstone with that guest's name on it. As each dish came out of the kitchen, the guests found themselves eating course after course of food that had been dyed entirely black.

It must have been a pretty tense dinner party. (Most guests assumed they were going to die.) Domitian spent the entire evening talking about the meaning of life and death and then, when they had all eaten and finished their dinners, he simply sent each of them home with their own tombstone as a party favor.

THE FOOD THAT WOULD HAVE BEEN EATEN at such a dinner was completely different from the food of Rome or Italy today. Indeed the flavor profiles of ancient Roman cuisine possess little in common with the peninsula's modern culinary tradition. The Romans loved garum, which was like their hot sauce or ketchup—they put it on *everything*. The closest modern equivalent to garum would be Asian fish sauce. But this very salty, fish-forward flavor was balanced out in Roman cooking with heavy doses of vinegar, honey, and lots of herbs, such as rue and lovage. Modern cuisine often focuses on the singularity of a strong herb or spice in a dish, or rather for the quiet syncopation of numerous flavors into a cohesive whole. The Roman chef was after an orchestral harmony of flavors and scents, with little desire to illuminate his diners to the ingredients included, instead inspired by a trompe l'oeil (literally a "trick of the eye") approach. Or perhaps a *trompe gout* approach.

A piece of lamb didn't necessarily have to taste like lamb, or even look like lamb. In sources on ancient Rome, we read about entire meals where foods were shaped into different animals, or where everything served was made out of one food, such as zucchini or, more astonishingly, jellyfish. Dishes were constructed out of ingredients that are unfamiliar to us today: flamingo, ostrich, sow's womb, or even omelets made with brains and rose petals. A standout specialty of the day? Dormice. Which were not sourced from the corners of the kitchen, but were actually farm-raised and mass-produced.

It is also important to note, as we are still in the initial stages of our culinary journey through space and time, that while products from across Asia, the Middle East, North Africa, and Europe were available in Rome through that empire's immense trade network, the foods of the Americas had not yet made their presence known in Roman cuisine. Therefore, the food of the Roman Empire was *pre-Columbian* (named for, you guessed it—Christopher Columbus). All the foods from the Americas that would become a part of European, Middle Eastern, Asian, and African cuisines *after* the European colonization of the globe, such as tomatoes, potatoes, corn, and chocolate, did not yet exist in our ancient urban metropolis.

The kind of ostentatious wealth that existed during the empire is perhaps nowhere better memorialized than in the first-century fictional work *Satyricon* by Petronius. In it there is a character, a formerly enslaved man, now freed, named Trimalchio, who has become fabulously wealthy by questionable means and subsequently famous for his elaborate dinner parties. Trimalchio has become such an icon for this sort of mysterious and inconceivable wealth that F. Scott Fitzgerlad's original title for *The Great Gatsby* was actually *Trimalchio in West Egg.*

At one such party thrown by Trimalchio, a group of diners are treated to the kind of lavish, ultra-rich party that seems incredible in a vacuum, and then horrendous when compared to how the majority of human beings are living nearby.

Trimalchio serves his guests dishes such as roasted birds in eggs made of pastry, dormice rolled in honey, and fish swimming in rivers of sauce. Still-life scenes are created out of edible materials; roasted piglets are dressed up as human characters. But the dinner reaches its height of theater and ridiculousness when a roasted pig is wheeled out to the diners. Trimalchio drunkenly inspects the beast and proclaims upon examining its protruding belly that the animal has not been properly gutted before being cooked.

"Call the chef in here!" he commands.

A nervous and cowering chef comes out in front of all the guests, where Trimalchio publically lambasts him for not having cooked the pig properly. He then has him stripped naked by two men with whips. The guests, beginning to feel rather uncomfortable, step in, begging Trimalchio to forgive the absentminded cook.

"Oh, fine!" Trimalchio concedes. "Gut the pig then," he orders, a smile emerging on his face.

The cook takes his knife and cuts the pig's stomach, opening it from one end to another—the room holds its breath—and out topple perfectly cooked, steaming sausages and black puddings.

Trimalchio begins to laugh, applauding this theatrical preplanned skit. All the guests cheer and laugh, while the poor cook is given a cup of wine in reward for playing along.

DINNER FROM HELL

THE SQUASH STEWED with Chicken and Varro's Beets can be combined and "blackened" to make the Black Dish, served at Emperor Domitian's legendary Dinner from Hell.

It is not known what ingredient was used to blacken the many dishes at Domitian's fateful dinner. There are many examples where dishes referred to as one color or another were merely close to these colors. Cameline or carmeline sauce (page 173) was called "red" when made with large amounts of cinnamon; another example would be the "white" meat of chicken. However, it is very probable that many dishes were blackened with squid ink or ash, both of which are commonly used for the same purpose in fine dining restaurants today. It is equally probable that various inks of differing degrees of toxicity were used, potentially harmful food additives having a long and terrifying history. If you want to produce the black versions of these dishes, I generally suggest using food-safe gel colors, which you can buy at any cake supply store. The gels will not alter the taste of the food.

Varro's Beets

BETACEOS VARRONIS

SERVES 4 TO 6 *Attributed to the great Roman scholar Marcus Terentius Varro, this recipe is in* Apicius, *sandwiched between two recipes for laxatives. Thankfully, I have not found it to have this effect.*

½ lemon

1 stalk salsify

12 ounces beets (2 to 3 small)

1 medium parsnip

1 leek

1 tablespoon extra-virgin olive oil

Large pinch of kosher salt

3 cups white wine

1 teaspoon honey

2 cups low-sodium chicken or vegetable stock

½ to 1 teaspoon red wine or sherry vinegar (optional)

Bull's blood beet shoots or other beet microgreens, for garnish

SQUEEZE the lemon into a bowl and add cold water just to cover the salsify (about 2 cups). Salsify tends to turn brown quickly, so put it in the lemon-water until you are ready to use it. Peel the beets, parsnip, and salsify and cut into thick slices.

TRIM the leek and discard all but the white part. Cut it lengthwise, then slice into half-moons, about ¼ inch thick. Wash thoroughly.

IN a saucepan, sauté the leek over medium-low heat in the olive oil. Season with the salt and sauté until translucent. Add the wine, honey, and stock. Cook until reduced by half.

ADD the beets, parsnip, and salsify and simmer until tender but not mushy, 12 to 15 minutes. Remove the vegetables with a slotted spoon and cover the saucepan. Reduce the remaining liquid over medium heat until it coats the back of a spoon, about 15 minutes. Return the vegetables to the saucepan and warm through. Check the seasoning and adjust salt at the end of the reduction process. Add the vinegar, if using. Transfer to a bowl and garnish with beet shoots.

Squash Stewed with Chicken

CUCURBITIS CUM GALLINA

SERVES 4 TO 6 *This fragrant stew combines complex and powerful flavors with the subtleties of squash, truffles, and peaches. It is another dish that showcases Roman cuisine's skillful combination of boldness and refinement.*

1 (3- to 4-pound) chicken, quartered

Kosher salt

2 teaspoons freshly ground black pepper, plus more for seasoning

2 to 3 tablespoons extra-virgin olive oil

4 ribs celery, roughly chopped

Leaves of 1 bunch cilantro, a few reserved for garnish

Leaves of 1 bunch watercress, a few reserved for garnish

2 tablespoons ground cumin

2 teaspoons caraway seeds

2 teaspoons dried mint

2 teaspoons asafoetida

4 cups white wine (such as Pinot Grigio)

2 tablespoons garum or fish sauce

1 pound kabocha squash, peeled, seeded, and cut into ½-inch cubes

2 to 3 cups frozen sliced peaches

1 tablespoon plus 1 teaspoon sherry vinegar

2 tablespoons truffle oil or 1 fresh black truffle

LIBERALLY season the chicken with salt and pepper. Add the olive oil to a deep stew pot and set it over medium-high heat until the oil is shimmering. Brown the chicken in the pan on both sides until deeply colored, about 5 minutes per side, then remove. Reduce the heat to medium and sweat the celery, seasoning it with salt and pepper, until just translucent. Add the cilantro and watercress and sauté for another minute or so, until just wilted. Stir in the cumin, 2 teaspoons black pepper, caraway, mint, and asafoetida. Add the wine, bring to a boil over high heat, and reduce the heat back to medium. Make sure to scrape any browned bits from the bottom of the pan. Add 2 cups water and the fish sauce and simmer over medium-low heat for 10 minutes.

RETURN the chicken to the pot, add the squash, and cook over medium heat for 15 minutes. Add the peaches and cook for another 5 to 10 minutes, until the chicken is fully cooked and the squash is fork tender. Stir in the sherry vinegar and truffle oil (or shave in half of the truffle), turn off the heat, and let the stew rest for a few minutes. Taste and adjust seasoning and garnish with the reserved cilantro and watercress leaves (and shave in the remainder of the truffle, if using).

Trimalchio's Pig

SERVES 8 TO 12 *Petronius's* Satyricon *was, as the name implies, a satire that combined comic and erotic elements. One object of the author's scorn was the vulgarity of newly wealthy Romans. A famous scene involves a decadent banquet given by Trimalchio, who was meant to embody the tasteless and nouveau riche Roman. This was a critical satire, but it also was a testament to the creativity of an already extraordinary cuisine, as we see in the recipes of Apicius. One of the courses was a magnificent pig that, when served, seemed to be improperly prepared and, in fact, not even gutted. However, upon carving it what at first glance appeared to be the offending guts of the animal were instead revealed as delicious sausages! Here's the good news: Roasting a suckling pig is way easier than you think. And a caution: Make sure that your oven can accommodate the size of your pig.*

FOR THE ROAST:

A generous amount of kosher salt

1 (15- to 20-pound) suckling pig

About 2 pounds Lucanian Sausage (page 10)

FOR THE OPTIONAL AROMATICS:

10 cloves garlic

1 bunch thyme

2 tablespoons dried mint

2 tablespoons whole black peppercorns

20 dried bay leaves

FOR THE BASTING LIQUID:

2 cups honey

2 cups white wine vinegar

SALT the pig liberally inside and out the night before you plan to roast it. Do not worry about being overly thorough; salt is your friend. Refrigerate overnight and wipe off the residual salt before cooking.

PREHEAT the oven to 300°F.

PLACE the pig on a baking tray or roasting pan. Prick the sausages and stuff them into the body cavity of the pig. Generally, you don't have to sew it closed: a couple of small skewers will do the trick. For added drama, you can tie a long piece of butcher's twine around the ties in the sausages that you then use when you pull the sausages from the roasted pig in front of your astonished guests. Add any or all of the optional aromatics to the cavity.

ROAST until an instant-read thermometer inserted in the deepest part of the shoulder and into the sausages reads 160°F, 3 to 4 hours. Whisk together the honey and vinegar and, while the pig is roasting, occasionally baste the outside with this mixture using a large brush. It is extremely hard to overcook a suckling pig because it has a ton of collagen (that turns to lip-sticking gelatin when roasted), so don't worry about erring on the far side of the time if necessary. You just don't want it to roast for so long that the sausages inside the cavity burst.

WHEN the internal temperature reaches 160°F, remove the pig from the oven and crank the temperature up to 500°F or as high as it will go. When the oven is fully heated, put the pig back in and roast until the skin is crisp, 20 to 30 additional minutes.

AFTER delighting your guests by revealing the sausages inside, there are two basic ways to carve your pig. You will find that a well-cooked suckling pig comes apart surprisingly easily. Using a very heavy chef's knife or cleaver-style Chinese knife, separate the head from the body. Don't be scared—there is wonderful eating there, especially the cheeks. Then flip the roast on its back and divide it down the spine into two halves. If you want to be super technical and fancy, divide the fat and skin from the meat, then pare the fat from the skin, cut the skin into squares, and serve it separately. Then cut each side of the body into four pieces. Alternatively, you can simply chop off the legs, then hack and slash along every other rib.

GARUM

MANY PEOPLE have now heard of garum, the ubiquitous Roman condiment, and virtually all of them are immediately horrified by its very description. It was, and is, a concoction made almost exclusively from salt and the fermented innards of fish, often anchovies. Indeed, rotten fish guts.

It is striking that, even today, people are still shocked by this, as they finish their delicious Thai dinners and savor the rich umami of fish sauce. Because that's what fish sauce is: small fish, including their guts, eyes, brains, everything, fermented with salt for months, filtered, and enjoyed. *Months* is the key. Just as you might not want to eat half-rotten barley or corn mash, you still savor a fine pilsner or the distilled, aged bourbon that it finally becomes. Fermentation is varied and magical, and the Romans knew it and enjoyed their garum with relish. Garum was mass-produced in factories located across the empire: in Italy, Spain, Turkey, and Libya. There were different grades and qualities of garum, as there are today for soy sauce. One particularly prized garum was made from mackerel in southern Spain, while Jewish citizens of the Roman world could even find kosher garum.

Fortunately, you can now easily order artisanal garum online, although fish sauce is a solid substitute.

Peas Supreme Style

PISA FARCILIS

SERVES 4 TO 6 *"Supreme style" refers to the extraordinary complexity and sophistication of this recipe, a magnificently layered terrine with a lush sauce. It is worth taking a moment to reflect on the two thousand years that have passed between its presentation to a Roman senator and its arrival on your dinner table.*

FOR THE TERRINE:

2 pounds frozen peas

8 ounces bacon

2 tablespoons extra-virgin olive oil

2 teaspoons kosher salt, plus more for seasoning

2 pounds leeks (4 to 6)

4 cups low-sodium chicken or vegetable stock, or water

2 tablespoons dried lovage

1 teaspoon freshly ground black pepper

2 teaspoons ground ginger

2 teaspoons dried oregano

1 pound Lucanian Sausage (page 10) or other pork sausage

2 pounds boneless, skinless chicken thighs or boneless game birds, such as squab or quail

1 piece (large enough to line a loaf pan) caul fat netting (see Note, page 30)

1 cup toasted pine nuts

FOR THE SAUCE:

8 hard-boiled egg yolks

1 tablespoon ground white pepper

¼ cup plus 2 tablespoons toasted pine nuts

3 tablespoons honey

¾ cup plus 1 tablespoon good-quality white wine (something slightly acidic, such as a Friulano or Sauvignon Blanc)

½ cup plus 1 tablespoon low-sodium chicken stock

1 to 1½ teaspoons kosher salt

Vinegar to taste, if necessary

COOK the peas with a few strips of the bacon in 1 tablespoon of the olive oil, with a large pinch of salt. Discard this bacon and set aside the peas. Cut the white parts of the leeks in half lengthwise, then crosswise into 1½-inch sections. Wash thoroughly and make sure to separate the individual layers of leek. Rinse and save the green tops.

PLACE the chicken stock in a stockpot, add the 2 teaspoons salt, and bring to a boil. Blanch the leeks for 3 minutes, then remove with a slotted spoon or skimmer and set aside. Add the green stalks of the leeks to the stockpot with 1 tablespoon lovage,

½ teaspoon pepper, 1 teaspoon ginger, and 1 teaspoon oregano. Bring to a boil and reduce to a simmer, then simmer for 20 minutes.

MAKE a spice blend by tossing together the remaining 1 tablespoon lovage, ½ teaspoon pepper, 1 teaspoon ginger, and 1 teaspoon oregano.

STRAIN the simmered stock through a fine-mesh sieve into a bowl and return the liquid to the stockpot. Over medium heat, blanch the remaining bacon in the liquid, remove with a slotted spoon or skimmer, and reserve.

If using standard pork sausage, cut it on the bias into oblong medallions, blanch them in the liquid, remove with a slotted spoon or skimmer, and reserve. (Lucanian sausage does not need to be blanched.) Blanch the chicken thighs or game birds in the liquid until barely cooked, about 10 minutes. Remove and set aside.

PREHEAT the oven to 350°F. Grease a 9 x 5-inch loaf pan or 4 x 12-inch terrine mold with the remaining 1 tablespoon olive oil. Line with the caul fat netting. Gently crush the pine nuts in a mortar and pestle or pulse a few times in a food processor fitted with the metal blade. Make an even layer of pine nuts in the pan. Make an even layer of about half of the peas on top of the pine nuts. Season with a bit of the prepared spice blend. Make an even layer of the blanched bacon on top, season with a bit more of the spice blend, and add an even layer of the cooked white part of the leeks and season that as well. Shingle the sausage slices over the leeks and season with a bit more of the spice blend. Layer the cooked chicken evenly over the sausages. Sometimes it helps to trim the thighs at an angle or to cut them into thick strips on the bias to make the layer even. Season with the remaining spice blend. End with a final layer of the remaining peas. Gently but firmly flatten the layers into the pan with the flat of your hand or a spatula. Fold the caul fat over the top to enclose the contents. Bake until the caul fat is nicely browned and the chicken thigh layer reaches 165°F on an instant-read thermometer, about 45 minutes.

MEANWHILE, make the sauce: In a blender combine all of the ingredients except the vinegar and blend until smooth. Transfer to a small saucepan and cook over low heat until thickened, 3 to 5 minutes. Taste and adjust seasoning. If you feel it needs a little acidity, stir in a splash or two of vinegar.

LET the terrine cool in the pan for 20 minutes, then invert onto a tray and unmold. Some liquid will be released, so let it drain. Carefully transfer to a serving platter with a long, wide spatula. Cut into ¾-inch slices and ring with some of the sauce. Serve the remaining sauce alongside.

NOTE: Caul fat, the fat netting that surrounds the internal organs, can be obtained from a quality butcher. It will both hold the terrine together more firmly and add visual appeal and porky richness to the dish. If you cannot find it, you can omit it and this recipe will still be extraordinary, but it is worth going the extra mile to look for it.

Ham in Pastry

PERNAM

SERVES 6 TO 8 *This dish is both succulent and incredibly elegant. The decorative case is limited only by your imagination and your knife skills.*

FOR THE FILLING:

1 carrot

2 ribs celery

½ red onion

3 cups white wine (such as Pinot Grigio)

4 cups low-sodium chicken stock or pork stock

8 ounces dried figs

4 dried bay leaves

1½ teaspoons kosher salt

½ teaspoon whole black peppercorns

3 pounds boneless pork shoulder, skin on

½ cup honey

FOR THE DOUGH:

5 cups all-purpose flour

2 teaspoons kosher salt

1⅓ cups extra-virgin olive oil

1 large egg, for egg wash

PREHEAT the oven to 300°F.

CUT the carrot roughly in half. Add the carrot, celery, half onion, wine, stock, figs, bay leaves, salt, and peppercorns to a casserole or large Dutch oven with a tight-fitting lid. Bring to a boil over high heat. Remove from the heat and add the pork shoulder, which should be covered by the liquid. (Add a little water or more stock if necessary to cover.) Cover and braise the pork in the oven until an instant-read thermometer reaches 160°F, the skin is soft, and a knife slides easily through the flesh, about 2 hours, then remove to a cutting board.

RESERVE the figs and either strain the liquid through a fine-mesh sieve into a medium saucepan and reduce it to make a sauce for the dish or discard it.

WHEN the pork is cool enough to handle, run a knife under the skin, peeling it back as you go. You want to remove the skin in a single piece, if possible. Turn the skin over on your cutting board and shave off the fat on the underside using a sharp chef's knife with the blade almost parallel to the skin. Discard the fat you remove.

PLACE the warm, trimmed skin in a bowl with the honey and toss to fully coat the skin with the honey. Refrigerate for 1 hour.

PREHEAT the oven to 375°F.

TO make the dough, add the flour and salt to the bowl of a stand mixer fitted with the paddle attachment and mix on low speed for 10 seconds. With the mixer running, add the olive oil in a thin stream and mix until combined, scraping down the bowl once or twice. Slowly add 1 cup cold water, with the mixer running, again scraping down the sides to make sure everything is thoroughly combined. Form the dough into a disk, wrap in plastic, and refrigerate for 30 minutes.

TRIM the braised ham into a generally uniform oblong shape. (Sharp edges and corners make it harder to wrap the pork in the dough and then the dough can break while baking.

It doesn't have to be perfect, the figs will fill in some space on the top, and the bottom will be out of sight.)

ON a large piece of parchment paper, roll out the dough about ⅜ inch thick

REMOVE the pork skin from the honey. Reserve the honey and cut the skin into squares, diamonds, or whatever shape strikes your fancy. Arrange the pieces of skin on the surface of the dough, cover with another piece of parchment, and roll over the surface gently to embed the pieces of skin in the surface of the dough. Place a board or baking sheet on this surface and invert so that the skin pieces are on the bottom of the dough.

RESERVE a few figs for garnish and cut the rest in half, flattening them. Place these in the center of the rolled dough to cover an area approximately the size of the top of your braised pork. Now invert the pork on

top of the dates. Remember, the fig side will be the top! Use the parchment to wrap the dough around the pork. Fold up one long side first, then the other, and fold up the narrower ends last. Cut away and discard any large amounts of excess dough, particularly at the narrow ends. Press the dough together to seal it.

INVERT the pastry-wrapped ham onto a baking sheet. The decorative skin pieces should now be on top. Briskly whisk the egg with the reserved honey and brush the mixture on top of the pastry and skin.

BAKE until golden brown, 40 to 50 minutes. Cool for 10 minutes, then use a serrated knife to cut into 1-inch slices. Garnish with the reserved figs and if you reduced the braising liquid to make a sauce, serve it on the side.

SUMPTUARY LAWS

ROMANS DOMINATED the world and believed their supremacy came from being tough and stoic warriors. Periodically, they worried that they were becoming morally and spiritually weakened by the luxuries they enjoyed. They attempted to address this by passing "sumptuary laws" that attempted to regulate these pleasures. Laws were passed that limited the number of diners at a banquet, what foods could be served, and the wearing of purple garments, which was considered pretentious. Serving fowl other than chickens was prohibited, as was the fattening of the chicken itself. Fattening animals or raising delicacies, including even the private ownership of fishponds, was often ridiculed as soft and effete. Serving dormice that were fattened on chestnuts and hazelnuts was banned, along with shellfish and imported foods, especially wines and exotic birds such as peacocks. It is easy to see the parallels between these laws and various other prohibitions against alcohol, various drugs, or dancing throughout history, and generally, they were roughly as successful. The citizens of Rome made the laws, promptly broke them, and made them again. And . . . you get the picture.

OF BREAD AND CIRCUSES AND DOCTORS AND GODS

JUVENAL WROTE IN HIS TENTH SATIRE that the Romans had abandoned their interest in politics and desired, "Two things only: bread and circuses." He is of course referring to the gladiatorial games that have become one of the most stereotypical hallmarks of ancient Rome. Gladiatorial games had existed since the days of the Roman Republic, but during the empire they were increasingly used by those in power to manipulate the populace—keeping the people fed and placated with entertainment.

During the Republic there were fifty-nine games a year. By the reign of Claudius in 41 CE, there were almost a hundred. Multiple times per week the citizens of Rome would file into their local amphitheater, grab their free bread, and settle in to watch the blood spill, as humans fought humans, animals fought animals, or some gruesome combination of the two. Gladiators were slaves, prisoners of war, criminals sentenced to death, or persecuted Christians and Jews (Rome wasn't into monotheism yet). The descriptions of the barbaric acts that took place in the Colosseum are horrendous, and perhaps not fit for the pages of a cookbook.

It is difficult to understand a cultural entertainment that is so abhorrent by our own standards. Humans watching other humans fight to the death, for fun—it is some twisted stuff. But it highlights an important point: it is often very tricky to understand the humans who came before us, because their societies operated in ways so different from our own. All you can do is be aware of your own framework, and then for a moment, try to walk in someone else's shoes with the information you have about them. After all, while we may question the morality of these bloody spectacles, violence in sports is still very popular today. Someone two thousand years from now might look at boxing, mixed martial arts, or American football—often brutal displays—watched by millions of teeth-gnashing fans, eating and drinking and cheering . . . and feel, well . . . similarly disturbed.

PERHAPS THE MOST FAMOUS PHYSICIAN OF ANCIENT ROME is Galen of Pergamon. He was born in the second century and came from a well-to-do family in Greece. He studied medicine and the works of Hippocrates, arriving in Rome just in time for the world's first recorded plague, which began in Rome in 166 CE, the Antonine Plague, also known as the Plague of Galen (because he wrote such descriptive accounts of it). So many humans had never lived so close to one another or been so well connected over such great areas. Cities and roads are vectors for more than just goods: they carry disease.

Galen's skill and knowledge as a physician immediately landed him gigs working as a private physician for the Roman elite, and eventually emperors, like Commodus and Septimus Severus. His work dissecting both humans and animals advanced the study of anatomy. But for our epicurean purposes, it was his work expanding on Hippocrates's Theory of the Humors that is most relevant.

The Theory of the Humors stated that the human body was made up of four humors (or substances): yellow bile, black bile, phlegm, and blood. Each of these humors corresponded to a temperament—yellow bile to a choleric disposition, phlegm to being phlegmatic, black bile to a melancholic disposition, and blood to a sanguine personality. An imbalance in any of these humors would result in its corresponding temperament. So if you had an excess of black bile in your body that would theoretically explain your presumed melancholic state. Galen believed that procedures such as bloodletting could help balance your humors. But also that food itself could ease your ills. Cold and dry foods were believed to produce an excess of black bile, so in order to fight off that depression you would be prescribed a diet of warm and moist foods.

THE FOUR HUMORS

YELLOW BILE	BLACK BILE
TEMPERAMENT:	TEMPERAMENT:
Choleric	Melancholic
STAY AWAY FROM:	STAY AWAY FROM:
warm and dry foods	cold and dry foods
PHLEGM	**BLOOD**
TEMPERAMENT:	TEMPERAMENT:
Phlegmatic	Sanguine
STAY AWAY FROM:	STAY AWAY FROM:
cold and moist foods	warm and moist foods

The Theory of the Humors explains centuries of medicine systems and theories of health and well-being, which were built off this foundation. The concept of humors was not just a Western phenomenon; we find similar systems in India with Ayurvedic medicine and the doshas. In the Middle East, the great philosopher of medieval Baghdad, Avicenna, would expand greatly upon Galen's work, producing *The Canon of Medicine*, used as the standard medical textbook throughout the Middle East and the Western world up to the eighteenth century. We will see this idea of humors, of who could and should eat what, run through the entire course of our culinary history.

TEMPLES, ALTARS, AND SHRINES TO THE GODS were littered and strewn about the forum and throughout every neighborhood in Rome. Religion was woven into daily life. Both the political and private spheres were controlled and defined by religious practices, procedures, and beliefs. But daily life wasn't just about religious beliefs; it was about tradition—tradition that held a vastly diverse empire together through myth and legend.

On the forum grounds, "The Navel of the City" (*Umbilicus Urbis Romae*) was the point at which the living world was in contact with the underworld. This kind of spiritualism has inspired modern pop-culture interpretations of Rome where emperors seek advice from Vestal Virgins, where gods take human form and act in the story, where the divine and the divine right to rule blur into a highly stylized historical fantasy. Perhaps a better way to understand the spiritualism of Rome is to think of Hinduism, with its thirty-three million gods and hundreds of holy days and shrines spread throughout India.

When Christians entered the scene, they were met with hostility. From the crucifixion of Jesus Christ by Pontius Pilate until the fourth century, Christianity was a heretical religion. Christians were regularly crucified and many met horrible deaths in the gladiatorial pits. The anti-Christian sentiment that existed in Rome becomes easier to understand when we consider differing attitudes regarding identity. Romans were Roman first. They were citizens of a great empire. Christians were Christian first. They were focused on the next life, not this one. They didn't care about serving in the military or contributing to Roman culture. In a society with immense civic pride, this was a contentious belief to hold. Christians stood in direct juxtaposition to everything Rome stood for.

But Christianity would keep growing. And by the fourth century, when Rome really began to fall apart, Christian religious authorities were ready to claim power over the West for themselves. The Church would maintain this supremacy for another thousand years. And in the millennia that followed, in an incredible reversal of roles, the Christians themselves would come to persecute, outlaw, torture, and murder their original oppressors, the pagans.

Poached Pear Custard

PATINA DE PIRIS

SERVES 8 *I have always loved the elegance of wine-poached pears in modern prepara-tions, and this clever technique of incorporating the poached pears in a delicate custard elevates them even further.*

4 Bosc pears

½ cup raisins

¼ cup plus 3 tablespoons honey

3 cups white wine (such as Moscato)

½ teaspoon ground cumin

¼ teaspoon freshly ground black pepper, plus more for finishing

2 large eggs

3 egg yolks

¼ teaspoon kosher salt

PEEL and halve the pears. Divide each half into four long slices. Cut along the inner edge of each of these slices to remove the core and the hard central line that runs from core to stem. Put the pear slices in a stockpot with the raisins and ¼ cup of the honey. Pour in the wine. Bring to a boil and then reduce the heat to a gentle simmer and poach until the pears have softened but retain some firm-ness, 25 to 30 minutes.

PREHEAT the oven to 325°F. Reserve 8 pear slices.

MEASURE 2½ cups of poached pears with their poaching liquid. The best way to do this is to fill a measuring cup with approximately 2½ cups of the pears, then top it off with the liquid. Add 1 tablespoon raisins from the poaching liquid. (Reserve any remaining poached pears and raisins for another use.) Place the 2½ cups pears and liquid and the 1 tablespoon raisins in a blender or a food processor fitted with the metal blade, along with the cumin, ¼ teaspoon black pepper, eggs, yolks, 3 tablespoons honey, and salt. Blend or process until smooth.

FILL eight 6-ounce ramekins with the mix-ture, leaving a bit of room at the top. Trim the reserved 8 pear slices to fit snugly in the ramekins and then gently place one on the surface of the custard mixture in each rame-kin. Bake until just set, about 15 minutes. Cool the custard and finish each with a pinch of pepper.

Honey Nut Sweets

ALITER DULCIA

MAKES 18 TO 25 PIECES, SERVING 6 TO 8 *It is interesting that the* Apicius *text takes pains to note that* dulcia, *or sweets, can be homemade. Rome, a thriving metropolis, had many street food vendors selling sweets, because apparently, just as today, many people who were comfortable cooking savory foods shied away from attempting to make pastry. These, first fried and then soaked in honey, have a lot in common with Indian pastries, such as* laddu *or gulab jamun.*

½ cup pine nuts

½ cup hazelnuts

½ cup spelt flour

½ teaspoon rue (see page 10)

¼ teaspoon kosher salt

½ cup port wine

½ cup whole milk

1 large egg, beaten

Canola oil for frying

4 cups honey

Freshly ground black pepper or ground "sweet" spice, such as allspice, nutmeg, or cinnamon for sprinkling

PULSE the pine nuts, hazelnuts, flour, rue, and salt in a food processor fitted with the metal blade until the nuts are chopped but still retain some texture. Transfer to a small saucepan, add the port wine (a stand-in for raisin wine) and milk, and cook over medium heat, stirring constantly, until the wine and milk are almost totally absorbed, 5 to 8 minutes. Remove the pan from the heat, add the egg, and stir vigorously to combine. Return the pan to medium heat, stirring constantly with a rubber or silicone spatula, until the mixture forms a thick dough with the consistency of thick peanut butter. It is fine if some of the mixture sticks to the bottom of the pan, as long as it doesn't burn and the egg is fully incorporated.

TRANSFER the dough to a piece of parchment paper on a clean sheet pan. With a metal offset spatula, spread the dough in a square ¼ to ⅓ inch thick. Allow the dough to cool completely, uncovered. With a sharp knife or cookie cutter, cut it into 1½- to 2-inch squares.

PLACE several inches of oil for frying in a heavy pot with high sides and heat it to 300°F.

IN a medium saucepan, gently heat the honey over very low heat until hot but not boiling. Working in batches to avoid crowding, fry the dough pieces in the oil, stirring and turning gently with a wire-mesh skimmer, until they rise to the surface and are golden brown but not burned. They should just barely be bubbling in the oil—this indicates that the dough is not too wet inside and will absorb the honey more fully. As the pieces are cooked, remove with the skimmer and immediately transfer them to the warm honey.

ALLOW them to soak in the hot honey until they have absorbed it, 8 to 10 minutes. Remove the sweets from the honey, drain briefly on a rack, and sprinkle them with a pinch of spice. Serve warm or at room temperature.

WHAT'S FOR DESSERT?

DESSERT AS we know it is a modern invention. However, the tradition of ending a meal with a specific dish or type of dish has a long tradition and goes back to Greek, and thus Roman, ideas about which foods properly "close the stomach" and aid in digestion. Sweet dishes, although appreciated throughout history, were usu- ally interspersed through the meal or, in many cases, were included in the large number of dishes placed all together before diners, but often sepa- rated into courses of multiple dishes. Romans formally dined in three courses, the *gustatio*, *primae mensae*, and *secon- dae mensae*, and sweets were usually served, along with other dishes, in the third. For our modern palates, I have gen- erally grouped items that we would now recognize as des- serts at the end of each chapter for convenience. However, par- ticularly if you have a large and sturdy table, I encourage you to set out a complete meal at once and play the emperor.

THE FALL

THE GREEK HISTORIAN POLYBIUS in his work *The Histories* tells a story of the early days of Rome, before the empire before the Republic, when Rome was ruled by a king named Tarquin. One day an old woman appeared before the palace doors of King Tarquin, carrying nine books. She offered to sell these books to Tarquin for a hefty sum. The king, disregarding her as some crazy old lady, refused and sent her away. The old woman burned three of the books. The next day she came back to the palace, now offering to sell Tarquin the remaining six books. He refused. She burned another three books. The next day she reappeared for a third time and offered to sell him the remaining three books. Tarquin, spooked by her persistence and maybe a little curious about what was in these books, finally agreed to buy them. Once Tarquin purchased the books, the old woman disappeared forever.

Tarquin found that within these books were the prophecies of Rome and that the old woman had been a sibyl, a prophetess. Though six books containing the future of Rome had been burned as a result of King Tarquin's arrogance, the remaining three still contained precious insight into Rome's future. Deep within the pages lay the ultimate prophecy, how Rome would come to meet its end. "Not foriegn invaders, Italy, but your own sons will rape you . . . punishing you, famous country, for all your many depravities, leaving you prostrated, stretched out among the burning ashes." Rome would be its own downfall.

Since the collapse of Rome in 476 CE, historians have occupied themselves with the question, "Why did Rome fall?" And there are 210 theories out there attempting to provide answers to the proverbial question. Broadly speaking, the consensus is that Rome was growing too big for its britches, and there were a whole bunch of barbarians knocking at its door as well as some environmental factors like a mini Holocene Ice Age and the plague. Although the barbarians were also driven by environmental factors—motivated by severe drought in central Asia, they were climate change refugees in search of greener pastures.

Perhaps we search so desperately for an answer to this question because in the fate of Rome we are met with a reflection of our own futures. For if Rome serves as our origin myth, then surely her fall will tell us something of our own.

I often wonder how it felt to live in Rome during its collapse. Did the city decay slowly? As people dispersed and left the once bustling city, did weeds and vines take their place, slowly growing over walls and up through cracked surfaces, reclaiming the bathhouses and amphitheaters like some ancient Chernobyl? Did the people who stayed move into decrepit villas, abandoned by their wealthy owners? How long did it take for the forum to cease to be the center of city life? For the marketplace to be abandoned? For the taps of the bathhouses to run dry?

As Rome plunged into its "Dark Ages," the knowledge, art, and culture of Rome grew quiet in the West. The Christian Church assumed the throne. The science and philosophy of the classical world, its gods and goddesses, were censured, burned, and condemned.

But all was not lost. To the East there was light. The works of Galen, Hippocrates, and others passed through many hands that still saw their value and found them a safe haven in the Middle East—in Baghdad, specifically, a city that was just coming into its Golden Age as Islam stretched its hands forth from the Arabian deserts and firmly grasped all that was before it.

DAD

BAGHDAD
8TH to 13TH centuries

T HE SUN HAD SET behind the arid hills. The tallow candles were burning down, pools of wax collecting at their bases. The dozens of plates laid out before the dinner guests, once piled high with sweet and fragrant stews, now contained only morsels, streaks of sauce not successfully mopped up with bread, alternating in random curves and swirls with the shiny silver of the plate beneath. Soft music was playing from the corner where a group of musicians were set up. Some of the guests began to recline, full, satiated, and perhaps a bit relieved.

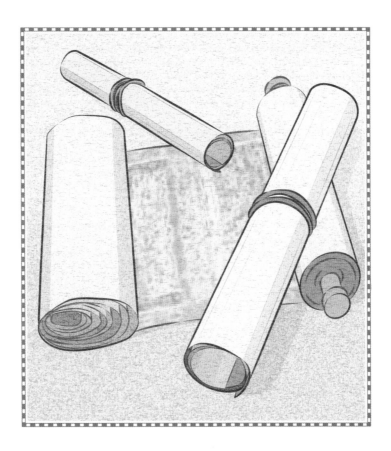

It was June 22, of the year 750 CE, in the Palestinian town of Abu-Futrus. The Umayyad family, recently defeated as the ruling caliphate of the Islamic world, had been invited to a conciliatory dinner by the victors of the revolution, the Abbasids. After the last Umayyad caliph, Marwan II, had been killed in the fighting, the surviving eighty royal Umayyads were eager to seek a truce and a guarantee of their safety.

Toward the end of the night, one teenage Umayyad prince named Abd al-Rahman stood up to relieve himself. As he parted the curtain and stepped into the next room al-Rahman observed the backlit shadowy file of numerous armed guards, knives unsheathed, making their way into the banquet hall. His heart began to race. He rushed to conceal himself. What followed were screams. The voices of his family members begging for their lives as the Abbasid guards descended upon them.

By some divine act of fortune, luck, or fate, Abd al-Rahman managed to escape that banquet of blood. The rest of his family were not so lucky. The Abbasids had wiped out their enemy in a single stroke. Or so they thought.

Many years later this runaway Umayyad prince would pop up in the least likely of places—Spain, where he would go on to found his own caliphate: the Umayyad caliphate of al-Andalus, which would last for centuries. But that is another story, for another time (and another chapter). This story is about the Abbasids. The new rulers of the vast and magnificent Islamic Empire.

When the Abbasids took power in the mid-eighth century, the Islamic Empire was bigger than Rome's had ever been. In just over a hundred years, Islam, as both a religion and a political power, had swept forth from the deserts of Arabia and moved with lightning speed across the Middle East and North Africa, pressing as far west as Europe and as far east as the borders of India and China. How had this new religion and political entity made such enormous strides in such a short period of time? There are many answers to this question. But perhaps we should consider that, after the fall of both the Roman Empire in the West and its eastern contemporary, the Sasanian Empire, power vacuums proliferated like weeds, from the Atlantic Ocean to Central Asia. Islam filled much of this void.

The subjects of the Islamic Empire were diverse. Certainly they were not all Muslim, though many converted. Religious tolerance was a hallmark of this period of Islamic rule. Christians, Jews, and Zoroastrians were not ostracized outsiders in a predominantly Muslim culture. Non-Muslims held powerful positions throughout society and were given protection by the caliph through paying *jizya*, a tax for those who did not adhere to the teachings and verses of the Koran.

Throughout this chapter (and when we rejoin Abd al-Rahman in Spain in Chapter Six), we will see the religious tolerance, diversity, and openness that defined Isalmic society in the medieval period. This unique cultural moment created the condition for an unparalleled synthesis of ideas, perhaps only to be rivaled by the Enlightenment in the seventeenth and eighteenth centuries, or the technological revolution of the twentieth and twenty-first centuries. By understanding Baghdad's role in the grand narrative of human intellectual achievement, we can understand a crucial piece of the puzzle, a fundamental part of the timeline that historians endeavor to lay out: how did we get from there to where we are now?

Rolled Sandwiches, Baghdadi Style

BAZMAWARD MADINI

MAKES 8 TO 12 SLICES, SERVING 6 TO 8 *These rolled, sliced, and baked sandwiches are rich and savory and make a perfect hors d'oeuvre. They can also be used to accent a larger platter of dishes. This recipe is sourced, as are all the recipes in this chapter, from* The Annals of the Caliphs' Kitchens *by Ibn Sayyār al-Warrāq, written in the second half of the tenth century.*

2 pounds lamb leg or beef chuck or top round, cut into ½-inch cubes

2 tablespoons vegetable shortening, plus more for assembly

1 medium red onion, roughly chopped

2 tablespoons fresh cilantro leaves

2 tablespoons fresh parsley leaves

1 teaspoon rue (see page 10)

2 teaspoons ground coriander

1 teaspoon freshly ground black pepper

2 teaspoons ground caraway

1 teaspoon ground cumin

4 cloves garlic, roughly chopped

1 large egg

2 teaspoons kosher salt

4 to 6 thin flatbreads, such as lavash

8 large eggs, hard-boiled and peeled

Murri, for serving (recipe follows)

PREHEAT the oven to 325°F.

ADD the lamb or beef, the 2 tablespoons shortening, and all the remaining ingredients except for the flatbreads, hard-boiled eggs, and murri to the bowl of a food processor fitted with a metal blade and pulse, scraping down the bowl a few times, until it forms a smooth paste.

ARRANGE one of the flatbreads flat on a work surface and spread a thin layer of shortening on it, then apply a thick layer of the paste with a spatula. The filling should be ¼ inch to ⅓ inch thick. Depending on the width of your flatbread, place 4 to 6 hard-boiled eggs in a line on the paste and carefully roll the flatbread up into a tube, like a burrito but open at both ends, overlapping by at least

a half-roll. It should be tight with no large air pockets. Add a little bit more filling at either end to seal the roll and spread additional shortening on the outside of the roll. Traditionally, it would now be wrapped in clean intestines—if you have some lying around, or if you have already begun forging a bond with your local artisanal butcher, go for it.

PLACE the roll on a nonstick sheet pan and bake until golden and just crisp on the outside and fully cooked through to an internal temperature of 160°F, 35 to 40 minutes.

COOL, slice into 1½-inch pieces (aim to slice through the centers of the eggs for visual appeal), and serve with murri.

ONE THOUSAND AND ONE NIGHTS OF UMAMI

VIRTUALLY EVERY elevated cuisine seems to have developed, and loved, its own fermented condiment. Soy sauce from fermented soybeans is ubiquitous in Asian cuisine. Southeast Asia and ancient Rome, as we have seen, have various umami-rich sauces made from fermented fish. European cuisine, from its development in the Middle Ages, has various vinegars, also produced through complex processes of fermentation. Perhaps the least known in our age is *murri*, made from fermented barley flour and often accented with additional ingredients, such as raisins, carob, and spices, to create a rich, salty, savory paste that was vital to the exquisitely balanced cuisine of the Islamic Empire.

The process of making murri involved wrapping barley flour dough in fig leaves for forty days. This was then ground and mixed with salt, water, more flour, and sometimes additional spices and other ingredients, and left in a warm place for another forty days, until it transformed into the final product. Fermentation is both an art and a science, and it takes years to master. Murri, like soy sauce, fish sauce, and garum, is an amazing artisanal product showcasing humanity's genius for culinary creation.

Murri

(FERMENTED BARLEY CONDIMENT)

MAKES ABOUT 1⅓ CUPS *One of the most difficult decisions in the creation of this book was what to use as an acceptable substitute for this vital ancient condiment. I consulted with my favorite fermentation ninjas, dug into the literature, generally lost sleep, and tore out my hair. While there are indeed ancient recipes from the period for "false" murris, these are substitutes for the heavily spiced and seasoned versions, not for the umami-rich original. True murri was a thick paste that could be thinned. Finally, through the above sleep- and hair-defeating process and quite a bit of trial and error, I settled upon the recipe below.*

1 cup Marmite

⅓ cup soy sauce

ADD the Marmite and soy sauce to a small bowl and whisk thoroughly. This mixture, like the products it is made from, will last almost indefinitely when kept tightly sealed at room temperature.

THAT'S it! And this substitution actually makes sense if you consider that true murri is the product of intensely fermented barley using naturally occurring yeast and mold.

Soy sauce is the refined result of the molded fermentation of soy and wheat, while Marmite is a paste made from the byproducts of yeast fermentation, originally from beer. All of these produce rich, complex flavors that are similar due to the high concentrations of glutamates, the source of the fundamental savoriness of umami.

Cold Dish of Carrots

BARIDAT JAZAR MAHSHI

SERVES 6 TO 8 *These aromatic carrots, served cool, make a perfect counterpoint to heavier dishes, such as stews. The colored heirloom carrots also offer visually appealing contrast with fresh herbs. Remember, it's all about the carrots, so buy fresh, firm carrots without cracks or small stringy rootlets. You want to feel like they are bursting with their inner carrotness.*

3 pounds rainbow carrots

1 teaspoon kosher salt

3 to 4 stalks fresh parsley, plus 1 tablespoon roughly chopped for garnish

3 to 4 stalks fresh cilantro, plus 1 tablespoon roughly chopped for garnish

3 to 4 stalks fresh mint, plus 1 tablespoon roughly chopped for garnish

¼ cup plus 1 tablespoon extra-virgin olive oil

1 small yellow onion, finely chopped

1 small red onion, finely chopped

½ teaspoon ground cinnamon

¼ teaspoon freshly ground black pepper

½ teaspoon ground ginger or galangal

½ teaspoon ground coriander

¼ teaspoon ground caraway

Pinch of ground cloves

¼ cup red wine vinegar

¼ cup white wine vinegar

½ teaspoon Murri (page 51)

Pinch of rue (see page 10)

PEEL the carrots and slice into ¼-inch rounds.

BRING a large pot of water to a boil over high heat and add the salt. Prepare a large bowl of ice water. Add the carrots to the water and let it return to the boil, then cook for 3 minutes, until just tender, so the tip of a sharp knife penetrates easily but with some resistance. Immediately use a slotted spoon or skimmer to transfer the carrots to the ice water to stop cooking. Drain and set aside in a large heatproof bowl.

MAKE a sachet of the parsley, cilantro, and mint stalks by folding them together in a piece of cheesecloth and tying it with

kitchen twine. Heat the ¼ cup olive oil in a small saucepan over medium heat. Add the yellow and red onions and the herb sachet and cook until the onions are translucent and the herbs are wilted, 3 to 4 minutes. Add the spices and cook for 30 seconds. Add both vinegars and ¼ cup water, then add the murri. Bring to a boil, then reduce the heat to a gentle simmer and simmer for 15 minutes. Pour this mixture over the carrots, add the rue, and toss with a small rubber spatula until the carrots are fully coated.

COVER and marinate for at least 1 hour, then garnish with the chopped herbs, drizzle with the remaining 1 tablespoon olive oil, and serve.

Fried Eggplant

BADHINJAN BURAN

SERVES 6 TO 8 *Eggplant recipes are so commonly associated with Middle Eastern cuisine that it is hard to imagine that eggplants were once rejected in the region—and all over the world—as harmful and even poisonous. It took the approval of a powerful caliph's wife, Buran, whose name is alluded to in the title of this dish, to popularize them. Here, they are fried, spiced, and wildly aromatic.*

4 small Italian eggplants

Kosher salt

2 leeks, white parts only

1 cup fresh cilantro leaves

1 teaspoon ground ginger

1 teaspoon ground cinnamon

¼ teaspoon rue (see page 10)

2 cups olive or canola oil, or another neutral oil for frying

3 tablespoons extra-virgin olive oil

1 tablespoon sesame oil

2 cinnamon sticks

1-inch-piece fresh ginger or galangal, peeled

½ to 1 teaspoon Murri (page 51)

½ cup chopped walnuts

CUT each eggplant lengthwise into thick rounds or planks and crosshatch both sides of each with a sharp knife. Salt liberally and set aside in a colander for 30 minutes.

CUT the leeks lengthwise, then into half-moons. Toss them to separate, wash and dry them thoroughly, and set aside. Roughly chop the cilantro leaves. Whisk together the ground ginger, ground cinnamon, and rue in a small bowl and set aside.

PLACE the 2 cups oil in a medium saucepan and bring to 300°F. Fry the leeks until crisp, about 2 minutes; remove with a slotted spoon or skimmer. Set aside a few whole cilantro leaves for garnish and fry the rest until crisp, 20 to 30 seconds.

HEAT the extra-virgin olive oil, sesame oil, cinnamon sticks, and fresh ginger in a large skillet over medium heat until the oil is hot and shimmering. Add the eggplant to the pan, working in batches if necessary to keep from crowding the pan, and fry until deeply browned on the bottoms, 7 to 8 minutes. Flip the eggplant slices and sprinkle liberally with some of the ground spice mixture. Drizzle a little murri over each slice. (Murri has a very strong flavor, and more can be served on the side, so be conservative!) Continue to fry until well browned, 5 to 7 additional minutes. Remove the pan from the heat, and flip the eggplant slices again, sprinkling the other sides with spice mix and drizzling with murri. Remove the eggplant to a platter and sprinkle with the walnuts. Season with salt. Cover with a kitchen towel and allow to rest for 2 minutes. Top with the fried leeks and cilantro and the reserved fresh cilantro and serve.

BAGHDAD:
THE GOLDEN AGE

IN THE YEAR 632, Prophet Muhammad, leader of the Muslim community, passed away. As he died without a son—or, as some believed, a clearly designated successor—the question of who should succeed the Prophet, both as a political and spiritual figurehead, began to fracture the young religion. One contingent of followers (which we know as the Sunni branch of Islam) believed that power should fall to an individual agreed upon by several senior members of the community. They chose Abu Bakr for this role, a man who had been the Prophet's closest friend. Another group believed that Muhammad had already appointed a successor on his deathbed, his cousin and son-in-law, Ali (we know this group as the Shi'a branch of Islam).

In the end it was Abu Bakr who assumed the position of leader, or *kalipha* (later caliph) of the Muslim community. His rule and that of the three caliphs that followed him, was known as the Rashidun, or the "Rightly Guided," caliphate. It ended with the rule of Ali (yes, that Ali), who was assassinated in 661.

The Sunni-Shi'a divide within Islam goes right back to the death of Muhammad and continues to this day. Wars have been fought over it and people have died for what they believe. A short explanation here, between recipes for vegetables and slippery pasta, surely will fail to do justice to the complexity of the Sunni-Shi'a divide. But an understanding, however basic, is important.

When Ali was assassinated, the Rashidun caliphate, the first caliphate of the Islamic world, came to an end. The Rashidun, who had been based in Arabia, were followed by the Umayyads. The Umayyad caliphate shifted its center to Damascus in Syria. But then after a revolution and one murderous dinner party, the Abbasid caliphate came to power in 750.

The Abbasids were originally from Khorasan, in modern-day northeastern Iran. They were not Arab like their Umayyad predecessors but instead Persian. The Persian culture they brought with them to the highest strata of power defined the new court culture and came with a rich tradition of the arts, poetry, and architecture and an elaborate haute cuisine. Suddenly the capital city of Damascus felt dated, too Umayyad. It was the second Abbasid caliph, al-Mansur, who decided he needed a new city from which to rule. Baghdad was about to come to life.

IN 762, AL-MANSUR BEGAN THE CONSTRUCTION OF BAGHDAD. To determine the most auspicious location for his new capital city, he took to the water and looked to the stars. He sailed down the Tigris River searching for a location that was well positioned for trade and protection from enemies and in a fertile area for growing food. He found a small village located on the western banks of the Tigris; it had a decent market, several Nestorian Christian monasteries, and numerous canals. Al-Mansur consulted his trio of stargazers—a Jewish, Christian, and Zoroastrian astrologer—who, upon examining the placement of the stars and the phases of the moon, agreed that this was indeed the place.

The city was not called Baghdad at first. Al-Mansur tried unsuccessfully to call it Madinat al-Mansur ("the city of al-Mansur"), after himself, but that name never stuck. Instead, Madinat al-Salam ("the city of peace") took hold. As did a few other nicknames, among them al-Zawra, meaning "crooked," because of the imperfect bend in the river upon which the original city was built. But it was the Persian influence of the Abbasids that won in the end: *bagh* meaning "God" and *dadh* meaning "founded." Baghdad. Founded by God.

At the center of al-Mansur's City of Peace was the caliphal complex, the "Round City," aptly named for its perfectly round walls. This circular fortification that encompassed the heart of Abbasid power contained four gates; the Gate of Khorasan, the Gate of Basra, the Gate of Kufa, and the Gate of Damascus. Above each gate was a gatehouse from which the entire city and beyond was visible. Sweeping views in every direction made it a formidable fortress, protecting, at its center, the caliph's palace and the Great Mosque.

No archeological remnants of the Round City survive. Al-Mansur's palace did not withstand the devastating Mongol invasion of 1258 (which we'll visit in the following chapter). However, when the prolific Moroccan traveler of the fourteenth century Ibn Battuta visited Baghdad, he named the Great Mosque among the city's jewels. At some point between Battuta's visit and the early twentieth century, the remains of the mosque slipped away into the recesses of history. Today in Baghdad there is a park called Al-Zawra (a reference to the city's old nickname), in a spot that appears to be very close to the original location of the Round City. It has a zoo and a Ferris wheel, and is a popular place for families to picnic on sunny spring and autumn days. Though nothing remains of al-Mansur's masterpiece, at the northwest corner of the park, ostensibly where the Gate of Damascus used to stand over one thousand years ago, is the "Al-Mansur Gas Station."

Tenth-century Baghdad was a dazzling place for visitors, even those from other impressive cities. When Michael Toxaras and John Radinos the Patrician visited Baghdad in 917 as ambassadors on behalf of the Byzantine empress Zoe, they were stunned by the city they encountered. They traveled from Constantinople (at the time the biggest city in the West, and the capital of the Byzantine Empire) to discuss peace terms with Caliph al-Muktadir, after years of warring on the borderlands between the two empires. Though Constantinople was not a one-horse town, Toxaras and Radinos were awestruck by one of the first palaces they visited (out of a whopping twenty-three), that was so grand they assumed it must belong to the caliph himself.

They visited palaces draped with thousands of curtains embroidered with gold, decorated with images of elephants, lions, and camels; with carpets so rich and luxurious that some were hung upon the walls, too precious to walk upon. They were led through hallways lined on either side with chained and muzzled lions, accompanied by a handler. They saw elephants covered in peacock feathers. They visited the Park of Wild Beasts, an insane tenth-century petting zoo of exotic animals. Toxaras and Radinos admired the beauty of the Palace of the New Kiosk, which contained a small lake. Boats floated on the lake, which was surrounded by palm trees and fruit tree groves. In the Palace of the Tree, they encountered a giant tree made entirely out of silver and gold. Its branches and colorful leaves swayed as though in the wind, and tiny mechanical birds were perched throughout.

Beyond the palaces and spectacular gardens, was the city, sprawling out into various districts, cut up into tiny islands by the city's numerous canals. Indeed one can't help but think of Venice when looking at a map of Abbasid Baghdad.

The waters of the Tigris River were harnessed to create an incredible system of canals that spread throughout every quarter of the city like the fine lines of a spider's web. These waters supplied neighborhoods, allowed for the transportation of people and goods, and, crucially, irrigated the lands of the alluvial plain to the west and south of the city. As a result, the land was rich and fertile; agriculture and the raising of domesticated animals thrived. Grains, legumes, and vegetables, including leeks, eggplant, spinach, and asparagus, and herbs such as cilantro, as well as fruit such as lemons, melons, apricots, and pomegranates abounded, keeping the population of the City of Peace fed.

FAMOUSLY KNOWN AS THE CALIPH from *One Thousand and One Nights* (also known as "Arabian Nights"), Harun al-Rashid is perhaps the Abbasid caliph whose name has transcended the boundaries of regional historiographies. In the fabled legend Harun frolics around the city getting into adventures with his sidekicks Jafar the Barmakid and the poet Abu Nuwas. This collection of folktales is also home to famous fictional character—including Aladdin and Sinbad—but Harun, Jafar, and Abu Nuwas were three very real men who lived in Baghdad during an extraordinary time.

Harun's rule began in 786 and lasted for twenty-three years, a reign considered to be Baghdad's "Golden Age." Culture flourished, new scientific discoveries were made, and an energy of collaboration and artistic inspiration took hold of Baghdad, making it, for a time, the proverbial center of the world.

The thing I have noticed about so-called Golden Ages is that they never last. They are ephemeral in both their longevity and in their ability to be re-created. In fact, they cannot be re-created. Because what makes a Golden Age so special is that it is a singularly unique set of circumstances; the timing, the people, the chance meetings and events that weave together to produce a moment in time so spectacular, the likelihood of all these factors coming together again is nonexistent. And in this sense, I believe a good way to spot a society in decline is to find one that is trying to reenact or re-establish its "Golden Age" (which more often than not ends up taking shape in perverted nationalistic forms).

Even Harun's contemporaries knew they were living through a special time. In the late tenth century, the Baghdadi historian al-Masudi wrote in his history *The Meadows of Gold* that Harun's reign had been a "honeymoon." So what made Harun's rule so . . . golden? As far as his political abilities went, he was a talented statesman and a shrewd politician. Baghdad's status as one of the biggest trading hubs in Asia meant there was not only an influx of goods but also money, and therefore disposable income for the elite. The caliphal coffers were used to build extraordinary palaces and fund extravagant lifestyles—but they were also used for intellectual and cultural pursuits.

Possessing a deep desire for knowledge, Harun was intensely curious about the world. He invited the greatest philosophers, scientists, physicians, mathematicians, and astronomers to Baghdad, becoming a patron of their work and setting the stage for a transcultural exchange of ideas that would spark the greatest intellectual progress since the days of Aristotle, a thousand years earlier.

Harun did not possess an unflinching attitude of cultural superiority. He recognized the immense value of the great thinkers of the ancient Greek and Roman worlds. He regularly sent envoys to the West—not in search of jewels or gold or land but books. These men were paid handsomely to visit the crumbling libraries of Europe to seek out any Greek or Latin texts they could find by the likes of Plato, Hippocrates, Galen, or Aristotle, and to bring them back to Baghdad. At the center of the Islamic world, these texts were translated into Arabic and studied voraciously by the intellectual elite. This process is known as the "Translation Movement," and, in time, would help to set the stage for the European Renaissance of the later Middle Ages.

Art flourished under Harun's reign, and poets and musicians enjoyed an almost rockstar-like status in Baghdadi society. They performed for wealthy patrons at their homes or in *majlis* (salons) and could make sizable fortunes from their art. One musician of the period, a woman named Arib who was born into slavery, was sold to Harun's boat master, who expected her talent for singing and music to be on full display. Arib composed over a thousand songs, played the lute and wrote poetry, and possessed a famously sharp wit. She did well for herself financially, and presumably bought her freedom. As a free woman, she lived the rest of her life in a luxurious villa in the city.

An enslaved woman performing music was one thing—a noble or royal woman performing was quite another. Harun's half-sister Ulayyah learned the art of song composition from her concubine mother and had a true talent for it. But she wasn't allowed to sing her songs publicly because of her noble status. Instead, members of the royal family passed her songs on to other musicians, who could perform them. In doing so a convenient workaround was achieved: Ulayyah could still compose her songs while maintaining expected societal standards. Her determination to find a way to pursue music in spite of restrictions has parallels to the consumption of alcohol in the Islamic world at this time. Technically the Koran forbade it, but those who really wished to imbibe could always find a way to do so.

The city's numerous monasteries provided an almost speakeasy-like safe haven for the tipplers of Baghdad. Monasteries were allowed to produce alcohol (as monasteries all over the globe often do) and to serve it to the public in what were essentially drinking taverns. After the sun set and the moon was high in the sky, Harun, Jafar, and Abu Nuwas would throw on their cloaks and descend into the bowels of the city, often in disguise, to visit a monastery's wine bar—where the wine flowed freely and tales of indiscretions rarely left the premises.

Perhaps after a heavy night of drinking, Harun and his friends, stumbling back to the palace with the rising sun, would have ordered the chef to make them something savory and delicious, a dish capable of mopping up those last dregs of wine, and lulling the bon vivants into a heavy-lidded sleep . . .

THE POETRY

ONCE YOU have recovered from the sophistication and precision of the recipes contained in this thousand-year-old cookbook, there is one more thing that sets them apart from, truthfully, every other cookbook I have ever encountered. That is the poetry. And I am not speaking of poetry in a metaphorical sense, or saying that the language of the recipes is poetic. No, these recipes are very often separated and enhanced by poems reflecting on the sensuous pleasures of the dishes and their ingredients.

Eggplant was initially thought to be unhealthy, but a recipe for it is immediately followed by a poem describing it as "like a lover whose love I won" with "a taste like saliva a generous lover freely offers. / A pearl in black gown, with an emerald set from which a stem extends."

This is just one poem among a great many, but every poem, whether about the joy of the hunt, the visual beauty of a dish, or the frank sexuality of asparagus (!), has one simple theme: pleasure. This is a beguiling celebration of food, of language, and of the heights of an extraordinary culture.

Slippery Pasta with Meat and Dipping Sauce

LAKSHA WITH MA' WA MILH AND SIBAGH

SERVES 4 TO 6 *This hearty dish demonstrates the parallel evolution of pasta in yet another location. We may have grown up hearing that Marco Polo brought pasta back to Europe from his travels in China, but noodles of all different shapes and sizes made from wheat, rice, buckwheat, and other starches and grains were actually invented independently in various places throughout history. The only constant is the singularly comforting satisfaction pasta delivers in all its guises.*

FOR THE DIPPING SAUCE:

3 cups buttermilk

½ cup garlic cloves (about 10 cloves)

½ cup walnuts

¼ teaspoon kosher salt

¼ teaspoon ground ginger

¼ teaspoon ground coriander

¼ teaspoon ground cinnamon

FOR THE PASTA:

3 cups all-purpose flour

1 tablespoon cornstarch

¾ teaspoon kosher salt

FOR THE MEAT AND BROTH:

2-inch-piece fresh ginger or galangal (about 1½ ounces), peeled

1 teaspoon kosher salt

2 pounds thick, well-marbled steak, such as New York strip, or lamb loin

1 tablespoon olive oil (optional)

2 quarts low-sodium beef stock

2 cinnamon sticks

1 bunch dill

¾ teaspoon ground cinnamon

1¼ teaspoons ground coriander

¾ teaspoon freshly ground black pepper

SET a sieve over a bowl and place a coffee filter in the sieve. Add the buttermilk, refrigerate, and let drain for at least 8 hours to produce 1 cup whey. Reserve any remaining whey and the solids for another use.

TO make the pasta, combine the flour, cornstarch, and salt in the bowl of a stand mixer fitted with the dough hook on medium speed. Add ¾ cup plus 3 tablespoons warm water and mix for 5 minutes on medium. The mixture will seem a little dry and may not come together. Remove from the bowl

and knead by hand. If the mixture still refuses to come together, add water, about 1 tablespoon at a time, until it does. When the dough has come together, form it into a ball, wrap it in plastic, and refrigerate for 30 minutes.

USING a rolling pin or a pasta machine, roll out your pasta into a sheet a little thicker than regular pasta, about twice as thick as an average spaghetti strand. Cut the dough into 2-inch strips, and then cut the strips into triangles.

COMBINE the 1 cup whey and the remaining sauce ingredients in a small saucepan and bring to a rolling boil over high heat. Transfer to a blender and process until smooth. Return the mixture to the saucepan and simmer over very low heat, stirring occasionally, 10 to 12 minutes, until thickened and any raw garlic smell is gone.

TO prepare the meat and broth, cut the ginger into thick planks. Salt the meat on both sides. To help keep the meat from sticking, add the olive oil, if desired, to a deep stockpot and place over medium-high heat. When the oil is shimmering, or the pan is well heated, 1 to 2 minutes, add the meat and brown on both sides, 3 to 5 minutes per side. Remove the meat and add the stock, planks of ginger, cinnamon sticks, dill, ½ teaspoon of the ground cinnamon, 1 teaspoon of the coriander, and ½ teaspoon of the black pepper. Bring to a boil and then reduce to a simmer and simmer for 10 minutes. Strain the stock through a fine-mesh sieve into a bowl and return it to the stockpot. Bring to a rapid simmer over medium heat.

CUT the steak into 1-inch cubes and add to the simmering stock. (Using a pasta basket or strainer makes it easy to remove the meat.) Cook until tender and just pink in the center, 4 to 5 minutes. Remove from the stock and sprinkle with the remaining ¼ teaspoon ground cinnamon, ¼ teaspoon coriander, and ¼ teaspoon pepper. Cover and keep warm.

WORKING in batches, cook the pasta in the stock until al dente, 3 to 4 minutes. As the pasta is cooked, transfer it to a bowl, adding a little stock to keep it from sticking.

ADD 1 cup of the stock to the dipping sauce. Bring to a gentle boil and simmer, stirring constantly, until reduced by about one-third, to the consistency of thin oatmeal, about 10 minutes. Taste and adjust seasoning.

SERVE each portion in a wide bowl, adding a ladle of stock to the pasta and topping with the meat and a bit of the dipping sauce. Serve the remaining dipping sauce on the side.

Whole Fish Three Ways

SAMAKA, RA'SUHA MASHWI, WA WASATUHA MATBUKH, WA DHANBUHA MAQLU

SERVES 6 TO 8, DEPENDING ON SIZE OF FISH *This intricate and amazing recipe uses a remarkable technique to simultaneously achieve three different textures in the same whole fish. The fish is partially wrapped in layers of cloth or paper to alter how different sections cook. As a result, the head is roasted, the shielded midsection is braised, and the thinly wrapped tail, heavily oiled, is fried. This was originally done with an extremely large fish, but for those of us limited by the moderate size of a conventional oven, I have adapted a technique from a Chinese fish recipe to finish the dish. The fish can be left bone in or butterflied by your friendly fishmonger. Remember to specify that you want the head—sometimes it is removed. Each of the three sauces for the fish three ways is thick, and each sets off the fish in a different way. It is not necessary to pair each sauce with a particular area. Each of the three pairs with the three parts of the fish in complex and different ways.*

1 (4- to 5-pound) whole, head-on meaty white fish, such as striped bass

Peels of 4 apples

1 bunch thyme

¼ cup lime or citron leaves

1½ teaspoons rue (see page 10)

Kosher salt

Extra-virgin olive oil for drizzling

½ cup canola or avocado oil, plus more for brushing

Fresh parsley and cilantro leaves, for garnish

1½ cups Raisin-Walnut Sauce for Fish (page 66)

1 cup Whey-Walnut Sauce for Fish (page 67)

1½ cups Sauce for Fresh Fish (page 67)

PREHEAT the oven to 375°F.

CUT a piece of parchment paper slightly larger than the fish and place the paper on a wire rack set on a rimmed sheet pan. (This will make it much easier to transfer the fish to a serving platter, especially if you are using a larger fish.) Place the fish on the paper.

ROUGHLY chop the apple peels, thyme stems, and lime leaves. Place in a bowl, add the rue, and mix thoroughly.

LIBERALLY salt the inside and outside of the fish and drizzle with a little olive oil. Stuff the body cavity and gill area with the apple peel mixture.

FOLD a sheet of parchment paper along its length so that it is roughly the size of the center portion of the fish. (You want the head area, center area, and tail to be about the same length.) Wrap the center area of the fish three times with this paper. (In other words, if the paper is folded in half and wrapped around three times, there will be six layers of paper around the center of the fish.)

Generously brush the tail area with canola or avocado oil and press a single sheet of parchment tightly around it. Heavily oil the paper over the tail as well.

ROAST the fish in the preheated oven until the center section reaches 140°F to 145°F on an instant-read thermometer, 20 to 25 minutes.

REMOVE the sheet pan from the oven and carefully remove the wrapping from the fish. Heat the ½ cup canola oil in a small pan over high heat to 425°F. Pour it over the tail section. Garnish the center section with parsley and cilantro. Transfer to a platter and serve with the three sauces.

Raisin-Walnut Sauce for Fish
Taken from Ibrahim bin al-Mahdi
SIBAGH, AL-ZABIB

MAKES ABOUT 1½ CUPS *This sauce, combining the sweetness of raisins with vinegar and redolent with spices, is a delight for the senses.*

1 cup raisins

1 cup red wine vinegar

2 cloves garlic, peeled

½ cup sherry vinegar

¼ cup walnuts

2 tablespoons Dijon mustard

½ teaspoon asafoetida

½ teaspoon ground cinnamon

½ teaspoon ground caraway

½ teaspoon ground aniseed

½ teaspoon kosher salt

PUT the raisins and the red wine vinegar in a medium bowl and refrigerate overnight. Place this mixture in a blender and blend until smooth. Combine 1 cup of the blended raisin-vinegar mixture with the remaining ingredients and again blend until smooth.

TRANSFER this mixture to a bowl and set aside until ready to use. Discard any remaining blended raisin-vinegar mixture.

Whey-Walnut Sauce for Fish
SIBAGH AL-JAWZ WA-L-MASL

MAKES ABOUT 1 CUP *This recipe is dense, pungent, and deceptively tricky. It yields a thick and powerful sauce that generates deep umami in a remarkable and unexpected way, but demands care and attention.*

1 cup whey from draining yogurt or buttermilk (see page 62, step 1)

½ cup walnut pieces

½ cup garlic cloves (about 10 cloves)

2 tablespoons olive oil

1½ to 2 teaspoons Murri (page 51)

COMBINE the whey, walnuts, and garlic in a blender and blend while gradually increasing the speed from low to high. Place the olive oil in a small saucepan and add the blended mixture. Simmer over very low heat, stirring constantly, until a thick sauce with the consistency of applesauce forms, 15 to 20 minutes. (Don't skimp on cooking time or the raw garlic will be too pungent, and don't stop stirring or it may burn and turn bitter.) If the sauce seems to be getting too thick before it is fully cooked, you can thin it with a little water and continue to cook. This can be repeated if necessary. When fully cooked, stir in 1½ teaspoons murri and taste. Add another ½ teaspoon murri, if needed.

Sauce for Fresh Fish
SIBAGH AL-SAMAK AL-TARI

MAKES ABOUT 1½ CUPS *A perfect contrast to the other sauces that accompany our fish, this is bright, herbaceous, and marvelously balanced.*

1 cup chopped fresh parsley stems and leaves

½ cup chopped fresh mint stems and leaves

1 cup white wine vinegar

1 teaspoon rue (see page 10)

1 tablespoon fresh thyme leaves

½ teaspoon freshly ground black pepper

1 teaspoon ground cumin

1 teaspoon ground caraway

½ teaspoon ground cinnamon

2 teaspoons turbinado sugar

½ teaspoon kosher salt, plus more to taste

VERY roughly chop the herbs, stems and all. Combine all ingredients in a blender and blend until smooth. Taste for salt and add a little bit more, if necessary. The sauce is herbaceous and powerfully sour from the vinegar, so it is often better to taste the sauce with a bit of fish or even a piece of bread to evaluate it. It can be thinned with a few tablespoons of water or olive oil, if necessary.

Stuffed Whole Fish Cooked Three Ways

SAMAKA MAHSHU, RA'SUHA MASHWI, WA WASATUHA MATBUKH, WA DHANBUHA MAQLU

SERVES 6 TO 8 *Believe it or not, there is an even more intricate and sophisticated version of the whole fish dish. For this recipe, the idea is to fillet the fish, retaining the skin, then make a forcemeat by grinding the fish flesh with spices, stuff that under the skin to recreate the shape of the fish, and again cook it simultaneously three ways! Obviously, you can have your trusty fishmonger prepare the bass for you, but be very precise in your instructions: a) you want to retain the skin in one piece, b) you want the head and tail, and c) you want the fish filleted and deboned. You can use the apple peel stuffing from the previous recipe in the head of this fish as well.*

1 (4- to 5-pound) whole, head-on meaty white fish, such as striped bass, to yield about 3 pounds fillets

2 large eggs

2 teaspoons sugar

½ teaspoon ground cloves

1 teaspoon ground cinnamon

1 tablespoon plus 1 teaspoon ground ginger

2 teaspoons freshly ground black pepper

1 teaspoon ground cumin

1 teaspoon ground caraway

1 teaspoon kosher salt

2 teaspoons Murri (page 51)

¼ cup extra-virgin olive oil

¼ cup almond flour

¼ cup sesame seeds

½ cup canola or avocado oil, plus more for brushing

IF you choose to butcher the fish yourself, first make a cut behind the gills and the fin. Cut down until you reach the bones but don't cut through them. Cut along the backbone of the fish, toward the tail. Lift the fillet up gently as you go to let your knife move smoothly over the ribs. Don't cut through the tail—this will make it easier to remove the skin. Turn the fish over and, holding on to the tail, insert your knife between the skin and the meat of the fillet. Keeping your knife flat against your cutting board, run it completely between the meat and skin until the fillet is free. Wiggling the tail slightly will make this easier. Try to keep the skin as intact as possible. Repeat the procedure on the other side. You should now have the head and tail with skin attached to the tail, connected by the backbone. If you want, you can simply cut away the backbone, retaining it, the head, the tail, and the skin. Otherwise, you can cut the ribs from the backbone with kitchen shears. Now, place the fillets on your cutting board and, using fish tweezers, remove any remaining bones. Cut the filets into large chunks. You will need 3 pounds fillet; if you are using a smaller fish, you may have to add some additional fish.

COMBINE the chopped fillets and all remaining ingredients except the sesame seeds in the bowl of a food processor fitted with the metal blade and pulse into a smooth paste. Add the sesame seeds and process to combine. Stuff this forcemeat between the head and tail, rebuilding the body of the fish. Smooth the skin over the forcemeat and tie in place with kitchen twine. If you have separated the head and tail and discarded the backbone, use a pair of wooden dowels or stalks of lemongrass to provide structure.

PREHEAT the oven to 375°F.

FOLLOW the instructions for oiling and wrapping the fish in parchment from the Whole Fish Three Ways recipe (page 65), using this fish in place of the whole fish. Roast this version in the preheated oven until it reaches 150°F on an instant-read thermometer. Transfer to a platter and serve with the three sauces.

Vinegared Stew

SIKBAJAT

SERVES 4 TO 6 *I was going to begin by saying, "There is a famous story about* sikbajat,*" but in truth, there are a great many famous stories about this beloved vinegar stew. Perhaps the most instructive is also the simplest: The caliph held a cooking contest, instructing all the entrants to cook their best dishes. Of course, all of them cooked sikbajat. And no one was really surprised. Sikbajat has been described as the queen of all dishes, and was beloved by caliphs and commoners alike. There is a lot of variation in sikbajat recipes, and additional meats, especially chicken, game hens, and organ meats, can be included. The dish can be served with Rolled Sandwiches (page 49) and Cold Dish of Carrots (page 52), and, as al-Warrāq advises, it can be garnished so that it looks "like a flower orchard embellished and ornamented with all kinds of adornments, like an illustrious bride or a decorated sword."*

⅔ cup white sugar

⅓ cup packed brown sugar

2 pounds leg of lamb or blade chops

2 pounds boneless beef short ribs, cut into large chunks

Kosher salt

1 tablespoon extra-virgin olive oil

1 tablespoon coriander seeds

1 large yellow onion, roughly chopped (about 2 cups)

½ bunch watercress stems and leaves (about 1 cup)

½ bunch parsley stems and leaves (about 1 cup), plus more leaves for garnish

½ bunch cilantro stems and leaves (about 1 cup), plus more leaves for garnish

2 tablespoons dried mint

Leaves of 12 to 15 sprigs thyme (about 2 tablespoons)

8 cloves garlic

1½ cups red wine vinegar

1½ cups sherry vinegar

4 cups low-sodium chicken stock

½ teaspoon saffron

Chopped fresh mint leaves for garnish

IN a small saucepan, combine the sugars with 1 cup water and bring to a boil. Whisk to make sure all sugar is dissolved and set aside.

ALTHOUGH traditionally the meat would simply have been braised, searing your meat first will deepen the final flavor and enhance the dish. Salt the meat liberally on both sides. Place the olive oil in a large deep pot with a lid, add the meat off the heat, then place the pot over medium-high heat and sear the meat until well caramelized, about 8 minutes per side. You may have to sear in two stages to avoid crowding. Set the seared meat aside.

ADD the coriander seeds and cook until fragrant, about 1 minute. Add the onion, season with salt, and cook until translucent, about 5 minutes. Add the watercress, parsley, cilantro, dried mint, thyme, and garlic. Cook until the greens are wilted, about 5 minutes. Add the vinegars and the chicken stock, bring to a boil over high heat, then reduce to a simmer and cook for 20 minutes. Strain through a fine-mesh sieve into a bowl and discard the solids. Return the liquid to the pot, add 1 teaspoon salt and ½ cup of the sugar syrup.

ADD the meat to the braising liquid and bring to a boil over high heat. Cover the pot and cook over medium heat for 1 hour. It is best to leave the lid slightly ajar, as you want the liquid to reduce slightly as it is cooked. Then add the saffron and continue to cook for 30 minutes. When fully cooked, the meat should be fork tender. Taste for seasoning, adding more salt, if necessary, and more sugar syrup if a sweeter flavor is desired. Generally, the more you reduce the braise, the more powerful it will become. When the braise is prepared to your liking, garnish with fresh parsley, cilantro, and mint, and serve with rolled sandwiches, sausages, pastries, all kinds of vegetables and herbs, and and and and . . .

THE ART OF SOURNESS

THE PEOPLE of the ancient Middle East were connoisseurs of sourness. They delighted in vinegars, the juice of unripe grapes, yogurt, buttermilk, and the clear whey drained from these dairy products. There is another level of sourness hidden in the deep, umami-rich complexity of murri, and the lactic acid ferments of their dairy products were further incorporated in grain ferments to produce a kaleidoscopic array of subtly and powerfully soured condiments and sauces. So many of their sauces, whether for fish, meat, or vegetables, play with contrasts of acidity and sharpness. Many great cuisines have a focus that sets them apart. Chinese dishes have fine gradations of texture; French foods play with richness, Mexican with heat, and Indian with a rich complexity of spices. Of course, this is a simplification, and all cuisines play with some of the same elements in ever-changing variations. But in my mind, the Baghdadi palate for sourness is unmatched.

Vinegar plays a part in many recipes in this book, and generally I suggest vinegar types in broad categories: red wine, white wine, sherry, cider, balsamic, rice wine . . . But, of course, there are Merlot, Chardonnay, French, Italian, Greek, Chinese, filtered, and unfiltered vinegars aged in a thousand variations. Quality vinegars should possess both power and subtlety in a small bottle. They elevate any dish and, within reason, you do get what you pay for. I have only two simple pieces of advice. Experiment. And splurge.

THE HOUSE OF WISDOM

COOKBOOKS FROM THIS PERIOD OF BAGHDAD are nothing short of incredible. *The Annals of the Caliphs' Kitchens* by Ibn Sayyār al-Warrāq, from which all the recipes in this chapter have been sourced, is a culinary artifact of the highest order. It is not only a cookbook but also a dietary guide, a health manual, and a guidebook on table manners and etiquette. It is filled with stories, anecdotes, and poetry that brings the entire period to life. The roughly five-hundred-page tome is an extraordinary work, not just by the standards of its own culture but of any culture, anywhere in the world at this time. In fact, it is safe to say that one will not encounter a cookbook as sophisticated as al-Warrāq's until perhaps eighteenth-century France.

Annals was likely written in the second half of the tenth century, when al-Warrāq was commissioned to compile this collection of dishes for an elite audience. It contains 132 chapters, 615 recipes, and 80 poems. Though many of the dishes require ingredients beyond the reach of the average Baghdadi in this period, there are some classics within its pages that transcended class barriers. Like *judhaba*, a dish that could be prepared with a number of different flourishes (apricots, bananas, and honey for example) but essentially involved roasting a chicken over bread and letting the juices soak in. Judhaba was eaten by common people and caliphs alike. Al-Warrāq regales readers with a story of the caliph al-Ma'mun (son of Harun al-Rashid) dressing in disguise so he can go to a local neighborhood eatery that specializes in judhaba. When al-Ma'mun's officials react with horror to the notion that he would deign to eat in such a "common" hole-in-the-wall, he responds, "The commoners drink cold water like we do. Should we abandon it to them?"

Al-Warrāq's culinary compendium also includes dishes for Christians who are fasting during Lent (such as instructions on how to make yogurt from coconut milk instead of cow's milk!). This serves to remind us of the large Christian community that existed in Baghdad. While Christianity spread west to Europe from its birthplace in the Middle East, it also spread farther into the Asian continent and remained firmly rooted in Middle Eastern culture for centuries.

A heavy Persian influence is notable throughout these recipes. The Abbasids were from Khorasan in northeastern Iran, and the court culture they established in Baghdad had visible roots in Persian traditions—like the round walls of the city, which were inspired by the urban design of the

Sasanian Empire. Many recipes feature that classic sourness that is characteristic of Persian cuisine (often achieved with tart fruits, vinegars, and fermented dairy products) as well as liberal uses of dried fruits and nuts sprinkled throughout. When we note the cultural influences on specific food cultures, we begin to understand the history of that society: where its people come from, who they have been conquered by, who they trade with.

Spices like saffron, cassia, galangal, asafoetida, coriander, caraway, pepper, and cinnamon are littered throughout *Annals*. For those who could not afford to spice their food, cooking might have involved fewer ingredients but was by no means less delicious or complex. Vegetables, legumes, bread, and cheap cuts of meat made up the average person's diet. Just like in ancient Rome, there were takeout options for the people of Baghdad. The city's *ta'am al-suq* (eateries) offered pre-cooked or prepared dishes for travelers, those who did not wish to cook, and even for those whose rudimentary dwellings might not have contained a kitchen.

Galen (the doctor from ancient Rome) and his theory of the humors finds its way into al-Warrāq's *Annals*, no doubt as a result of the Translation Movement. The basic principles are the same, though al-Warrāq expands upon them, creating an even more detailed and complicated tableau of how to maintain good health. Al-Warrāq writes about the age-related temperatures of people (children are moist, because they need moisture in order to grow; the elderly are cold because they have more earth element; women are cold because their bodies excrete more fluids due to their inherent humidity). These temperatures are linked to a balance of the humors (black bile, yellow bile, blood, and phlegm) in the body. And, just like Galen, al-Warrāq advises that people consume certain foods (all of which have properties of their own) to achieve balance and therefore a healthy body. In his guide, he made extensive notes on the humoral properties of various fruits, vegetables, and meats, such as camel, antelope, ibex, and horse, as well as the nature of sweet, sour, pungent, bitter, and greasy foods.

While European monarchs scarcely knew how to boil water, the Abbasid caliphs were not hesitant to get into the kitchen. Caliph al-Ma'mun and his brother al-Mu'tasim (who would succeed him as caliph, from 833 to 842) enjoyed having cookoffs. In one of these events a commoner was plucked off the street to judge the cooking of al-Ma'mun and two of his courtiers: a court official only listed as "a Greek," and the chief judge Yahya ibn Aktham. Luckily this man, who had been randomly chosen to act as a blind taste-testing judge for a royal cooking competition, chose the caliph's dish as his favorite. This luck—and his playful sense of humor—landed him in the caliph's service.

WHEN HARUN AL-RASHID PASSED AWAY IN 809, a dispute about succession between two of his sons, al-Amin and al-Ma'mun, turned into a bloody civil war that lasted until 813. Al-Amin, whom Harun had designated to rule first, was deposed and executed. Al-Ma'mun subsequently took the throne and under his reign the Translation Movement reached new heights. He might have killed his brother, but in this one regard, he certainly would have made his father proud.

One of the centers of the Translation Movement in Baghdad was the wonderfully named *Bait al-Hikam* (House of Wisdom). Part library, part university, this hub of knowledge was likely located within the Round City and built during al-Ma'mun's reign. From al-Ma'mun's patronage came one of the most accurate world maps that had ever been made to date. Translators who were sent to Constantinople to search for ancient Greek and Roman texts were paid handsomely to do so, making up to five hundred dinars a month, roughly equivalent to about $24,000 today. Works weren't just translated, crucially, they were expanded upon, advancing the study of chemistry, physics, astronomy, mathematics, and medicine.

Almost every scholar in Baghdad had studied Ptolemy's *Almagest* (dating back to the second century CE), which was first translated into Arabic by the Jewish astronomer and physician al-Tabari. The *Almagest* is the text in which Ptolemy lays out his geocentric model of the universe (the theory that the Earth is at the center, and the planets and stars revolve around it). This baseline of astronomical knowledge led to the building of observatories in Baghdad and Damascus. Ptolemy's model of the universe was predominant for over a thousand years, until the sixteenth century, when Nicolaus Copernicus's model of the universe placed the sun at the center instead of the Earth.

As astronomy developed out of astrology, so chemistry developed from alchemy. Geber the alchemist, aka Jabir ibn Hayyan, lived during the reign of al-Ma'mun and created the oldest known classification of chemical substances, the earliest precursor to the periodic table. His name is also the origin of the word "gibberish," presumably coined by Westerners who struggled with Arabic and referred to Jabir's words as such.

Abu Bakr Muhammad ibn Zakariyya al-Razi, or al-Razi, is known as the greatest physician of the Middle Ages. Among his numerous accomplishments, he ran the psychiatric ward of a hospital in Baghdad and wrote about his patients' mental health. His work was studied in Europe for centuries. In fact, in the seventeenth century, students at Oxford were required to study

Arabic so they could read the works of Islamic scholars in their original tongue. Al-Razi's most controversial stance was his dislike of Galen's humoral theories. He saw deep flaws in Galen's views about how the human body functioned and on health. He believed that just because Galen had been read for thousands of years did not mean his work was irrefutable. Unfortunately for al-Razi, another Arabic scholar, Avicenna, would publish works that built on Galen's theories and pushed al-Razi's criticisms to the wayside—and slowed the spread of medical innovation for hundreds of years.

A man named Sahl ibn Harun is believed to have been the chief librarian of the House of Wisdom in the early ninth century. He was also sent by al-Ma'mun to Byzantium to find texts. One cannot help but wonder what his trip must have been like. Had he been to Constantinople before? Did he have contacts with whom he had arranged meetings? Or did he show up in this Christian city at the edge of the Islamic world and begin seeking out rare-book sellers, antique merchants, other librarians willing to swipe a manuscript for a secret exchange of cash? Did he know what he was looking for? Or was he willing to purchase whatever he could find?

We would not be wrong to assume that Sahl ibn Harun was purchasing copies of books and manuscripts written by Aristotle himself. But actually very few of the texts we now possess from the ancient world are actually ancient. The only original physical texts that survive from before 500 CE are a couple of scrolls from the Herculaneum archeological site and papyrus fragments that were found on a pile of trash in Egypt. The rest have been lost, destroyed, or perhaps have simply disintegrated over the centuries. All we have left are copies of copies, transcribed from one subjective hand to the next over the course of millenia, with all those individuals' thoughts, beliefs, views, and ideas either directly baked into them, or subtly so.

Pastry for the Elite

SHAKMIYYAT AL-KHAWAS

SERVES 6 TO 8 *This is a rich, honey-soaked bread that is stuffed with dried fruits and nuts. Apricots, dates, and almonds are suggested, but feel free to use your favorite nuts and dried fruits.*

2 cups all-purpose flour

1 teaspoon active dry or instant yeast

¼ teaspoon kosher salt

3 egg whites

¼ cup sesame oil, plus more for coating bowl

⅓ cup blanched almonds

⅓ cup dried apricots or other dried fruit

⅓ cup pitted dates

½ cup lard or vegetable shortening, at room temperature

1½ cups honey

Confectioners' sugar for finishing

1 tablespoon rose syrup

ADD the flour, yeast, and salt to the bowl of a stand mixer fitted with the paddle attachment or dough hook and mix for 1 minute to combine. Add ¾ cup lukewarm water and mix until the dough comes together in a ball, then mix for 1 additional minute to develop gluten. Add the egg whites and mix until fully incorporated, 5 to 8 minutes. Transfer to a lightly oiled bowl, cover, and set in a warm place for 1 hour to rise.

ROUGHLY chop the almonds and dried fruits but keep them separate.

PREHEAT the oven to 375°F.

THICKLY grease a 6 x 12-inch loaf pan with the shortening. It will seem like too much, but it will be absorbed as it bakes. Add the sesame oil to the bottom of the pan. Transfer the dough (which will be very runny) into the pan using a bowl scraper. Try to keep it in one piece.

BAKE for 15 minutes; it should be firmly set. Remove the pan from the oven (leave the oven on) and, using a small pastry ring or cutter, the tip of a pointed spoon, or the end of a dowel, punch a parallel series of 8 to 12 holes in the loaf. Be careful, as the dough will be quite hot! Fill each hole with the nuts and dried fruits, alternating them so that they stay separate. Pour the honey over the top and tilt the pan gently so the honey covers the surface and runs down the sides. Return the pan to the oven and bake for 20 additional minutes.

LET the pan cool on a rack for at least 10 minutes. Carefully (the honey will still be very hot) remove the pastry from the pan and transfer to a serving tray. The pastry can be served warm or you can allow it to cool. Sprinkle with confectioners' sugar and drizzle with the rose syrup just before serving.

Latticed Fritters

ZALABIYA

MAKES 8 TO 12   *These are the ancestors of* jalebi, *a very popular treat in modern India. When cooked properly, the batter forms delicately crunchy hollow spirals that burst with honey. Getting a batter that will give you the perfect texture can be a bit finicky. In fact, the original recipe, written over a thousand years ago, lists various causes for issues, ranging from bad yeast to watery honey to the weather, and all of these are true. Because it may require some effort to get the batter just right, I have built a testing method into the recipe. Keep trying and making small adjustments and you will get there!*

1 cup all-purpose flour, plus more if needed

1 tablespoon cornstarch

1 tablespoon instant or active dry yeast

Pinch of kosher salt

3 cups honey

About 3 cups vegetable oil or clarified butter for frying

COMBINE the flour, cornstarch, yeast, and salt in a bowl and whisk in ⅔ to ¾ cup water until it forms a smooth batter. Let the batter ferment at room temperature for 50 minutes. The fermented batter should show some frothiness from the yeast, but it should not be bubbly.

PLACE the honey in a saucepan, bring to a boil, and then leave on the lowest possible heat. Place the oil in a large pot with high sides (it should come about 2 inches up the sides) and heat to 325°F.

PLACE a small amount of the batter in a piping bag or squeeze bottle. Squeeze batter into the hot oil in a 2- to 3-inch-diameter spiral, with the rings overlapping slightly. When the fritter is just fried and the oil has

almost stopped bubbling, use a skimmer to remove it from the oil and transfer it to the hot honey. Let it absorb the honey for a few minutes. Allow the fritter to cool, but taste it when it is still warm. It should be thin, crispy, and entirely soaked through with honey. If it is leathery, the dough may be too thick or may not have fermented enough. Whisk in a bit of water and wait a few minutes. If the dough breaks apart, it is too wet or overfermented. Whisk in a bit of flour. Test and repeat! You will soon get into a rhythm, and the memory of your first perfect zalabiya will last forever. When you are satisfied with the batter, place half of it in the piping bag or squeeze bottle and make more fritters, then refill with the remaining batter.

THE END OF THE
GOLDEN AGE

AS THE CENTURIES PROGRESSED, the Abbasid caliphs began to find it difficult to maintain their enormous empire. Rising regional caliphates in Spain, Egypt, and Morocco fractured the once united empire and then, just as the Abbasids were facing an ideological crisis over the very meaning of the "Islamic World," the Mongols appeared on the scene.

Genghis Khan had already conquered huge swaths of Asia by the time his grandson Hülegü set his sights on Baghdad. And unfortunately for Baghdad, Caliph al-Mustasim, who reigned from 1242–58, was not exactly the guy you wanted running the show in the face of a ferocious Mongol army numbering in the hundreds of thousands. He didn't mobilize the army quickly enough, his arrogance led him to underestimate how much of a threat the Mongols really were, and he was generally considered to be a rather ineffective ruler—one who was more committed to having a good time than leading his people. On February 10, 1258, Hülegü's army poured into the city. It was a bloodbath. Hundreds of thousands died. Buildings burned. Bodies piled up in the streets. There is a famous saying about the Mongol invasion of Baghdad: "At first the Tigris River ran black with ink from the city's libraries and then red with blood."

The Abbasid caliphate never really recovered from this event. Caliphs increasingly became puppets, figureheads who merely held symbolic power, while court officials and various families with grand political ambitions manipulated the strings behind the scenes. But the Mongol destruction of Baghdad was also a huge blow to the psyche of the Islamic world at large. People simply could not comprehend how one of the most spectacular cities of the medieval world was brought to its knees by nomadic horsemen. Though the Mongols would help to rebuild the city they had destroyed, Baghdad was never the same. In 1650 when a traveling Frenchman passed through the city and happened to jot down a rough map of Baghdad; it depicted a town, not a metropolis, that looked eerily similar to the map the British drew when they occupied Baghdad—in 1917.

Just as the Islamic world preserved and advanced the knowledge of the ancients during the "Dark Ages" in Europe, so the roles would reverse as the Islamic Empire faced its own contraction. Slowly, the books and manuscripts that the Mongols had not destroyed trickled into Europe via merchants, travelers, and traders. Entering ports. Exchanging hands. Making their way into the private libraries of the elite and into the minds of the intellectual class, where ideas simmered and took hold before boiling forth and triggering the Renaissance, the rebirth of classical culture.

I wonder why we have forgotten this connection: That our collective knowledge is a universal human achievement, one that transcends borders, arbitrary boundaries on a map, or the fortified walls of one city. It belongs to all of us.

Sleepless, I watch the heavens turn
Propelled by the motions of the spheres;
Those stars spell out (I don't know how)
The weal and woe of future years.
If I flew up to the starry vault
And joined the heavens' westward flow
I would learn, as I traveled the sky
The fate of all things here below.
—*Caliph al-Ma'mun*

THE SIL

K ROAD

THE SILK ROAD

13TH to 16TH centuries

T HE SILK ROAD EMERGED over two millennia ago. As the Han Dynasty in China expanded its power westward, trade networks began to appear. They grew slowly at first, joining with desert roads in central Asia, routes tracing north from kingdoms in India. Then they began to shoot off rapidly from a central core, the Persian Empire, the Caucuses, Arabia, and beyond came together, linked by long tendrils expanding north and south, spreading over the Asian continent like the nervous system of a forest floor.

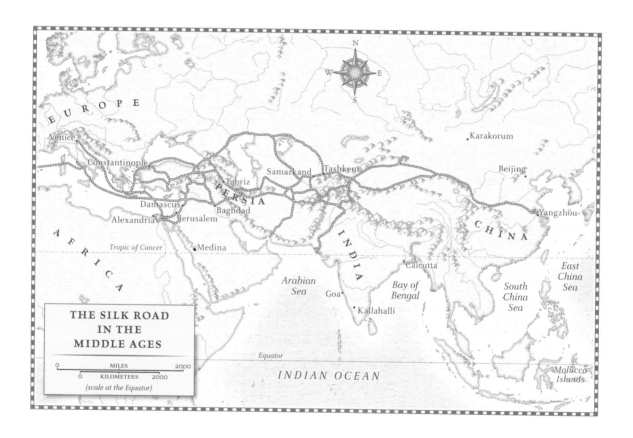

The name "Silk Road" is somewhat misleading. Rather than one long road stretching from China to Europe, it is in fact a series of both land and sea routes, spanning seven thousand miles from Asia through the Middle East, parts of North Africa, and into Europe. But the designation "Silk Road" also invokes a kind of folkloric journey through great kingdoms long gone and camel caravans whose tracks the sand has washed over a thousand times since they were first made.

In many ways, the Silk Road was the world's earliest highway, named in 1877 by the German explorer and geographer Ferdinand von Richthofen. Silk, of course, was traded along this route—not just as a luxury item but also as a kind of currency. Producing enough coinage to keep up with the expanding empires of the ancient world proved difficult, but a recognized luxury product like silk held universal value.

But it wasn't just silk being traded. Jade, porcelain, emeralds, rubies, amethysts, ivory, bronze, silver, gold, camels, horses, furs, and spices like pepper, cinnamon, nutmeg, cloves, ginger, and frankincense were all common goods along the Silk Road, as were enslaved people from East Africa, the Caucasus, and the Balkans. Slavic people were enslaved in such large numbers the word "Slav" is the origin of the very word itself. These captured people were bought and sold in slave markets from Baghdad to Prague, from Marseilles to Venice. As humans, both free and enslaved, moved across deserts and through mountain passes and oasis towns, their cultures and their religions were transported and diffused: the spread of Christianity, Buddhism, Islam, Hinduism, and Judaism are products of the Silk Road as well.

Few people traveled the full length of the seven-thousand-mile-long Silk Road (only a single Roman voyage made it to China in 166 CE). Rather, goods were moved from one city, town, or outpost to another, where they would be transferred to another merchant who would carry them on to the transfer point, the products changing hands dozens of times before reaching their intended destination. Most of these merchants had no idea what lay beyond their well-traversed path from point A to point B. Only rumors and tales provided any kind of information.

Goods made spectacular journeys to end up in what seem like the unlikeliest places. The king of France sprinkled pepper from India on his dinner plate. Merchants in Venice sold nutmeg from Indonesia to the city's wealthiest residents. Dirhams (the currency of the Islamic world) minted in Samarkand were circulated in Germany. Abbasid coins from

Baghdad were used in early medieval England. We may not think of the medieval world as being particularly connected, but it was. In fact, the world has been intricately connected for a very long time.

DISHES FROM INDIA

THE FOLLOWING RECIPES FOR Stuffed Eggplant and Jackfruit, Mango, and Bitter Melon Salad are drawn from the *Soopa Shastra*, from 1508, and the *Manasollasa*, from 1129. The *Soopa Shastra* was written on palm leaf and contained six chapters comprising 450 poems, or recipes. The author was Mangarasa III, the Jain ruler of what is now Kallahalli in modern-day India. These vegetarian dishes are redolent with the spices of southern India and reflect the ingredients that thrived in the climate there, such as jackfruit, coconut, and raw plantain. The *Manasollasa*, by King Someshvara III, goes far beyond cooking and covers topics from art to medicine as well. Indian cookbooks were often composed in classical verse, and instructions on the preparation of food were even included in works meant for the education of kings, manuals on topics as distinct as economics and the training of elephants!

Stuffed Eggplant

BHARVE BAINGAN

SERVES 4 TO 6 *Historically, eggplant is part of that interesting group of foods, including potatoes and tomatoes, that are today considered staples but were once thought to be poisonous in the West. In Italy, they were believed to cause insanity. This is a delicious dish that can be served whole or sliced as an appetizer. I have found that the best eggplant-to-stuffing ratio is obtained with smaller or narrower varieties like Japanese or Thai eggplant. A neat trick for coring Japanese eggplant is to use a power drill with a large bit, or just the bit itself. I have a bit in my kit just for this purpose.*

2 Japanese or 8 Thai eggplants

¼ cup unsweetened flaked coconut

¼ cup cooked chickpeas

¼ cup breadcrumbs

1 tablespoon peeled and minced fresh ginger

1 medium yellow onion, roughly chopped

6 fresh curry leaves, minced (available at most Indian markets)

2 tablespoons chopped fresh cilantro

1 tablespoon freshly ground black pepper

1 teaspoon ground cumin

2 teaspoons ground fenugreek

1 tablespoon sesame seeds

1 teaspoon sugar (raw sugar or jaggery is best)

2½ teaspoons kosher salt

4 tablespoons unsalted butter

Oil or ghee for frying

CUT off the tops of the eggplants and reserve them. Hollow out the bodies of the eggplants and set aside. Grind the flesh removed from the eggplants and the remaining ingredients except the butter and oil for frying in a mortar and pestle or pulse them in a food processor fitted with the metal blade, scraping down the sides a couple of times. Do not grind into a paste—you want some texture, especially from the coconut and onion. Melt the butter in a skillet over medium heat and cook this mixture, stirring occasionally, until fragrant and well combined. Stuff the mixture into the eggplants. For Japanese eggplants it is easier to use a piping bag.

REPLACE the tops of the eggplants and fix them in place with toothpicks. Fry the eggplants in several inches of oil or ghee until soft, then drain briefly.

Jackfruit, Mango, and Bitter Melon Salad

KATHAL, AAM, KARELE AUR KELE SALAT

SERVES 4 TO 6 *Fresh jackfruit is sweet and fragrant. It can be found in Asian or Indian markets, as can canned jackfruit, an acceptable alternative that may come in handy given the relatively short season. Bitter melon is sort of like jackfruit's evil twin; where one is soft, the other is delightfully crunchy, and where jackfruit is wonderfully sweet, bitter melon really lives up to its name.*

FOR THE SALAD:

1 bitter melon (you will probably use only about ¼)

2 tablespoons kosher salt

3 to 4 pounds ripe jackfruit (see Note)

2 ripe mangos (see Note)

2 ripe plantains, peeled and cut on the bias

FOR THE DRESSING:

2 tablespoons black mustard seeds

¼ cup sugarcane vinegar or apple cider vinegar

2 tablespoons sesame seeds

Large pinch of kosher salt

1 cup canola or olive oil

½ teaspoon sesame oil

Maldon sea salt for finishing

TRIM the ends of the bitter melon and cut it in half lengthwise. Scrape out the white center section, leaving only the green, making two long half moons. Cut these into slices about ⅛ inch thick. Place them in a bowl and toss with the salt. Cover, refrigerate for 30 minutes, then blanch in boiling water for 1 minute and shock in ice water. Drain and set aside. Cut the jackfruit flesh into ¼-inch strips.

TOSS the jackfruit and mango together in a bowl and add the bitter melon in small amounts. A good ratio is about equal parts jackfruit and mango and about one-eighth of that amount of bitter melon. Taste and adjust the ratio to your liking.

TO make the dressing, grind the mustard seeds in a mortar and pestle or spice grinder. Transfer to a medium bowl and mix with

the vinegar; let stand for 30 minutes. Whisk in the sesame seeds, salt, and the canola and sesame oils and dress the salad lightly. (You may not need all of the dressing.) Finish with Maldon sea salt to taste.

NOTE: Most places sell jackfruit in quarters or even smaller pieces. Jackfruit happens to be the world's largest fruit, so this is reasonable. You want only the luscious yellow flesh. First, pare away the thick white surrounding tissue and then remove the flesh with a spoon or your fingers. (You can also save the seeds, which are edible and can be roasted or even stewed in a curry.) The 3 to 4 pounds jackfruit in the above recipe will yield about 1 pound when prepared.

A mango has a wide flat pit. There are a number of ways to cut it, but I suggest imagining the seed in the center and cutting

parallel to it. You don't need to peel the mango. Next, take each of the mango halves and cut a crisscross pattern through the flesh and down to the skin. Now turn the sides inside out so they are convex and cut away the flesh from the skin. It should come away in convenient chunks. To get the remainder of the fruit around the pit, cut away the skin on the periphery, then pare the remaining flesh away from the pit.

DISHES FROM BAGHDAD

AS WE HAVE LEARNED from the previous chapter, Baghdad was one of the most important cities of the medieval world, so perhaps it is not surprising that it was also one of the epicenters of the Silk Road. It was a massive trading center, where rice and wheat from Egypt met spices from India, frankincense and myrrh from Arabia, fruit from Syria, silk from China, and slaves from Eastern Europe. While the city itself faced near total destruction when the Mongols invaded in 1258, Baghdad still retained symbolic importance for Muslims as the home of the old caliphs and retained cultural value for its art, architecture, literature, discoveries in the sciences, and, of course, its food.

These dishes come from *Kitab al-Tabikh*, or "The Book of Dishes." It was originally written in 1226 by Muhammad bin Hasan al-Baghdadi (d. 1239 CE). Out of all of the ancient cookbooks, this one perhaps most clearly underlines the difference between the highly literate East and decidedly less so West, where recipes were often no more than a list of ingredients without weights, measures, or instructions beyond "Cook it and serve it forth." It is fair to say that these Middle Eastern cookbooks were a solid four to five hundred years ahead of their Western counterparts, and a book like this one reads much like a French or English cookbook from the 1700s (except with a great deal more poetry, which is a wonderful thing).

Walnut-Stuffed Fish

SAMAK MASHWI

SERVES 4 TO 6 *A stuffed whole fish is a delicious and elegant centerpiece to a meal. Served on a bed of saffron rice, it will wow your guests, whether they are nobles visiting the court of Harun al-Rashid or Uncle Mike from Minneapolis.*

½ teaspoon kosher salt, plus more for seasoning fish

¾ cup well-stirred tahini

1 cup crushed walnuts

6 cloves garlic

1 teaspoon ground ginger

2 teaspoons sugar

1 tablespoon plus 1 teaspoon freshly squeezed lemon juice

1 teaspoon ground cinnamon

½ teaspoon freshly ground black pepper

1 teaspoon ground sumac

2 medium trout, butterflied (see Note)

Lemon wedges for serving

PREHEAT the oven to 400°F.

PLACE the ½ teaspoon salt and all the other ingredients except the fish and lemon wedges in a food processor fitted with the metal blade and process to a smooth paste, scraping down the sides periodically. Open the fish and liberally fill the bodies with equal amounts of the filling. Close the fish and tie with twine. It doesn't have to be fancy—you can simply wrap the fish in four or five turns of twine and tie it off. Don't tie too tightly, as you want to secure the fish for baking but not damage the flesh. Place the fish on a parchment paper–lined sheet pan and salt liberally.

BAKE in the preheated oven until the flesh is flaky, about 15 minutes. Let rest for a few minutes, then remove the twine with shears. Serve the fish with lemon wedges.

NOTE: You should be able to get your trout butterflied by your local fishmonger. I have seen many instructions on how to do this yourself, often with as few as four simple steps, which is roughly like explaining how to carve a nineteenth-century four-masted schooner from a block of wood with, "Simply cut away everything that doesn't look like a nineteenth-century four-masted schooner." That said, it's very satisfying to do this kind of finesse work yourself.

The basic method is as follows: You will need a thin, flexible, and genuinely sharp knife and a pair of kitchen shears. First, arrange the cleaned fish on your cutting board with the belly toward you. Remove the belly and back fins with shears or a knife. Now, the tricky part. Open the fish and cut through the ribs along one side of the spine. Cut only through the ribs, avoiding cutting through the fish. Do the same on the other side and open up the fish. Now, using your knife or kitchen shears, cut through the spine by the head, and then cut beneath the spine down the length of the trout. You should now be able to lift out the entire spinal column of the fish. Next, starting from where the ribs connected to the backbone, use the tip of your knife to separate the ribs from the flesh. It is better to do this with multiple small cuts, keeping your knife against the ribs. Separate the ribs all the way down to the belly and you should be able to pull the ribs away as a flap. Repeat this procedure on the other side. Run your finger down the center portion of the fish to feel for any tiny bones that were attached to the spine and remove them with fish tweezers. Gently check the rest of the fish to find any remaining bones and remove. You are a champion!

WHY SPICE?

OUT OF ALL INGREDIENTS, few appeal to a single sense—smell—as much as spice. And of all the senses, none is more evocative of emotional memory than smell; merely opening a jar of cloves is enough to conjure many Americans back to childhood and holidays. If there is something about the smell of spices that hints at faraway lands, it is important to remember that even for people of the Indian subcontinent, whose cuisine is redolent with cinnamon and cardamom, many of these spices still came across vast distances, some from islands in the Indonesian archipelago, to reach them. This was even more true for the peoples of China, and fantastically so for the Europeans, where nutmegs and black pepper were extraordinarily valuable. Equally fantastic, in the minds of those rich enough to afford them, were the magical and healing properties ascribed to spices that could balance their bodily humors and cure disease, and it is not hard to see why these rare commodities, prime among them the financial juggernaut of black pepper, dominated international trade and transport for millenia.

Walnut-Lamb Patties

MAQLUBA

MAKES 8 TO 12 PATTIES, SERVING 4 TO 6 *This is a lovely starter with layers of brightness from the citrusy sumac and lemon and subtle depth from the nuts and spices. It traditionally relied on a technique of braising until the water evaporated, which requires a very precise knowledge of the pan and the heat source, and pounding the lamb almost into a paste (using a food processor makes this process infinitely easier).*

¼ cup ground sumac

3 teaspoons kosher salt

1½ pounds lamb blade chops

2 lemons

1 tablespoon plus 1 teaspoon dried mint

2 teaspoons ground cumin

1 teaspoon freshly ground black pepper

1 teaspoon ground cinnamon

2 large eggs

1 cup walnuts

¼ cup sesame oil

¼ cup canola oil

COMBINE the sumac, 2 teaspoons of the salt, and 3 cups water in a medium saucepan and bring to a boil. Cover tightly and let stand for 20 minutes. Strain out the sumac through a fine-mesh sieve into a bowl and return the liquid to the pan; discard the sumac. Add the meat and simmer for 3 hours on medium-low heat until the bones are easily removed. Drain the meat and place on a sheet pan. Grate the zest of 1 lemon directly onto the meat, distributing the zest evenly. Squeeze the juice of ½ lemon over the meat and let rest, uncovered, for 30 minutes.

PROCESS the meat in a food processor fitted with the metal blade until it is almost a smooth paste. Add the zest of the other lemon, the remaining 1 teaspoon salt, the mint, cumin, pepper, cinnamon, and the eggs and pulse to combine. Add the walnuts and continue to pulse, paying close attention to the texture. You are looking for a texture resembling a mixture of peas and rice. Form small, thin patties of the mixture 2 to 3 inches in diameter.

COMBINE the sesame and the canola oils in a medium skillet. Heat over medium-high until shimmering. Fry the patties until browned and crusty on both sides, turning once, about 2 minutes per side. Serve hot.

BEYOND OCCIDENT AND ORIENT

PART OF THE SILK ROAD'S MYSTERY was that even though goods from the West ended up in the East and goods from the East ended up in the West, for a long time neither had any direct knowledge of the other. The distance didn't just seem insurmountable (traveling by camel only averaged seven to ten miles per day); what lay beyond was simply unknown.

There were a few individuals who lived to tell the tale of what it was like to make the entire journey from East to West or vice versa. The most famous is Marco Polo, the thirteenth-century Italian merchant who left Venice in 1271 and spent seventeen years at the court of Kublai Khan in China before returning home in 1295. Ibn Battuta, a fourteenth-century Moroccan, was just as illustrious a traveler; he developed serious wanderlust after making the *hajj* to Mecca and subsequently spent twenty years traveling through the Middle East, India, Asia, and North Africa, racking up some pretty impressive travel stories in the process. He worked as an ambassador for the sultan of Delhi for a decade, was kidnapped in Calcutta, traveled to the Mongol court in China, and was even given the honor of accompanying the Byzantine princess Euphrosyne Palaiologina from her husband's court in the Caucasus to her hometown of Constantinople to give birth.

For the West, there was a mythology surrounding the East. There were even rumors circulating in medieval Europe that there was a Christian King named Prester John who ruled over an entire kingdom of Christians, somewhere in the depths of the East. Prester John first entered the Western narrative when a letter, supposedly authored by him, found its way to the Byzantine emperor Manuel I Comnenus in 1165. In the letter Prester John claims to be descended from one of the Three Magi (the Three Wise Men present at the birth of Jesus), and he describes an earthly paradise filled with spices, lush gardens, and strange creatures. Prester John asked for help against the Muslim armies that were pressing in around his land from all sides. The letter was enough to inspire Pope Alexander III to send a mission east to find Prester John. For centuries missions left Europe hoping to find a lost Christian kingdom in Asia. None ever did and most were never heard from again—most likely because the king and the Christians they were actually searching for were not east but south, in the Christian kingdom of Ethiopia (but we'll get to that in Chapter Eight).

The idea that unparalleled wealth, sumptuous courts, and exotic luxuries all originated in the East is demonstrated in the opening lines of Euripedes's fifth-century BCE play *The Bacchae*, when Dionysus declares that he has arrived in Greece from "the fabulously wealthy east." We see it in Delacroix's nineteenth-century Orientalist paintings depicting excess and orgies of the flesh. But perhaps the writer Edward Said summed it up best when he wrote, "The Orient was almost a European invention, and had been since antiquity a place of romance, exotic beings, haunting memories and landscapes, remarkable experiences." (Though in recent times the West has seemingly destroyed its own constructed mythology of the East through its repeated wars of imperialism, reducing any preconceived notions of opulent grandeur to a new vision of bombed-out rubble.) The sheer size of space between the two served as a kind of shroud, veiling understanding of the other but also constructing a hazy perception that was rooted as much in myth and legend as it was fact.

For Westerners it is easy to fall prey to the trap that they have been conditioned to believe in: that the West is the civilized culture that went forth and conquered the Earth. But if we think of Alexander the Great, one of the greatest conquerors in history—he did not look to the West to expand his empire, to add to his riches, to embolden his power—he looked to the East. And centuries later, as Rome came to be one of the most dominant players on the scene, its power stemmed not from conquering Gaul or Britain but from its land grabbing in the East. We have forgotten that Rome, the supposed arbiter of Western civilization, was mostly based in what we would now call the Middle East.

And as much as the culture of the East certainly influenced the West, it truly went both ways. Greek tragedies written by giants of the Western world like Sophocles and Euripides were studied and read as far east as the Indus Valley in modern-day India. The *Aeneid* (a first-century BCE epic poem by Virgil) likely derived inspiration from the *Mahabharata* (an even earlier Sanskrit epic of ancient India). There is more influence at play that explains the similarities between ancient cultures that we have traditionally thought had no direct contact with one another.

If ancient India's *Ramayana* could actually have been inspired by Homer's *Iliad* and the *Odyssey*, these heroic stories that lie at the bedrock of so many cultures across Eurasia reveal that they are not flowers blooming alone in the desert but rather perennials growing in tandem, with hundreds of others, across a great and magnificent vine.

IN 1206 ON A FREEZING PLAIN IN CENTRAL ASIA, an enormous crowd gathered as arctic winds blew in from the northwest. A large black carpet had been laid out on the cold earth. A young man named Temujin stepped onto it. The carpet, with Temujin upon it, was lifted up above the heads of the crowd, as shamans rhythmically beat drums, chanting to the gods. The onlookers bowed to their knees. Temujin stepped off the carpet as Genghis Khan. The thousands watching turned their hands, palms up, toward the sky in unison and in so doing confirmed Genghis Khan's new status as emperor of the great Mongol nation.

Over the next fifty years the Mongols would carry out one of the bloodiest campaigns of territorial expansion in human history. They conquered lands and massacred people from the Pacific coast of Asia to the borders of Poland and Hungary. The Mongol Empire was one of the largest empires in history (only to be outsized by the British Empire in the twentieth century).

While Genghis Khan traditionally has the reputation of being the Mongol who carried out this infamous campaign, the truth is much of the credit is owed to his son and successor Ogedei. Genghis was ruthless and incredibly successful in expanding Mongol territory in a way it never had been before, but the campaigns of his lifetime focused mainly on China and northern Asia. It was Ogedei, who became the new supreme khan in 1229, who led the Mongols to conquer the Middle East, Russia, Korea, Pakistan, northern India, and parts of eastern Europe.

As the Mongols set forth from the steppes, the timing could not have been more perfect. The Islamic Empire, which had rapidly expanded from Arabia to include the entirety of the Middle East and North Africa in the centuries before, was beginning to crack under the pressure of maintaining such a massive territory. As fissures grew and the Islamic Empire broke into smaller caliphates and kingdoms, this weakness provided the Mongols with the ideal moment to sweep in.

The accounts of their violence are nothing short of legendary. Entire cities were decimated. Men, women, and children were murdered. Survivors wrote of babies being ripped from the wombs of their mothers, of mountains of human bones being mistaken for snow-capped hills, of stray cats and dogs being slaughtered, of the earth stained red with blood. Millions were killed.

But violence was not used the same way everywhere the Mongols went. As they pushed westward they would commit horrific atrocities in one town, with the specific goal of terrifying the next town over to open their gates and submit peacefully to avoid a similarly horrifying fate. And for the most part, this strategic violence worked. Interestingly, the spared (though there weren't many of them) were artisans, crafts makers, and intellectuals. And after the devastation was over the Mongols would typically invest heavily in the rebuilding of whatever town or city they had destroyed by injecting huge cash flows into the promotion and creation of local culture.

Perhaps the most important outcome of Mongol rule for the Silk Road was the Pax Mongolica, a period of peace, which ironically followed the previous period of unimaginable violence. Unification under the Mongol Empire meant looser trade restrictions, increased travel, a more seamless flow of goods, ideas, and peoples. The Pax Mongolica set the stage for the Silk Road's Golden Age. There was a saying at the time that the roads under Mongol rule were so safe, a virgin girl could walk with a basket of gold on her head from one end of the empire to the other, without being bothered. An exaggeration for sure, but you get the sentiment.

As so many empires throughout history have found, however, ruling over half the earth proves, well, tricky. Empires break down into smaller, more manageable territories, usually in the aftermath of a succession feud. The Mongol Empire proved no different and subsequently split into four different *khanates* or kingdoms, all ruled by various family members and descendents of Genghis Khan: the Golden Horde (Russia, Caucasus, and parts of eastern Europe), the Ilkhanate (basically the Middle East, ruled by our friend Hülegü from Baghdad's destruction in Chapter Two), the Chagatai khanate (the heartland of central Asia), and the Yuan dynasty (essentially modern-day China). While each khanate had its own unique culture, the Yuan Dynasty is particularly interesting, especially as it relates to food.

Kublai Khan, grandson of Genghis Khan, founded the Yuan Dynasty in 1271. It wasn't like the other khanates because, while it was Mongol by blood, in form and practice the dynasty took its cues from traditional Chinese culture. The food of the Yuan Dynasty became this new fusion cuisine, which is perfectly illustrated in the 1330 dietary guidebook, *Yinshan Zhengyao* or "Proper and Essential Things for the Emperor's Food and Drink," or as it has become more commonly known, *Soup for the Qan*. This dietary guide is essentially a fourteenth-century cookbook, or as close as we will get to one. It was written by the imperial dietary physician Hu Szu-Hui and presented to the emperor Ningzong, or Rinchinbal Khan (his Mongolian name), a descendent of the great Kublai Khan.

Soup for the Qan is a fascinating text because it incorporates foods from all the realms conquered by the Mongols, and seems to be a real attempt at creating a tangible record of Mongol culture as it stood in the early fourteenth century. The cuisine of the Mongols, prior to their conquering most of the known world, was pretty spartan. It consisted mostly of meat and milk, specifically mutton, lamb, and horse, and primarily fermented mare's milk, or *qumis*. But in *Soup for the Qan* we see recipes for dishes that are Chinese and Middle Eastern, and even influences from as far away as the Caucasus. While one could certainly still detect a heavy nomadic influence in the recipes (boiling meat was the preferred means of cooking), the food of the Yuan Dynasty now included the regional culinary influences of the formerly disparate places that had been unified by Mongol rule. Fusion cuisine was beginning to find its legs.

DISHES FROM MONGOL CHINA

THE FOLLOWING TWO DISHES, Lamb Spread and Turmeric-Colored Tendon, come from the fourteenth-century cookbook *Soup for the Qan*. The most important thing to understand about the sprawling Mongol empire, especially from a culinary point of view, is that it did not just conquer and steal—it mixed and matched, making the cuisine a fabulous mix of regional Chinese, Persian, and Turkic elements combined with their ancestor's nomadic diet of sheep's nose to sheep's tail and everything—yes, everything—in between.

Lamb Spread

ISHKANE

SERVES 4 TO 6 *I generally divide ancient recipes into two broad classes: those I read and immediately think, oh, this should be amazing, and those that I read, then reread, then think, well, I have no idea what this is going to taste like. This recipe falls solidly into the latter category, and though it was initially attempted with some apprehension, it yielded surprisingly satisfying results. Ishkane is a true syncretic dish. It was a spread enjoyed by the Mongol emperors on a flatbread that most closely resembles Indian naan. It also combines Chinese, Persian, and Turkic elements with Mongol staples. It has a fairly large number of ingredients, some of which can be a bit difficult to source, but I hope that is generally part of the enjoyment of these recipes. On that note, feel free to play around with the balance of ingredients to suit your own taste.*

8 ounces lamb leg or shoulder, cut into ½-inch cubes

Kosher salt

¼ cup lotus root cubes

3 tablespoons sheep-tail fat (available from halal butchers) or lard

½ large yellow onion, roughly chopped

¼ cup cooked sliced mushrooms (any mushrooms are fine—don't break the bank)

3 tablespoons roughly chopped cooked Swiss chard

1 tablespoon ground ginger

¼ cup finely chopped Chinese chives

2 hard-boiled egg yolks

1 tablespoon pickled ginger

1 ounce sweet melon pickle

2 tablespoons well-stirred tahini

2 tablespoons Chinese vinegar (black, red, or dealer's choice)

¼ cup crumbled feta cheese

BOIL the lamb in generously salted water until thoroughly cooked, about 15 minutes. Blanch the lotus root in a small saucepan of salted water and drain.

MELT the sheep-tail fat in a medium skillet over medium heat and cook the onions, seasoning with salt, until dark. Add the mushrooms and chard and continue to cook, seasoning with salt and adding the ground

ginger. Cook until most of the moisture has been released and evaporated. Cool completely, retaining all of the fat.

TRANSFER the mixture to a food processor fitted with the metal blade, add the remaining ingredients, and process to a relatively smooth paste, scraping down the sides of the processor bowl. Taste and adjust for salt.

Turmeric-Colored Tendon

JIANG HUANG JIAN ZI

SERVES 4 TO 6 *The combination of braising and batter-frying produces a richly flavored contrast in textures: crunchy on the outside and on the inside a dense chewiness that I adore. The most immediately obvious thing about this recipe is that it contains no turmeric. Instead, the name refers to the color imparted to the dish by the saffron, which was extraordinarily valuable at the time. The original recipe included both saffron and nuts from the gardenia flower; however the gardenia was intended only as coloring. If you're a stickler for authenticity, the nuts can be sourced through your local traditional Asian medical emporium, but I use annatto, an organic coloring agent that appears in many Latin cuisines. Beef tendon is sold in Chinese supermarkets, and you can buy it prepared if you want to skip the first step.*

8 ounces beef tendon	1 teaspoon fennel seeds
¼ cup soy sauce	Canola oil for frying
3 cinnamon sticks	Large pinch of saffron
5 star anise	1 cup all-purpose flour
1 teaspoon whole black peppercorns	½ teaspoon ground annatto
1 teaspoon Szechuan peppercorns	½ cup Chinese black bean paste
3 cloves	

CUT the tendon into 8 to 10 thick strips a few inches long (like double-thick bacon strips). Arrange tendon in a steamer basket or bamboo steamer over 3 cups water and the soy sauce and bring the liquid to a simmer. Place the cinnamon sticks, star anise, both types of peppercorns, the cloves, and fennel seed on top of the tendon and steam for 4 hours. Make sure to check the water level in the steamer periodically, adding more when necessary. Discard the spices.

PLACE several inches of canola oil in a heavy saucepan and bring to 325°F.

MEANWHILE, bloom the saffron in ¼ cup warm water for 90 seconds. In a medium bowl, whisk together the flour, annatto, bean paste, and bloomed saffron and its water. Slowly whisk in an additional ¾ to 1 cup water to create a batter a little thicker than the average burger joint milkshake. It doesn't have to be perfectly smooth—slight lumps actually add a bit of welcome texture.

DREDGE the tendon pieces in the batter and fry for a few minutes until crisp. Drain on a cooling rack and serve.

Bear Soup

XIONG TANG

SERVES 4 TO 6 *For the faint of heart or the budget conscious, beef or lamb stewing meat may be substituted for bear. If you can't find cubeb tailed pepper, another pepper can be substituted. In a pinch you can simply increase the quantity of black pepper, but including two different peppers adds to the complexity of the dish.*

½ cup canola oil

2 pounds bear meat, cut into 2-inch cubes

2 large yellow onions, diced

2 medium red onions, diced

2 tablespoons kosher salt

3 tablespoons cubeb tailed pepper

2 teaspoons asafoetida

1 tablespoon freshly ground black pepper

1 tablespoon plus 1 teaspoon ground turmeric

Large pinch of saffron

⅓ cup plus 2 tablespoons dark soy sauce, plus more as needed

THIS can be braised on the stovetop or in the oven. If you prefer to use the oven, preheat it to 300°F.

PUT 2 tablespoons of the oil in a large, deep pan with a tight-fitting lid on medium-high heat. Heat oil until smoking, then add the meat and cook until deeply seared. Remove the meat and reduce the heat to medium. Add the remaining ¼ cup plus 2 tablespoons oil to the pan and cook the onions with the salt until soft. Return the meat to the pan, add the remaining ingredients (except for the soy sauce), and cook until fragrant. Add 3 quarts water, which should just cover the meat, and bring to a boil.

COVER with the lid and either reduce the heat to a simmer or cook in the preheated oven until the meat is completely fork tender, about 3 hours. Adjust the final flavor of the broth with dark soy sauce to taste.

THE SPICE TRADE

PRESENT THROUGHOUT THE PAGES of *Soup for the Qan*, as seen in the previous recipes, is the use of spices—and lots of them. But the use of spices wasn't singular to the East. Western European cookbooks of the same period call for the use of just as many, if not an equal number of, spices. Spices were one of the main products traded along the Silk Road in part because there was a real demand for them in Christendom. Like a luxury sports car or a designer handbag today, spices like black pepper, cinnamon, cloves, nutmeg, and ginger were the luxury items of the day in medieval Europe. Kings, queens, and anyone who was anyone simply had to use these Eastern spices in the food they ate and served their guests because they demonstrated wealth. Spices were a status symbol.

The reason for their popularity is perhaps twofold. When Christian knights began to flood the Holy Land in the eleventh century in an effort to wrestle back Jerusalem from Muslim rule, entire generations of Europeans were exposed to a culture they had never known before. Among the many new facets of life in the "East" were new cuisines, many of which included

WOLVES AND OSTRICHES AND BEARS, OH MY!

THE MONGOL EMPIRE was many things, but perhaps most of all it was huge. Combined with the fact that it was "peaceful on pain of death" and vastly wealthy, it is not surprising that its cuisine drew elements from across its vast reach and often combined them into new dishes. Traditionally, the Mongols had been herdsmen, and so the most classic Mongolian dishes revolved around sheep—namely boiled sheep heads and organs cooked with hot stones in a sheep's stomach. The cuisine was transformed as the empire grew, however, and *Soup for the Qan* draws together delicately steamed crabs from China and aromatic spices from all along the trade routes. Some of these dishes, like *ishkane* (recipe on page 103), show obvious influence from one end of the empire to the other.

At the same time, imperial Chinese cuisine had a long tradition of rarity and exoticism, from jellied bear paws and bear stew to wolves's heads and pig embryos. This was a powerful ostentatious cuisine: they could have almost anything in the world, and they did.

the use of Eastern spices. When these crusaders finally returned home (if they did) they brought with them a taste for something new. Much like a twenty-first century traveler who ventures to a foreign land and experiences the scents and flavors of a new culture's dishes and wishes to recreate them back home, crusaders did the same. The origin story for mince meat pie (an English classic to this day, especially around Christmas time, and a recipe included in Chapter Five about the Tudors) finds its beginnings in the years after the crusades, when spices from the Holy Land—and their assumed religious connection by way of geography—found their way into an unlikely partnership in a new kind of holiday pie.

But another reason for the popularity of spices in Western Europe in the Middle Ages and their constant stream along the Silk Road during those centuries goes back to the idea of "Eastern exoticism" discussed previously. Europeans had little geographical knowledge of what lay beyond the Holy Land (this was the heyday of flat-earthers) and therefore spices that came from the East were inherently mysterious and exciting. They seemed to appear from a mystical place beyond the known world. In many ways, the allure of Asian spices in medieval Europe was not all that different from the popularity of "superfoods" found in the depths of the Amazon today.

Spices were ludicrously expensive, a gram's worth being equivalent to annual salaries. And the many steps involved in getting, say, nutmeg from the Maluku Islands off the coast of Indonesia to Amsterdam in the fourteenth century, was nothing short of extraordinary. But how were Venetian merchants who might purchase these spices in Alexandria, Egypt, with the intent of selling them back home, supposed to know how to judge the freshness and the quality of a product they had never seen in the wild?

There were all kinds of handbooks in circulation during this period that would help merchants with just such quandaries. According to one of these mercantile handbooks, black pepper could remain fresh for forty years, cardamom for ten years, nutmeg for seven years, while cloves would only remain fresh for one year. So, if you were purchasing pepper in Alexandria, chances are it was still good for consumption (unless you were being massively ripped off), but if you were purchasing cloves, you really had to know your product. And if you were part of the chain of traders moving cloves from Indonesia to the Mediterranean, you had to move very quickly against factors like weather, sickness, warfare, and unforeseen other obstacles.

DISHES FROM VENICE

THE RECIPES ON THE FOLLOWING PAGES, Apple Fritters for Lent and Cooked Wine, come from *Libro di Cucina*, written in 1430 by an anonymous Venetian, and are characterized by the same spices we have followed along this seven-thousand-mile path. While we may not immediately think of ginger, nutmeg, and cloves when we think of Italian cuisine, they were very much the dominant flavors in the fifteenth century, along with vinegar and verjus, the sour juice of unripe grapes.

THE MIRACLE SPICE!

PERHAPS ONE of the most maligned foods today is that pale demon: white refined sugar. But this was not always the case. In an age when far-off lands were truly believed to be inhabited by dragons and headless humans with faces on their chests, this spice (sugar was very much considered a spice) was a powerful force both in cuisine and in humoral medicine. Sugar is indigenous to the Indian subcontinent and its use there predates the rest of the bee-chasing, honey-sweetening world by millenia. There are sweets still consumed today in India that have not changed significantly in hundreds of generations. But it was not until the alchemy of the medieval Arabs that raw sugar, or jaggery, was refined into the white crystals so cheap and familiar today.

However, by the time this near magical substance reached Europe, through Venice, by a largely overland route covering thousands of miles and a secret chemical transformation, it had become incredibly valuable. Only the rich and powerful could prepare the recipes such as Apple Fritters for Lent (page 110), and the liberal use of sugar was conspicuous consumption of a high order.

Apple Fritters for Lent

FRITELLE DE POME PER QUARESSIMA

MAKES 8 TO 12 *These are meant to be the size of Catholic communion wafers, which are 1⅛-inch in diameter, but you can also leave them in larger slices. Braeburn and Jonagold apples work very well; Granny Smith are perfect if you prefer a little more tartness.*

FOR THE FRITTERS:

3 apples

Juice of ½ lemon

Large pinch of saffron

1¼ cups all-purpose flour

½ cup dried currants

2 teaspoons sugar

¼ teaspoon kosher salt

Canola oil for frying

FOR FINISHING:

3 tablespoons sugar

¼ to ½ teaspoon ground sweet spice such as ground cloves, ground cinnamon, allspice, or frankincense

TO make the fritters, peel the apples and cut them crosswise into slices about ¼ inch thick. Trim out the cores, then cut the apple slices into rounds with a fluted cookie cutter. Fill a large bowl with cold water, stir in the lemon juice, and place the slices in the water.

BLOOM the saffron in 1 cup water for 15 minutes, stirring occasionally. Put about half of the flour, the currants, the sugar, and the salt in a food processor fitted with the metal blade and pulse to combine. Add the 1 cup saffron water and pulse until incorporated. You can control the final texture of the currants to your taste. Add the rest of the flour and pulse

a few times to make a batter. How smooth you make the batter comes down to your personal preference. I prefer to barely incorporate the flour, as a slightly lumpy batter lends more texture to the final fritter.

PLACE several inches of canola oil a heavy pot with high sides and bring to 375°F. Drain the apple slices and pat them dry. Dip the slices in the batter and fry them, working in batches, if necessary, until crisp. Drain the fritters on a rack or paper towels. In a small bowl, combine the sugar for finishing with the sweet spice of your choice and sprinkle the mixture over the fritters. Serve hot.

Cooked Wine

VINO COCTO

SERVES 6 TO 8 *This recipe produces something like a cross between a port wine and a syrup. It is aromatic and intensely sweet and is a wonderful accompaniment to many modern dessert options, such as a British trifle, an Italian granita, or ice cream, or as the basis for a lovely cocktail.*

1 bottle (750 ml) strong red wine (such as Sangiovese)

½ cup honey

4 cinnamon sticks

4 pieces long pepper (see Note)

3 allspice berries

1 whole nutmeg

COMBINE all the ingredients in a medium saucepan. Bring to a simmer and cook until reduced by one-third. Allow to cool, then strain through a fine-mesh sieve into a glass or plastic bottle and serve at room temperature.

NOTE: Long pepper, is a truly wonderful spice that has notes of cardamom when whole and is closer to aromatic black pepper when ground. I hope to champion its culinary comeback. Cardamom can be substituted.

HEADING WEST

ALONG WITH THE SPICES that made their way west, travelers like Marco Polo, Ibn Battuta, William of Rubruck (a Flemish Christian missionary and explorer), and John of Montecorvino (also a Christian missionary, though of Italian origin) returned with tales of all they had seen in the East. When Marco Polo returned home to Venice in 1295, Venice and Genoa were at war with each other and Marco was taken captive by the Genoese before he even had a chance to set foot on land; he spent the next few years in prison. (Not exactly the homecoming one might be hoping for after twenty-four years on the road.) However, Marco Polo's own story only survives for us today because his cellmate was none other than Rustichello, a famous Italian writer, to whom Marco dictated his entire story. When Marco was released from prison in 1299 after the war, he faded into oblivion and was never taken seriously in his own lifetime. Supposedly, children used to chase him down the streets of Venice yelling, "Messer Marco, tell us another good story!"

The stories travelers told when they returned home perhaps seemed unbelievable because they were describing what no others had seen before. There was no way to verify anything, because there was so little knowledge of what was out there—in the beyond. But modern science and archeology have shown that Marco Polo had really seen and faithfully described the parts of the world through which he had traveled. On his deathbed, his last words were, "I have only told you half of what I saw."

As Marco Polo passed on from this world, ships laden with spices from the East continued to sail into Venice year after year. Creaking hulls packed with chests containing wildly expensive seeds, roots, and bark docked in the aquamarine waters of the floating city. The piles of spices were like piles of gold for those who traded in them, and as coins filled the pockets of men, this wealth in turn would come to fund the art of a new generation; a generation determined to bring the classical world back to life.

RENAISSA

NCE ITALY

RENAISSANCE ITALY
14TH to 16TH centuries

CHAPTER FOUR

RAVIOLI

SQUAB POTAGE OF FRESH FAVA BEANS

FLORENTINE-STYLE MEAT IN A BAKING DISH

GARNISHED (ARMORED) TURNIPS

OIL-BRAISED TUNA STEAKS

STUFFED LEG OF LAMB

*LOMBARD SAUCE, VERJUS GARLIC SAUCE,
BLACK GRAPE SAUCE*

CHERRY TORTE WITH ROSE PETALS

ZABAGLIONE

S HE BREATHED IN AS DEEPLY as her tight-fitting corset would allow, which was not much. She placed right foot in front of left foot, her dark satin dress swaying softly forward underneath her golden ermine-lined cloak. Deep folds of luxurious fabric kept her warm from the February chill that swept through the streets of Ferrara.

The crowd of five thousand, spectators who had amassed themselves to watch the wedding procession from the steps leading to the Great Hall of Della Regione, pulled their layers closer to their bodies in recoil to the icy wind.

Lucrezia Borgia climbed the final steps to the hall where her groom was waiting. She turned to smile at the crowd, a delicate wisp of blonde hair blew across her pale face. She beamed with the quiet determination of a woman who had lived far beyond her young years. Lucrezia was twenty-two. For a time, she would be the most powerful woman in Italy. She was the pope's daughter, after all.

Lucrezia Borgia and her relatives dominated the politics of Renaissance Italy alongside the infamous Medici, the Sforzas, the Orsini, and the Este families, among others. What is unique about the Borgias, of course, is that their power did not emanate from a dukedom, a kingdom, or a bank, but rather from the papacy and the Vatican itself. Lucrezia's father, Pope Alexander VI, sat at the very center of Christian power from 1492 until his death eleven years later.

As we turn back to Rome, almost a thousand years after the fall of the empire, Trajan's forum now lies in ruins. The taps of the bathhouses have run dry. But there is a spirit at work between the decaying remains of glories past and the new ones emerging. The Renaissance, the rebirth of classical civilization, is in full bloom.

The Borgias were intertwined with many branches of Renaissance life in Italy from their base in Rome. From their patronage of artists, to their chess moves in the games of Italian city-state politique, to their art of war—we find traces of their fingerprints on nearly every surface we can study from this period. Starting with the papacy.

We tend to think of the papacy and the Vatican as an austere yet ornate, surely celebate, definitely serious, and entirely male sphere. But during the reign of Alexander VI, the Vatican was like any other royal court in Europe, filled with intrigue and romance and violence. The women (daughters, lovers, family members) lived in a palace next door. They came and went through the Papal Palace via a connecting door in the Sistine Chapel. The halls of the Vatican were filled with children. Marriage alliances were proposed and broken. Declarations of war made. Truces sought. It wasn't just ecclesiastical decrees and the laws of God that were debated in these halls—politics were practiced here too.

What made the situation of the Italian city-states so different from every other European country during the Renaissance was the sheer power the papacy radiated out across the peninsula, preventing any form of unification. Italy, as a country or nation state, did not yet exist. In fact, "Italy," the country we know today, would not unify until 1871. However, for ease, we will refer to this geographic region as Italy.

So why Italy? Why did the Renaissance take off in Italy and not some other location? It is, as they say, all about location, location, location. The coastal position of many Italian cities baked seafaring into their DNA. Over the centuries places like Genoa and Venice grew from towns to cities to city-states (with their own unique government systems and legal codes). They thrived off the wealth their powerful merchant citizens brought home. Italy was, after all, one of the end points of the Silk Road. The merchants of Venice and Genoa, who brought spices, slaves, and luxury goods to Europe, delivered more than just the material. The works of the ancients, housed and expanded upon in cultural centers like Baghdad, found their way aboard wooden ships, bobbing across the seas and appearing on Italian shores.

There is something beautifully symbolic about the rebirth of classical civilization taking place where it was born; about Plato, Hippocrates, Galen, and Aristotle coming home to their metaphorical motherland to reintroduce themselves—after centuries abroad or shelved in the forgotten corners of dank monastery libraries.

Perhaps on the day one such manuscript arrived in the port of Naples, a wealthy member of the Cloth Guild went to pick it up from the merchant whom he had hired to find it. He would walk home from the merchant's port office, prized pages in hand, up the hill to his town house. At the kitchen table waiting for him would be a hot plate of ravioli made by his family's cook. Akin to dumplings from Asia, these tightly wrapped little parcels were filled with pork belly and capon, pepper from India, cloves from Indonesia, and ginger from China. Our worldly Neapolitan could not fully understand the lengths traveled to get the fillings for his supper, but he would understand they had come from far, far away. Topped with grated cheese and perhaps a little oil, each mouthful a burst of flavor from another world as he unfolded Avicenna's writings, holding in his hands what three hundred years earlier had sat upon a sun-drenched table in Baghdad.

Ravioli

RAVIOLI

MAKES 20 TO 30 RAVIOLI, SERVING 4 TO 6 *I see the roots of dishes twist and transform themselves through history: I can't help it. Here, from the anonymously authored pages of* The Neapolitan Recipe Collection, *in the late fifteenth century, we see dishes that we might begin to recognize. Filled pastas such as ravioli have a long history, although the term "ravioli" originally may have referred more to the size and shape of the dumpling than to any specific type of pasta. And we may have grown up hearing that Marco Polo brought pasta back to Europe from his travels in China, but pasta, regardless of shape, size, and whether made from wheat, rice, buckwheat, or any number of starches and grains, has been invented independently through history. The only constant is its singularly comforting satisfaction. If you do not feel like making fresh pasta, store-bought pasta sheets can be substituted.*

FOR THE PASTA:

2 cups coarse semolina flour (see Note)

½ teaspoon kosher salt

3 large eggs, beaten

1 teaspoon extra-virgin olive oil

FOR THE FILLING:

Kosher salt

4 ounces skinless pork belly, cut into 1-inch cubes

4 ounces chicken breast, cut into 1-inch cubes

6 ounces Parmigiano-Reggiano cheese

¼ cup ricotta

1 tablespoon roughly chopped fresh parsley leaves

½ teaspoon roughly chopped fresh mint leaves

¼ teaspoon roughly chopped fresh rosemary leaves

1½ teaspoons ground ginger

Pinch of ground clove

¼ teaspoon freshly ground black pepper

¼ teaspoon saffron

FOR FINISHING:

1 large egg, beaten

¼ cup grated Parmigiano-Reggiano

½ teaspoon ground ginger

½ teaspoon ground cinnamon

½ teaspoon freshly ground black pepper

2 quarts salted chicken stock

TO make the pasta dough by hand, whisk together the flour and salt and mound the flour on a clean work surface. Make a well in the center and add the eggs and olive oil. Using a fork or your fingers, gradually draw in the dry ingredients from the side of the well, then bring the dough together. It will still seem quite dry. Form it into a ball and begin to knead, pressing it down and forward with the heel of your hand in a folding motion and knead until smooth and supple, 8 to 10 minutes. If it is too dry, you can add a very small amount of water. Alternatively, place the flour and salt in the bowl of a stand mixer fitted with the dough hook or a food processor fitted with the dough blade. Mix or pulse to combine, then add the eggs and olive oil and mix or process until the dough comes together, 6 to 8 minutes for the stand mixer and less for the food processor. If the dough is too dry to form a ball, add ½ teaspoon of water at a time until it does. With either method, wrap the dough in plastic and let it rest in the refrigerator for 30 minutes.

BRING 4 cups salted water to a boil in a medium saucepan. Add the pork belly and cook on medium-high heat, 8 to 10 minutes, until cooked through. Remove with a slotted spoon and reserve. Add the chicken breast and cook 5 to 6 minutes, until cooked through. Remove with a slotted spoon and reserve.

ADD the cooked pork belly, cooked chicken breast, and all other filling ingredients to the bowl of a food processor fitted with the metal blade and pulse until entirely combined.

ROLL out the pasta sheets using a rolling pin or pasta machine and cut into 4-inch circles or squares using a cookie cutter. Put approximately 1 tablespoon filling in the center of each round or square. With a pastry brush, apply beaten egg around the edge of each piece of pasta and bring together to form a small pouch, carefully squeezing the edges tightly closed.

WHISK together the grated Parmigiano, ground ginger, cinnamon, and black pepper.

BRING the chicken stock to a boil in a medium saucepan. Add some of the ravioli and cook for 2 minutes. With a slotted spoon, transfer the ravioli to a bowl with a bit of the chicken stock. Cook the remaining ravioli in batches. Garnish with the Parmigiano and spice mixture.

NOTE: Semolina flour comes in two grinds, coarse and fine. Fine is used for bread and pastries and will make the pasta too gummy, so look for coarse semolina flour. All-purpose flour can be substituted.

Squab Potage of Fresh Fava Beans

POTAGIO DE FAVE FRESCHE

SERVES 4 TO 6 *For this delicate dish, from* The Neapolitan Recipe Collection, *it is important to use young fava beans that do not need peeling. Edamame can be substituted. A squab is a farm-raised pigeon and should be eaten medium or medium-rare. Renaissance Europe was largely a roasting, baking, and boiling culture, but I suggest searing the squab, for both taste and appearance.*

1 small bulb fennel

3 squab, semi-boned

1 teaspoon kosher salt

½ teaspoon freshly ground black pepper

1 tablespoon extra-virgin olive oil

3 tablespoons thinly sliced salt pork

8 fresh mint leaves, roughly chopped, plus more for garnish

1 tablespoon dry marjoram

½ teaspoon ground ginger

¼ teaspoon ground cinnamon

4 cups young fresh fava beans

CUT the fronds off the fennel bulb, roughly chop, and reserve. Trim the stalks off the fennel bulb, cut off the bottom, and cut the bulb in half. Make a V-shaped cut to remove the tough core of the fennel and then thinly slice against the grain. Finely chop the fennel.

SEASON the squab with ½ teaspoon of the salt and the pepper on both sides. Heat the oil in a medium saucepan over high heat. Working in batches, if necessary, sear the squab until deeply colored on both sides, about 3 minutes per side. Remove and reserve.

ADD the salt pork to the saucepan with just enough water to cover, about ¼ cup, and reduce the heat to medium-low. Let the water cook off, which will help render the fat and

deglaze the pan. Add the chopped fennel to the pan and cook until tender.

ADD 2 cups water to the saucepan with the 8 mint leaves, marjoram, ginger, cinnamon, and the remaining ½ teaspoon salt. Bring to a boil and add the squab breast sides up. Cook until the breasts are medium-rare to medium and somewhat firm to the touch, 3 to 5 minutes. They should read 125°F on an instant-read thermometer. Remove and reserve.

ADD the fava beans and cook, covered, until tender, about 20 minutes. Return the squab to the saucepan to reheat. Transfer to a serving bowl and garnish with the fennel fronds and mint leaves.

Florentine-Style Meat in a Baking Dish

CARNE IN TEGAMO ALLA FIORENTINA

SERVES 4 TO 6 *This is a rich, fabulous braise with the type of sweet and sour taste that we now associate with Asian or Persian cuisine, but that was very much the preferred flavor profile of the lucky Europeans who could afford it during the Renaissance. The recipe comes to us from* The Neapolitan Recipe Collection *(which deems it Florentine) and it makes use of a combination of wine and verjus (the juice of unripe grapes) combined with a gentle richness from spices and dried fruits. Verjus was often used in place of vinegar in this period. This dish can be prepared the day before, refrigerated overnight, and then reheated for even deeper flavor.*

1 medium parsley root

1 medium yellow onion

Kosher salt

2 pounds veal shank, beef shank, or beef short ribs

1 tablespoon canola oil

2 cups red wine

2 cups red verjus

1 cup veal stock

1 cup raisins

1 cup prunes

½ teaspoon whole cloves (about 15)

6 cinnamon sticks

1 teaspoon whole black peppercorns, plus 1 teaspoon freshly ground

Large pinch of saffron

2 tablespoons turbinado sugar

½ teaspoon ground ginger

½ teaspoon ground cinnamon

PREHEAT the oven to 325°F.

PEEL the parsley root and cut it into thick sections. Cut the onion into thick half-moon slices. Salt the meat aggressively. Add the oil to a heavy casserole dish with a tight-fitting lid and place over high heat until the oil is shimmering. Add the meat to the pan and brown deeply on both sides, 3 to 5 minutes per side. Add the onion and parsley root and cook until the onion is just softened, stirring often. Add the wine, verjus, and veal stock,

some additional salt, and the raisins, prunes, whole cloves, cinnamon sticks, whole peppercorns, and saffron.

BRING to a boil and cover with the lid. Transfer to the preheated oven and cook until the meat is fork tender, 45 minutes to 1 hour. Transfer to a serving platter or shallow bowl, or leave the braise in the casserole. Whisk together the sugar and ground spices and sprinkle over the meat. Serve hot.

RECOVERING THE DEAD

FERDINAND GREGOROVIUS, A HISTORIAN who wrote seminal works on medieval Rome, once described Lucrezia Borgia as "the most unfortunate woman in modern history"—a rather bold statement considering the breadth of human misery and depravity in the last five hundred years. But it would be fair to say that how Lucrezia has been remembered is rather unfortunate.

Her father, Rodrigo Borgia, became Pope Alexander VI in 1492. This is already confusing because, well, a Catholic pope isn't supposed to have children. Far be it for the pages of a cookbook to ruin a successful two-thousand-year-old ruse, but it's true: popes most certainly have procreated over the centuries; some just made more of an effort to conceal it than others. Alexander VI made no effort to conceal his children. In fact, he not only recognized them but also bestowed titles and lands and fortunes upon them. He was head of the Christian Church, God's chosen representative on Earth, after all. Who could tell him what to do?

Pope Alexander VI's four favorite children were born to him by Vannozza dei Catanei, with whom he had a long relationship. Lucrezia and her brothers, Cesare, Gioffre, and Giovanni, would benefit from their father's ascension—and suffer terribly. Like any ruler, Alexander VI had great hopes for the future of his dynasty. His children's marriages were strategic. Lucrezia, known for her beauty and smarts, was a particularly valuable chess piece.

Three times her father arranged marriages for her. The first ended in divorce when her father decided the groom was no longer useful. Her brother, Cesare, had her second husband killed. Luckily for her third husband, he managed to outlive Lucrezia and his murderous in-laws. Lucrezia has gone down in the history books as one of the most cunning and evil femme fatales in Western history; accused of incest with not only her brother, Cesare, but also her father, she is said to have participated in outrageous orgies at the Vatican, among other crimes. The rumors of incest, the frequent murders that always seemed to trace themselves back to the Borgia doorstep, and their so-called unchristian behavior created a reputation that shrouds the family to this day.

But if we comb through the chronicles, poems, and letters of the day, beyond the surface-level stereotypes, a portrait of a very different Lucrezia Borgia appears: that of a young woman who was manipulated and used as a pawn by her father and brother for the advancement of their own power.

After she finally left her family in Rome to live with her third husband, Alfonso d'Este, in Ferrara, records show a very different portrait. They reveal her good deeds. Her piety. Her generosity to the people of Ferrara. She was finally free from the corrosive grip of her family.

ON DECEMBER 29, 1479, LORENZO DE' MEDICI attended the execution of a man named Bernardo Bandini Baroncelli in the Palazzo del Bargello in Florence. We must imagine he felt some sense of justice, revenge, and relief as the body of Bandini swayed from the noose, Bandini's long cloak hanging over his limp feet. Bandini had been involved in a plot to overthrow the Medici, resulting in the murder of Lorenzo's brother Giuliano in the Duomo of Florence on Easter Sunday. Lorenzo himself only narrowly escaped with his life. The rest of those involved in the plot had been executed; the search for Bandini sent Lorenzo's deep network of affiliates all the way to Constantinople, where the last conspirator was found, arrested, and extradited back to Florence. Now the entire city watched him die.

We know of two other people who were in the crowd that day. One of them was Niccolò Machiavelli. Just ten years old, he observed power being enacted—men deciding who lives and who dies. This event made such an impression on him that he would write about it many years later in his *Florentine Histories*. Also present that day was Leonardo da Vinci. At age twenty-seven, he may have been more seasoned to the temporality of life than young Machiavelli, but even he was moved to record this day; he drew a sketch of the dangling corpse, a visual legacy of what was, in reality, not a particularly extraordinary day at all.

A person executed in a public square: How many times has this happened throughout history? Hundreds of thousands of times? Millions? And yet we know about this particular day because three of the men present became legendary. But who else was in the square that day? What did the woman who ran the neighboring tavern think? Or the children playing in an alley nearby who would not grow up to reach Machiavellian levels of fame? Surely this event made an impression upon others present. But we will never know what they thought or how they felt because they do not exist to us.

And herein lies one of the biggest conundrums of trying to write history. The records we have—the voices that have survived—are just a tiny fraction of those who were present at the time. The poor, which was most of the population of the world really, are written about in large sweeping generalizations. The stories of women exist largely as addendums to the men in their lives. It's hard work to recover the voices of the voiceless. It is even harder when we don't know their names.

One name we should be thankful to have is Christine de Pizan. She was born in Venice in 1364, and spent most of her life in France after her father became the court astrologer for King Charles V. At fifteen, she was married to a young court notary named Etienne de Castel, and they appear to have been incredibly happy. She would later write that these early years of her life were ones of domestic bliss. But then in her early twenties, tragedy struck; her father and husband died one after another. And so at twenty-five, she found herself a widow with three young children and an ailing mother, and no financial means to take care of her family.

We would not be able to blame Christine if she had chosen to remarry and find a man to take care of her and her family. But Christine chose an entirely different path for herself, leading to an extraordinary and brilliant life. She got a job.

To be fair, she had a rather valuable skill: she was literate (thanks to her father) at a time when most people could not read or write. She found employment as a copyist in a workshop where books were produced. And as she toiled away at her office job during the day, in her time off, she began to write her own poetry—she was a writer with a day job.

Her work deals with themes of love and loss and, because of her father's former position at court, her writing became known in elite circles. Patrons and sponsors began to pay her for her poems. As Christine developed as a writer, the content of her work began to shift from poetry to social and political commentary. Yes, she still wrote about love, but from a feminine perspective. It's hard to overstate how remarkable this was. We're not just talking avant-garde art here; we're talking about the equivalent of Leonardo da Vinci designing a submarine five hundred years before they even existed.

Christine dismantled the way men wrote about women in courtly love stories of the time; she argued that the way women were described actually vilified them, which led to her involvement in what was essentially the medieval equivalent of a Twitter feud. Christine accused Jean de Meun, author of *Roman de la Rose*, one of the most popular books of the period, of being a misogynist—this, in the fourteenth century! Some pretty fiery letters were exchanged back and forth, in which de Muen attacked her and she held her ground and fought him right back. All of the letters were made public. Christine became the first woman of the period (of any period?) to call out a renowned intellectual man for making denigrating, disparaging, and sexist remarks against women.

In her most famous work, *The Book of the City of Ladies*, Christine imagines an alternative society for women—one without men—where they could find refuge from the abuse of a sexist world. The city is populated with great women of the past and present and built upon a foundation of "reason." Her last work, a biography of Joan of Arc, was the only piece written about Joan while she was still alive. It was completed in 1429; Christine may have died the following year. But we do not know for sure when she died. Even a famous woman of the day can vanish quickly from the historical archives. Perhaps if she had remarried, her death would have been recorded in her husband's family records. But like ink bleeding off wet paper, a woman's life rarely holds to the page.

Lucrezia Borgia, on the other hand, is a woman about whom we know a great deal. And despite being bandied about from marriage to marriage, she did have moments when she exercised incredible power. Just before her marriage to Alfonso d'Este, her father chose her to take his place while he was visiting the Papal States, literally putting her in charge at the Vatican. She was to open all correspondence concerning affairs of the state, finances, and diplomacy—though not correspondence concerned with ecclesiastical affairs. (I suppose the cardinals wouldn't sign off on that one.)

With finesse and confidence, Lucrezia installed herself in the papal apartments and took charge of the most powerful seat in Christendom. I like to imagine her working late into the night, poring over letters of state by candlelight, devising brilliant strategic responses to the sovereigns of Europe as she sipped red wine between alternating bites of a rich and hearty stew.

WHILE LUCREZIA BORGIA MAY have been unfairly remembered, her brother Cesare's legacy as a monster is no exaggeration. He was brutal and he was ruthless. Cesare began his career reaping the benefits of extraordinary nepotism as a cardinal, an ecclesiastical position that didn't really fit his five-year plan. Eventually released from the clergy by his father, he became the duke of Valentinois and ultimately a pseudo-military commander on behalf of the Borgia family, with aspirations of creating his own kingdom and uniting Italy. Cesare certainly had the name for a man intent on bringing back the Roman Empire. The inspiration for Machiavelli's *The Prince*, he is perhaps best summed up by Caterina Sforza, daughter of the noble Milanese family, who wrote of her year as Cesare's prisoner in 1500, "If I could write anything on it, I would stupefy the world."

You would not be wrong to assume the Renaissance must have been a period of peace. How could all this art have sprung from a time of war? But it did. For most of the Renaissance the Italian city-states were at war: with each other, with neighboring countries. Armies constantly roved the countryside. Towns and cities were regularly sieged. Treaties and truces were temporary. It was a violent time.

As Cesare raped and pillaged his way through northern Italy in the early years of the sixteenth century, he employed none other than Leonardo da Vinci as his master of war. Da Vinci is known for many things: painting the *Mona Lisa* and the *Last Supper*; designing a flying machine and a submarine; his studies on anatomy, engineering, and astronomy. He was a painter, a sculptor, an architect—a true Renaissance man. But he also created weapons of war for Cesare Borgia.

His notebooks, all written in his signature backward script, are filled with descriptions and designs for weapons. In one passage he describes how to utilize a bomb to inflict maximum destruction when invading a town:

> Again if you discharge a small bombard in a courtyard surrounded by a convenient wall, any vessel that is there or any windows covered with cloth or linen will all be instantly broken; and even the roofs will be somewhat heaved up and start away from their supports, the walls and ground will shake as though there was a great earthquake, and the webs of the spiders will all fall down, and the small animals will perish, and every body which is near and which is possessed of air will suffer instant damage and some measure of loss.

This coming from the man who described war as, "the most brutal madness," and who was a practicing vegetarian because he was deeply troubled by the butchering of animals (to be a vegetarian in the Middle Ages was very rare; this was a time when most people were just happy to have food to eat). Da Vinci's lived experience, contrasted with his legacy as a "Renaissance man," makes him a perplexing character. But I suppose humans are complicated. Beliefs and actions don't always align. Perhaps he was forced to work for Cesare Borgia? Or maybe I'm just searching for an explanation that doesn't exist.

While we will likely never know the interior workings of Da Vinci's mind, we do know he spent a good deal of time with another giant of the Renaissance at Cesare's court at Imola in 1502: Niccolò Machiavelli.

Author of the famed political treatise *The Prince*, Machiavelli worked for many years as an official in the Florentine government, writing numerous works on political science and philosophy during his lifetime. Machiavelli was sent to Cesare's court at Imola essentially to spy on him, though under the guise of "diplomacy." He had a miserable winter there. He found Cesare sinister and evil. The weather was bitterly cold, he got ill, and he felt like the whole trip was for nothing.

I wonder what Da Vinci and Machiavelli talked about that winter in 1502. Did they lament their time with Cesare? Did they talk about their lives in Florence? Did they ever make the connection that they had both been present at Bandini's execution so many years ago? Perhaps one chilly evening they shared a plate of roasted turnips, spiced with whatever was available. An accommodating dish for Da Vinci's diet and Machiavelli's delicate constitution.

Garnished (Armored) Turnips

RAPPE ARMATE

SERVES 6 TO 8 *This is a rich, heavy dish, similar to a sweet and heavily spiced gratin. It comes from one of the most famous cookbooks of Renaissance Italy,* Opera dell'Arte del Cucinare *by Bartolomeo Scappi, published in 1570. It is a massive, well-organized tome with about one thousand carefully explained recipes, as well as advice for building and organizing a kitchen. It was one of the first modern cookbooks in the West and by far the most impressive. I say in the West because, as we have seen, they were doing most of this in Baghdad five or six hundred years earlier! These sweet and savory turnips make a perfect side dish for a meat course and play well with the sharper sauces, like Lombard and Verjus Garlic Sauces (page 139).*

4 pounds turnips

Kosher salt

2 tablespoons sugar

2 teaspoons freshly ground black pepper

1 teaspoon ground cinnamon

½ teaspoon freshly grated nutmeg

1 stick (8 tablespoons) unsalted butter, melted, plus more unmelted for the baking dish

4 cups Parmigiano-Reggiano shavings

PREHEAT the oven to 350°F.

PEEL the turnips. Bring a pot of lightly salted water to a boil over high heat. Add the turnips, return to a boil, cover, reduce the heat to medium-low, and simmer until just soft enough to pierce with a paring knife, about 10 minutes. Shock in cold water to cool. Cut the turnips into slices about ¼ inch thick or a little less. The thinner the turnips are sliced, the richer the dish will be.

WHISK together the sugar, ½ teaspoon salt, and the spices. Heavily coat a deep 10-inch round or 9-inch square baking dish with butter. Arrange a layer of turnip slices like shingles in the bottom of the pan, overlapping slightly. Brush on a generous amount of the melted butter and sprinkle evenly with some of the sugar and spice mixture. Cover the turnips with a layer of cheese shavings. Continue adding layers of turnips, butter, spices, and cheese until all the ingredients are used up, ending with a layer of cheese on top. Bake until golden brown, 25 to 30 minutes. Let the turnips cool for 10 minutes before serving.

Oil-Braised Tuna Steaks

TONNO ALL'OLIO

SERVES 4 TO 6 *The elegant preparation of this fish dish from Scappi's* Opera dell'Arte del Cucinare *allows for great control of the cooking process. It works equally well for diners who enjoy their tuna cooked all the way through and those who like it rare. The original recipe calls for grape must, a very common sweetener in the period, made from the skins and solids left over from crushing grapes for winemaking, which were then reduced further to concentrate the sugars. Here, I substitute reduced grape juice.*

4 cups grape juice

2 cups white wine vinegar

2 cups white wine, such as Pinot Bianco or Verdicchio

3 cloves garlic, minced

3 tablespoons freshly ground black pepper

¼ cup freshly toasted and ground coriander

2 teaspoons kosher salt

2 pounds sushi-grade tuna steaks

4 to 5 cups olive oil

REDUCE the grape juice to 1 cup in a medium saucepan over medium heat. Whisk this reduction with the vinegar, wine, garlic, pepper, coriander, and salt. Transfer the reduction to a bowl, add the tuna, cover with plastic wrap, and refrigerate for 2 to 3 hours.

PREHEAT the oven to 325°F.

PLACE 2 cups of the marinade in a baking dish (reserve the remaining marinade), add the tuna, then add enough olive oil to cover the tuna completely. Roast in the preheated oven for 20 to 25 minutes, depending on

the degree of doneness desired. It is a good idea to periodically check the tuna with an instant-read thermometer: 125–130°F for rare, 130–140°F medium-rare, 140–145°F for medium, and 150°F for well-done.

IMMEDIATELY remove the tuna from the oil when it reaches the desired temperature or is a few degrees below it. Discard the cooking liquid.

WHILE the tuna is cooking, bring the remaining marinade to a boil and cook for 5 minutes. Serve the tuna with this sauce.

Stuffed Leg of Lamb

A EMPIRE UNA SPALLA, O ALTRO MEMBRO

SERVES 8 TO 12 *This recipe from Anonimo Toscano, an anonymous source, is not "stuffed" in the sense we think of today but "forced," meaning the meat is minced with other ingredients and reshaped around the bone and then encased in caul fat and grilled or roasted. It is a delicious showpiece at the center of a grand meal and pairs beautifully with the powerful sauces that follow. If you cannot source the caul fat, the recipe will still hold together but will lose some of its drama and unctuousness. All three sauces that follow match well with this dish; choose one or serve all three.*

1 (5- to 6-pound) leg of lamb

FOR EACH 1 POUND OF LAMB MEAT:

8 ounces skinless pork belly, cut into ½-inch cubes

¼ cup fresh parsley leaves

2 teaspoons fresh thyme leaves

¼ cup fresh mint leaves

¼ cup fresh sage leaves

1 tablespoon freshly ground black pepper

1 tablespoon ground ginger

1½ teaspoons ground cinnamon

½ teaspoon saffron

¼ cup ricotta

1 large egg

2 teaspoons kosher salt

2 to 3 pieces caul fat, to wrap completely

Canola oil for pan

FOR THE SAUCE
(CHOOSE ONE OR SERVE ALL THREE):

Lombard Sauce (page 139)

Verjus Garlic Sauce (page 139)

Black Grape Sauce (page 140)

PREHEAT the oven to 350°F.

FIRST, remove and save the central bone from the lamb leg. You are going to mince the meat, so you do not have to use any fancy techniques—just cut in straight to the bone, then peel the meat away with small cuts using the tip of your knife. Alternatively, you can go full swashbuckler and cut away the meat in large chunks. Regardless, reserve the bone and cut the meat into roughly 1-inch pieces. Weigh the meat and scale the ingredients accordingly.

TO prepare the lamb meat, put the lamb in a large bowl and mix in the pork belly, herbs, spices, ricotta, egg, and salt. Working in batches, mince the mixture in a food processor fitted with the metal blade. Line a roasting pan with oiled parchment. If you have a roasting rack, place it in the pan. Spread the caul fat on a work surface. Spread about half of the meat mixture thickly on the caul fat, leaving 1 to 2 inch margins around the edge. Place the bone in the center, with a few inches projecting out one end of the caul fat. Spread the other half of the mixture over the bone and form the mixture into the original shape of the leg. Bring the caul fat up around the sides to encase the "leg." Tie it in place with butcher's twine.

TRANSFER to the rack, if using, or place on top of the parchment in the pan. Roast in the oven until the internal temperature at the deepest part reaches 165°F on an instant-read thermometer, about 1½ hours. Serve with your choice of the sauces.

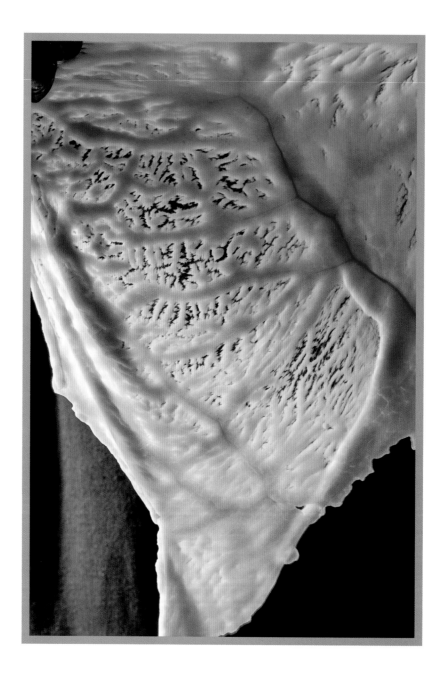

Lombard Sauce

SALSA LOMBARDA

MAKES ABOUT 1 CUP *This is a sharp, vegetal sauce similar to a chimichurri or gremolata. It pairs well with rich meat dishes and is also a great counterpoint to grilled or roasted vegetables.*

½ cup fresh parsley leaves

2 tablespoons chopped fresh mint leaves

2 tablespoons chopped fresh sage leaves

2 teaspoons fresh thyme leaves

1 leaf Swiss chard

3 cloves garlic

1 teaspoon freshly ground black pepper

¼ cup toasted breadcrumbs

½ cup white wine vinegar

¼ cup white grape juice

1 teaspoon kosher salt

ROUGHLY chop all the herbs and chard. Combine these and the remaining ingredients in a blender and blend until smooth. Let sit for 30 minutes to allow the flavors to marry. Taste for salt and acidity. If it is too sharp, add a little more grape juice. The sauce should be herbaceous, bright, and lingering.

Verjus Garlic Sauce

AGRESTO CUM AGLIO

MAKES ABOUT 2 CUPS *Verjus is fresh and light, which makes it a wonderful change from vinegar in sauces and dressings. This quality is brought out further in this sauce by the licorice notes of the fennel and the wonder of fresh basil.*

6 cloves garlic

½ cup chopped fresh fennel bulb

1 cup fresh basil leaves

1 teaspoon freshly ground black pepper

1½ cups white verjus

½ teaspoon kosher salt, plus more to taste

ADD all ingredients to a blender and blend until smooth. Refrigerate for 30 minutes and taste to adjust salt.

Black Grape Sauce

SAPORE DE UVA NEGRA

MAKES 1 TO 1½ CUPS *This is very much the flavor of the late Middle Ages and Renaissance. People are often surprised when I liken these flavors to those of Persian and Near Eastern cuisine, but the combination of sweet, sour, and aromatic spices makes this sauce a perfect example.*

1 pound seedless black grapes

⅓ cup breadcrumbs

½ cup grape juice

1 cup red verjus

1½-inch-piece fresh ginger, peeled and cut into planks

1 cinnamon stick

5 whole cloves

¼ teaspoon freshly grated nutmeg

Small pinch of kosher salt

ADD the grapes and the breadcrumbs to the bowl of a food processor fitted with the metal blade and pulse until fairly smooth, working in batches if necessary. Transfer to a large bowl and refrigerate for 1 hour. Drain through a fine-mesh sieve into a bowl, pressing out as much liquid as you can with the back of a large spoon or ladle. Combine this liquid, the grape juice, verjus, ginger, cinnamon stick, cloves, and nutmeg in a medium saucepan. Bring to a boil and add a small pinch of salt for balance.

LET the sauce reduce over medium-low heat until it coats the back of a spoon, about 25 minutes, then strain through a fine-mesh sieve into a storage container and discard the solids.

CHEFS, BANKERS, ARTISTS, AND DREAMERS

THE DISCERNING READER MIGHT HAVE NOTICED that this chapter, though about Italian food, does not contain one single tomato. This is not a stylistic choice, but a reflection of Italian cuisine as it really was at the time. There were no tomatoes to be found in sauces, stews, or salads because tomatoes did not yet exist in Europe. Tomatoes come from the Americas, Mexico specifically, where they were domesticated and farmed. Even when the Spanish conquistadors brought tomatoes back to Europe in the early sixteenth century they were largely grown as decorative plants and deemed unsafe to eat. It would be another century or so before they entered the kitchens of Italy.

Clearly Italian food has changed in the last five hundred years. And not just in terms of ingredients. Taste itself has changed. Wealthy medieval Europeans adored spices and lots of them, driving the spice trade and fueling the economies of city-states such as Genoa and Venice. Spices that today we might associate with desserts or sweets, like cinnamon, nutmeg, or cloves, were added to savory main course dishes with gusto—upon meats and in stews, with fish and vegetables. The resulting flavor for the modern dinner is different, yet familiar. Scents and flavors appear in unexpected places.

This period also sees a sort of Renaissance of cookbooks, or culinary manuscripts. These recipe collections were not written to be used in the kitchen, but to be consulted by the head of the household, who would look to these manuscripts for menu planning or even to consult as a dietary manual. Galen's humors were still the foundation theory for achieving good health. Sometimes a wealthy individual would commission a cookbook as a kind of living record of the types of dishes served in their home. Cooks would not regularly look to these recipes for guidance, the dishes and their methods would have already been committed to memory during their training and apprenticeship.

Perhaps the most famous cookbook of the Renaissance was Maestro Martino's *Libro de Arte Coquinaria*, "The Art of Cooking," which was published in 1465, the first-ever cookbook to be printed by a printing press. Martino's cookbook represents a culinary transition from the Middle Ages to the Renaissance. There are descriptions of how a kitchen should be set up; more details about weights and measures; and the recipes are sequenced logically, as a meal would be, in contrast to earlier hodgepodge collections.

From Martino's newly established tradition, we see more cookbooks emerge, such as *De Honesta Voluptate*, by Bartolomeo Sacchi (also known as Platina), from 1474, and the later fifteenth-century anonymous work now known as *The Neapolitan Recipe Collection*. Bartolomeo Scappi's *Opera dell'Arte del Cucinare* (known in English as "The Opera of Bartolomeo Scappi"), which was published in 1570, builds on Martino's tradition: highly organized and specific, it provides actual reasons for why things should be done a certain way. These books represent a kind of written culinary tradition in the West that had previously only been seen in the caliphal kitchens of Baghdad and the Middle East.

While these cookbooks demonstrated the food of the elite, lower and middling classes also had their own traditions and practices. Where one would need a large kitchen with numerous staff to execute most of the fantastical dishes of Scappi or Martino, those who had smaller urban kitch-

ART, ARTIFICE, AND FIRE-BREATHING PEACOCKS

HAVE YOU EVER SEEN a roasted pig with an apple in its mouth? It was probably in a movie or a cartoon, as whole roasted pigs are rarely served these days. But the apple is not simply a garnish—it is one of the last vestiges of a long tradition of artifice in food. The apple is supposed to make the pig look alive. Step back a few hundred years and the pig (or stag) may have been presented standing, made lifelike and held up by rods and wires. The roast could be presented alongside a "garden" sculpted from bread and pastry, with real fruits as well as fruits made of sugar. A grand centerpiece was a roasted or boiled peacock whose skin and feathers had been painstakingly removed whole and preserved, then replaced over the body. Sometimes, if the plumage itself wasn't spectacular enough, the feathers were gilded with gold and silver. A final touch was filling the beak with wool soaked in a flammable liquid that was then set alight.

The closest presentation we have these days is the serving of a large roasted turkey on a platter for Thanksgiving, or maybe certain forms of liquid nitrogen artifice in crazy fine-dining restaurants, but those are the tail end, not the beginning, of a tradition that was truly spectacular.

ens (or perhaps none at all) could rely on their city's or town's cooked food merchants for their meals, i.e., takeout. Almost as soon as cramped urban dwellings appear, so too do the structures to feed their residents. Taverns and even what we might now refer to as a restaurant (though slightly different in form) populated the Italian city-states. In his diary, the Florentine artist Pontormo wrote about meals he shared with fellow artist Bronzino at one of the city's taverns. One day it was ricotta crepes that "were marvelous to eat," along with dishes of small fried fish. Another day it was a salad, cacio cheese, an egg frittata, boiled lamb kidneys, and radicchio. On one Saturday, the meal consisted of ricotta, eggs, and artichokes. It was simple fare, leaning more toward eggs, fish, and vegetables, and representative of how the lower classes would have eaten.

THE MEDICI FAMILY TOWERS OVER THE RENAISSANCE. They ruled Florence for generations. They amassed fabulous wealth through their family banking business. They were patrons of the very best artists and commissioned monumental public works. But Florence was and is a postage-stamp-size city. How did these small Italian city-states rise to become some of the wealthiest cities in the world during the fifteenth and sixteenth centuries? The answer is trade, and not just commercial trade but the flow of ideas and culture.

Cosimo de' Medici was the one to elevate the family from bankers to de facto rulers of Florence in the mid-fifteenth century. Not only was Cosimo a talented banker, but he also understood how to forge relationships and alliances that would benefit his family. Close ties were established with the papacy, essentially allowing the Medici to become the bank of the Vatican. Cosimo also helped to lift others to positions of power, like Francesco Sforza. (Sforza's story is an extraordinary one of social mobility in its own right. Sforza was born to an illiterate peasant who was kidnapped as a young boy by a gang of adventurers and eventually rose through the ranks to become the leader of one of the most skilled mercenary gangs in Italy.) Cosimo recognized Sforza's potential and helped him become the duke of Milan in 1450, establishing the Milanese Sforza dynasty.

Beyond politics and money, Cosimo was an intellectual, a Renaissance man always on the hunt for classical texts and books from the East. He became good friends with Machiavelli, and the two even planned a trip to the Holy Land to find Greek manuscripts. (It appears they never made it.) With bank branches across Italy and Europe, Cosimo had a preexisting network of individuals who kept their ears to the ground for word of any Greek manuscripts found. Apparently German monasteries were especially fruitful locations, as their libraries contained rare works that the monks didn't recognize or value.

From London, Cologne, and Geneva to Lyons, Avignon, Bruges, Antwerp, Bologna, Rome, Naples, Pisa, and Venice, Medici banks were everywhere, funding businesses and merchants and even loaning money to kings. During Britain's War of the Roses, a thirty-two-year-long war in the middle of the fifteenth century, the Medici bank lent such huge sums of money to King Edward IV that it caused the London office branch to collapse. But the Medici banks didn't just deal with money and old books— they also supplied their customers with art, slaves, silk, tapestries, spices, sugar, olive oil, fruits, nuts, jewels, and once, for a particularly special client, a giraffe. They traded in every medium imaginable, and gained unbeliev- able power as a result.

Cosimo chose not his son but his grandson Lorenzo (aka Lorenzo "the Magnificent") to succeed him as head of the family business. Lorenzo was not quite as talented with finance as his grandfather, but he knew how to throw a party. He became famous during his rule, in part for the many fes- tivals, feasts, pageants, parades, and tournaments he held in Florence. His wedding to Clarice Orsini consisted of three days of feasting and dancing, three barrels of wine, and an astonishing five thousand pounds of sweet- meats. Lorenzo supported artists like Sandro Botticelli and Michelangelo, and he became so close to Michelangelo that the artist ended up living at the Medici palace for a number of years, essentially as Lorenzo's adopted son.

In 1557, Michelangelo received a letter from the father of a young art- ist, asking if he would examine some of his child's artworks. Michelangelo obliged and received a copy of one of his own works by a young woman named Sofonisba Anguissola. We don't know exactly what Michelangelo thought of Sofonisba's copy of his work but we do know that she was an incredibly skilled miniaturist (essentially creating small portraits that people could carry around of their loved ones, almost like pictures). Her portraits were so admired by such a wide audience that in 1560, Sofonisba became a lady-in-waiting to the queen of Spain and the court painter. Sofonisba spent the rest of her life as a working artist until she died at the old age of ninety-two.

Like Sofonisba, the Bolognese artist Lavinia Fontana was taught by her father, as the schools and academies of the period were closed to women. But Lavinia carved out an incredibly successful career for herself as an artist. In 1603, she became an official painter to the papal court, and the Habsburg royal family paid enormous sums for her paintings. She found herself so overwhelmed with commissions that her artist-husband, Gian Paolo Zappi, quit his own career to become a stay-at-home father, taking care of the children while Lavinia created exquisite pieces for the most discerning buyers of Renaissance art.

The work of female artists was not heavily commissioned nor given much attention by the Medici. This did not necessarily determine their success but proved to be the barrier to entry that posed the greatest challenge for aspiring female artists of the period, and is perhaps why there are not many records of them. However, women were clearly present in traditional female roles: from weaving fabrics, to making jewelry and harvesting the most luxurious spices and food items of the day, the hands of women were everywhere within the global trade network—their fingerprints have simply been wiped away.

THE BLACK DEATH FOUND ITS WAY TO ITALY VIA THE SILK ROAD. While the Pax Mongolica might have helped to open up the medieval world to global trade, it also provided the perfect system of transportation for the Plague. In the deep reaches of Crimea on the coast of the Black Sea, intrepid Genoese and Venetian merchants had set up outpost trading centers under grants from the Mongols. In one such Genoese trading post, the city of Caffa (now Feodosiya in modern-day Crimea), spices and goods from the East arrived for transport back to the Italian city-states. At some point in the 1340s, *Yersinia pestis* (the plague-causing germ) arrived on the backs of mice and rats from central Asia. Fast-forward a few years to October 1347, as a fleet of Genoese ships sailed into harbor in Messina, Sicily. As the ships got closer to the shore, the Sicilians noticed the eerie silence hanging about them. Upon inspecting the ships, they found barely any crew left alive. Corpses littered the decks. Those who were not already dead were close to death's door. Despite the Sicilians' attempts to kick the infected Genoese sailors out of the port, it was too late. The Plague had touched down in the Mediterranean.

As the disease swept through Italy, different cities responded differently to the catastrophe, mimicking in many ways our own modern world's response to the COVID-19 pandemic. Sienna chose to largely ignore the crisis and attempted to carry on life as usual. In Venice, strict lockdowns were enforced. Some city dwellers ran away to live in the countryside.

Others bunkered down in their homes hoping to wait out the storm. And some, believing the end of the world was nigh, partied as if there was no tomorrow. When faced with the unbelievable, humans' reactions prove to be as diverse as humans themselves.

Numerous theories abounded as to why people were dying at alarming rates. There were people who believed it was a punishment from God. One Parisian doctor claimed the Plague was due to the unusual conjunction of the planets on the afternoon of March 20. In many cities and towns throughout Europe, Jewish citizens were believed to be the source of the scourge. Jews were regularly rounded up and burned alive. The Plague kept killing Christians anyway.

In Giovanni Boccacio's *The Decameron*, set during Florence's devastating plague epidemic of 1348 and written just after it, Boccaccio writes of a group of young people who decide to escape the city. Seven young women and three young men, of affluent backgrounds, retreat to a series of country villas and estates to escape the Black Death and the doomy reality that had taken hold of their lives. They while away their days in luxurious gardens, dancing, singing, enjoying the sweet scents of flowers in bloom and taking turns telling one another stories. Each member of the troupe of ten tells a tale in the afternoon, about love, loss, intrigue, cunning deception, and grand adventures. Every evening they sit down to a sumptuous feast paired with fine wines and even more delectable desserts. They attempt to find comfort, amid so much loss and upheaval in what feels like the end times, in food and drink and stories. And in that sense, Boccaccio's young dreamers are not too dissimilar from ourselves.

Cherry Torte with Rose Petals

TORTA DE CERASE

MAKES ONE 9½-INCH TART, SERVING 6 TO 8 *There is a real elegance to this recipe. It is not too sweet, which is somewhat surprising for the dishes from this period—when they used sugar, they often really went for it! There is also a subtle depth from the cheese and interplay of spices. This is the type of dish that fine dining pastry chefs are always searching for.*

FOR THE CRUST:

2 sticks (16 tablespoons) unsalted butter, cut into ½-inch cubes, plus more for pan

2 cups all-purpose flour, plus more for pan

1 teaspoon kosher salt

FOR THE FILLING:

1 pound pitted cherries

1 cup packed rose petals (from 4 to 5 flowers), well rinsed and dried

1 cup ricotta, drained overnight

2 tablespoons grated Parmigiano-Reggiano

2 large eggs

1 teaspoon ground cinnamon

1 teaspoon ground ginger

¼ teaspoon freshly ground black pepper

½ cup granulated sugar

¼ teaspoon kosher salt

FOR FINISHING:

2 teaspoons rosewater

2 tablespoons confectioners' sugar

PREHEAT the oven to 350°F. Butter and flour a 9½-inch tart pan.

TO make the crust, add the 2 cups flour and the salt to the bowl of a food processor fitted with the metal blade and pulse a few times to combine. Add the cubed butter and pulse until fully incorporated. Add ½ cup cold water and continue to pulse until totally combined. Shape the dough into a disk, wrap it in plastic wrap, and refrigerate for 30 minutes.

ROLL out the dough to a circle ⅛ to ¼ inch thick and line the tart pan with it. Be sure to get the dough all the way down into the bottom of the pan by gently lifting from the outside and easing it in, not pushing from the inside, which will stretch the dough. Cut off excess dough and use it to patch any holes in the crust.

CLEAN the food processor and add all the filling ingredients to the work bowl. Pulse to combine completely. Pour this mixture into the tart, up to ⅛ inch from the top. Bake until the filling is set, about 1 hour 15 minutes, and let it cool in the pan on a rack. Unmold the tart, splash it with rosewater, sift the confectioners' sugar over it, and serve.

Zabaglione

ZABAGLONE

SERVES 6 TO 8 *I love this Maestro Martino recipe because it is both delicious and presents a clear connection to the modern version that (almost) shares its name. It has a powerful cinnamon kick, which reflects the tastes of the time. It pairs wonderfully with the preceding cherry torte.*

¼ cup plus 2 tablespoons sugar

1 tablespoon ground cinnamon

12 egg yolks

1 cup Italian dessert wine, such as Marsala

2 tablespoons unsalted butter

WHISK together the sugar and the cinnamon in a large bowl. Add the egg yolks and whisk together until completely combined.

IT is important to use a medium saucepan, a little bit larger than you would expect, because you will be stirring vigorously to incorporate air into the egg mixture as it cooks. Add the wine to the medium saucepan and bring it to a simmer over medium heat. Pour the wine into the egg mixture in a thin stream while stirring continuously and stir until completely combined. Return this mixture to the saucepan and continue to cook over medium heat, stirring very vigorously, until the mixture forms a frothy foam. Take the pan off the heat and add the butter while continuously stirring. Show that pan who's boss!

CAREFULLY transfer the mixture to ramekins or parfait glasses. Serve warm or refrigerate and serve chilled. If using as an accompaniment to the cherry torte, transfer to a dish and serve alongside.

ABSOLUTE POWER

IN 1492, RODRIGO BORGIA (aka Pope Alexander VI) took the throne in the Vatican and transformed the papacy. When he was still a cardinal, foreign kings and invaders could and did march on the city-states of Italy, almost unchecked. Alexander changed this. He militarized the papacy and let Cesare essentially become a warlord fighting on behalf of the pope's interests. He pawned his children off in strategic marriages to form alliances with various houses and countries, just as a king would. This is how we should view Pope Alexander VI. As a king.

We might think that Alexander's actions did not have consequences beyond Europe, but as we will see in Chapter Seven, Alexander played a decisive role in drawing the new borders of what would become "the Americas." In the early 1490s, when Spain and Portugal quarreled over which lands in the Americas belonged to whom, Alexander put forth the Treaty of Tordesillas. In it he neatly divided the world in two: everything to the east of the Cape Verde Islands belonged to Portugal, everything to the West belonged to Spain. The fates of millions of people who already lived in those lands, as well as the enslaved peoples brought to the Americas against their will, were quietly determined by one white man who had never left southern Europe.

As the papacy became more authoritative, the monarchs of Europe would rebel against it. In the following chapter, we will see Henry VIII of England struggle for a divorce from Catherine of Aragon (the same Aragon region where the Borgias are from), because of the power Alexander had established. This new uncheckable sovereignty of the papacy would ultimately force the monarchs of Europe to consolidate their own authority into pre-nation-state formations. The modern world was beginning to take shape.

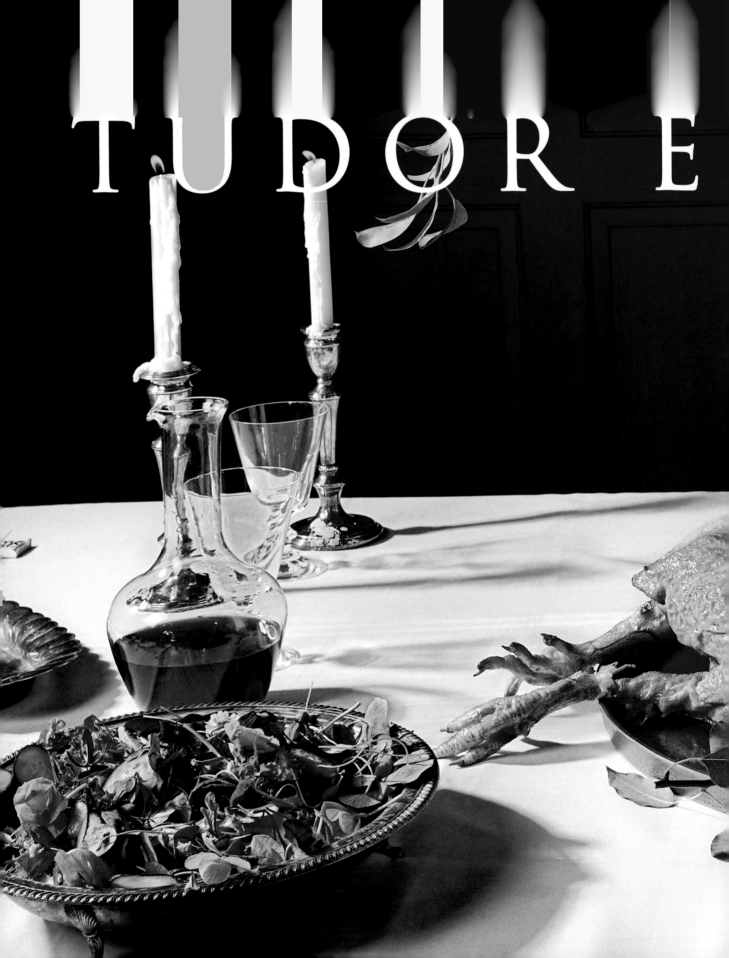

TUDOR E

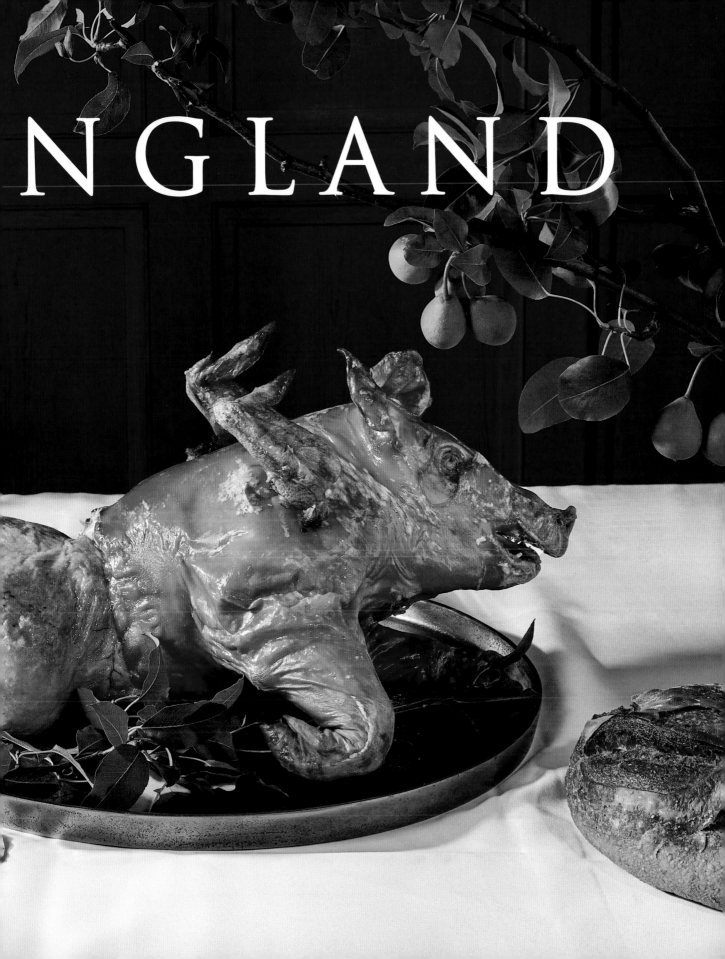

NGLAND

TUDOR ENGLAND
15TH to 17TH centuries

THE TUDORS WERE A ROYAL FAMILY that ruled nearly five hundred years ago, on a small northern island, for just a few generations. And yet they remain ever present in our popular culture. Much has been written about them. Their dramatic lives continue to serve as fodder for scripted television dramas, movies, documentaries, and podcasts. The Tudors seem to occupy a space in the cultural zeitgeist that I'm not sure any other dynasty throughout history ever has.

Why are we so fascinated with the Tudors? We know about Henry VIII and his seven wives—the divorces, the beheadings, the annulments. We know about Henry's infamous battles with Pope Clement VII (son of Giuliano de' Medici who was killed by Bandini and his conspirators in the Duomo in Florence) to secure the divorce he wanted from Catherine of Aragon. We know he did eventually get the divorce he so desperately wanted, resulting in England's separation from the Catholic Church and the creation of the Church of England. We know about England's spectacular defeat of the Spanish Armada under Queen Elizabeth I's rule. We know about Elizabeth's famed virginity, but also (maybe) her lifelong affair with Robert Dudley. Tudor rule is marked by all the sex, violence, political intrigue, and religious upheaval that makes any medieval tale a winner.

But the age of the Tudors was so much more than this. It was a period of transition—and of transformation—from a medieval feudal society into an early modern nation-state. And perhaps this is what makes this dynasty so poignant in the long arc of history and why we continue to tell their story.

Sure, the everyday lives of the Tudors looked different from ours, but we have a lot more in common with them than we do with say, thirteenth-century Britons. During Tudor rule the nature of foreign policy changed. Ties with Rome were broken, shifting the balance of power toward monarchs, not popes. As a result, the government became more centralized, structured, and bureaucratic. The way the aristocracy functioned changed. A civil service appeared. Technological advancements changed commerce. New economic opportunities allowed for more mobility within the rigid class structures. Art and literature flourished. This was the age of Shakespeare, one of the most famous writers of the Western world. All this while ships filled with English sailors charted the coast of North America, setting the stage for this small island nation to assume a new role on the world stage . . . a stage it would dominate in centuries to come.

But we're jumping ahead to the end here. Let's start at the beginning, shall we?

In 1485, a relatively unknown Welshman, Henry Tudor of the House of Lancaster, defeated King Richard III on the battlefield, officially ending the War of the Roses—a long, bloody battle for the throne of England (that also forced the London office of the Medici bank to go broke). By the time he assumed the throne as King Henry VII, the throne had changed hands by force six times in eighty-six years. Henry VII would be the last king of England to win his throne on the battlefield.

The reign of the Tudors was, in the grand scheme of things, relatively short. Five Tudor monarchs ruled over England for 118 years. Starting with Henry VII, followed by his son Henry VIII and then three of his children—all from different wives, all very different in character. The Tudor dynasty ultimately came to an end with Henry VIII's daughter Queen Elizabeth I, often referred to as "The Virgin Queen," who, perhaps not surprisingly given the nickname, had no offspring.

From the start, the Tudors needed to convince their subjects of their dynasty's legitimacy and permanence. Having fought his way to the throne, Henry VII did his very best to wipe out anyone with royal blood who might pose a possible threat. He also banned private armies, which meant that lords with grand aspirations and deep pockets could no longer stake their claim to the crown through uprisings and insurrection—a hallmark of the medieval world (and today a familiar Hollywood story—how many medieval dramas are about one powerful man trying to overthrow the other?).

Henry VIII continued his father's approach regarding the kingdom's power balance and the result was exactly what they had hoped for: fewer people with long aristocratic lineages who could claim the right to high office. The power of the aristocracy was diminished, and in its place a sort of Tudor civil service emerged. Most of the men who served Henry VIII had been raised by the king from the gentry class. One of the most stunning things about the Tudor era (from a modern perspective) was how lower-middle-class people were able to rise through the ranks.

Take Thomas Cromwell, for example. When we hear the name we assume that he must have been born into power, because he occupies so many pages of British history books. But he wasn't. Born the son of a blacksmith, Cromwell lived a life abroad in Europe, fighting as a mercenary. He returned to England in the early years of the sixteenth century to rise to the highest echelons of power, serving as chief minister to King Henry VIII from 1532 to 1540, when he was beheaded (not all meteoric rises end well). He was born into a vast sea of nobodies, and against all odds managed to climb his way to the top—and for a brief glorious moment, he held fast. Perhaps we can see some of our own modern conceptions of the "American Dream" or the rise and fall of celebrity in Cromwell's story.

Readers should not deduce from Cromwell's life story that Tudor England was some kind of free market economy where anyone with a strong work ethic and a desire to succeed would and could. Divisions between the classes were still very real.

There were unifiers across the classes, however, a certain beverage—ale—being one of them. In terms of Tudor booze consumption, ale was the most popular beverage for commoners until the sixteenth century. Then beer grew increasingly popular, as the use of hops in brewing made beer last longer than ale. This became especially important in the eighteenth century, when British sailors working for the East India Company started adding large quantities of hops to their beer so it would keep on the journey to India. And thus India Pale Ales (IPAs) were born.

But in Tudor time, beer wasn't just a beverage, it was also considered a food. Three pints of beer a day gave a growing Tudor boy a quarter of the calories he required, as well as nutrients like vitamin B. At times beer was actually cheaper than food, so for ordinary (read: lower class) people it became a vital part of their diet. If you feel, at any point in this chapter, the desire to drink like an ordinary Tudor, a craft beer or ice cold ale would go quite well with any number of the following savory recipes.

LENT

IN THE MODERN DAY, most of us know Lent as the thirty days preceding Easter, when observant Catholics give up something not particularly inconvenient, like chocolate or potato chips. In the medieval period Lent was that time, plus every Friday, plus a whole host of saints' days and whenever else the Church felt like it. (There are arguments to be made that fasting from February to March actually made sense in terms of food supplies, since Lent occurs when the food stores were at their lowest, just before the spring harvest.) Coupled with the fact that the Catholic Church has about the same number of saints as rappers have rhymes about the number of rhymes they have, fasting days could take place up to one third of the year. Lent and fast days generally meant no meat, dairy, or eggs. Fish was allowed. Thus, to be "out of Lent" was to be able to eat butter and cheese and everything rich and delightful again. The following *Tarte Owte of Lente*, is a perfect example of what people would have eaten after the Lent fast.

Spinach Fritters

FRITTERS OF SPINNEDGE

MAKES 12 TO 15 FRITTERS, SERVING 4 TO 6 *This recipe comes from the cookbook* The Good Huswifes Jewell, *written by Thomas Dawson and published in 1596, yet these fritters feel oddly familiar to us today. When we first tried them, there was an instantaneous memory connection to a type of gastropub food—something greasy and delicious yet elevated. But the spices set them apart from anything in our time period. They make an excellent pairing with Cinnamon Sauce (page 173) and your favorite assertive wine or rich ale.*

1¼ cups thawed frozen or fresh spinach

1½ teaspoons kosher salt, plus more for cooking water

1 tablespoon unsalted butter, softened

¾ cup panko breadcrumbs

1 tablespoon black currants

1 large egg, beaten

1 teaspoon ground ginger

1 teaspoon freshly ground black pepper or grains of paradise (see Note)

1 teaspoon sugar

3 to 4 cups canola or other neutral oil, for frying

1¼ cups all-purpose flour

1 to 1¼ cups beer or ale

IF using thawed spinach, drain it and squeeze out excess water. If using fresh spinach, blanch it in boiling salted water, then shock it in ice water. Squeeze the moisture out of the spinach and chop it finely. Place the spinach, butter, breadcrumbs, currants, egg, ginger, black pepper, ½ teaspoon salt, and the sugar in a medium bowl and mix thoroughly. Scoop out portions weighing about 2 ounces each and pat them flat between your hands into patties. There is no right or wrong way, but keep the overall thickness to ½ inch or less.

HEAT the oil in a deep pot with heavy bottom to 350°F. Place ¼ cup of the flour in a small bowl.

WHISK together the remaining 1 cup flour and remaining 1 teaspoon salt in a large bowl and whisk in enough beer to form a batter.

Some lumps are okay and actually give the fritters a nice texture.

WHEN the oil is hot, dredge the fritters first in the flour, then in the batter, and fry until golden brown, about 3 minutes. Cool briefly on a rack or drain on paper towels and serve.

NOTE: Grains of paradise—related to the ginger family and originating in West Africa—is included for historical accuracy not personal preference. The popularity of this spice, in my opinion, is due to one of the greatest examples of food branding in culinary history: when Eastern merchants realized they could charge Europeans a lot more money for a spice that apparently came from "paradise." A decidedly second-rate talent with an A-list agent, it is the Colin Farrell of the spice world.

Rich Cheese Tart
(for Meat Days)
TARTE OWTE OF LENTE

MAKES ONE 9-INCH TART, SERVING 6 TO 8 *The recipe for this dish comes to us from the 1490 cookbook* Gentyll Manly Cokere *and is perfect for your celebratory feast, Easter or otherwise: rich, delicious, and a great way to show off the subtlety of white pepper. If you would rather make a freestanding pie, use a springform pan or a round cake pan rather than a pie pan.*

FOR THE CRUST:

2 sticks (16 tablespoons) unsalted butter, plus more for pan

Large pinch of saffron

2¼ cups cake flour, plus more for pan

1 teaspoon kosher salt

2 egg yolks

1 large egg, beaten, for egg wash

FOR THE FILLING:

1 cup grated white cheddar cheese

⅔ cup heavy cream

1 large egg, beaten

2 egg yolks

1 teaspoon ground white pepper

¼ teaspoon kosher salt

TO make the crust, cut the 2 sticks butter into ½-inch cubes. Melt one-quarter of the butter cubes in a saucepan with the saffron. It should turn orange when bloomed. Put the 2¼ cups cake flour and the salt in the bowl of a food processor fitted with the metal blade and pulse a few times to combine. Add the remaining butter cubes and the saffron butter and pulse until entirely combined. This is a rich crumbly crust, not flaky, so combine fully. Add the yolks and pulse until mixed. If the dough seems dry, add a few tablespoons of ice water and pulse to bring together. Form the dough into a disk, wrap in plastic, and chill for 30 minutes.

PREHEAT the oven to 350°F. Butter and flour a 9-inch springform pan. Divide the dough into two equal pieces. Return one-half to the refrigerator and roll the other into a disk about ¼ inch thick. Gently place it in

the prepared pan, nudging the dough down into the bottom without stretching it. Trim around the top of the pan, leaving a ½-inch margin above the rim.

TO make the filling, combine the cheese, cream, egg and yolks, white pepper, and salt in a large bowl and fold together. Brush the lip of the bottom crust with the egg wash and gently fill the crust with the cheese mixture. Roll out the second half of the dough into a disk slightly larger than the pan. Cut a vent hole in the center of the disk. Fold the disk in half and then in quarters, position the hole in the center of the pie, and then unfold it. Crimp the edges to seal and trim any excess dough. Brush egg wash on the top.

BAKE in the preheated oven until the crust is a rich golden brown, 45 to 50 minutes. Serve warm or cold.

Mince Pie

SERVES 4 TO 6 *Mince pies have a long narrative in British culinary history, and they still find their way onto Christmas tables every December. But the original concept of the mince pie dates back to the twelfth century, when the Crusaders brought the concept of cooking meat with fruits and spices back to England from the Holy Land. The use of spices from the East was an obvious link to Christ's birthplace and the three wise men, so it became a dish traditionally eaten around Christmas. This specific recipe comes from* The Forme of Cury, *a collection of English recipes from 1490. It is the first known English cookbook to use spices from Asia such as mace and cloves.*

The most important thing to know about mincemeat is that it is meat. A mince pie is both a rich and delicious savory dish—and not a dessert—because a) it really is a meat main-course dish, and b) there was little or no distinction between hot, cold, sweet, and/or savory dishes in the Middle Ages. Dessert as a course wouldn't really be invented for around three hundred years. The second thing to consider is that the pie shell was usually made of an inedible paste of flour and water and functioned primarily as a cooking vessel rather than providing the lovely flakiness we now expect. The technique of baking meat, spices, and whole and dried fruits together in a more or less invulnerable and sterile shell, or "coffin," was an extremely effective strategy for preserving meat in an age without refrigeration. Do not, however, feel bound by this—feel free to use the rich crust from the Rich Cheese Tart (for Meat Days) on page 161 or your own favorite pie dough recipe, and enjoy.

FOR THE CRUST:

6 cups all-purpose flour

½ cup kosher salt

1 egg, beaten

FOR THE FILLING:

10 ounces lamb loin or leg, minced by hand

2 tablespoons beef suet or unsalted butter

1 tablespoon brown sugar

1 cup pitted prunes

1 cup dates

¾ cup raisins or currants

Finely grated zest of 1 orange

¼ cup plus 2 tablespoons freshly squeezed orange juice (from 1 to 2 oranges)

Finely grated zest of 1 lemon

1 teaspoon freshly squeezed lemon juice

1 teaspoon freshly grated nutmeg

1 teaspoon ground cloves

1 teaspoon freshly ground black pepper

1 teaspoon kosher salt

¼ teaspoon ground cinnamon

¼ cup plus 1 tablespoon sweet wine or sherry

2 teaspoons sherry or balsamic vinegar

TO make the crust, combine the flour and salt in the bowl of a stand mixer fitted with the paddle. Very slowly add 2 to 2½ cups water. You are looking for a claylike or Play-Doh consistency. It can take a little more time to hydrate than you might think, so add water slowly and gradually. Wrap the dough tightly in plastic wrap and let it rest in the refrigerator for 30 minutes to 1 hour. Then divide the dough into thirds. Roll one-third into a ½-inch-thick disk; this will be the base of your pie. Place it on a sheet pan. Roll another third into a thick rope about the width of your thumb. Build the wall of the pie by curling the rope around the edge of the base and pinching it into shape. (Any pottery experience will come in handy here.) Take your time and make sure it is sturdy.

ADD all of the filling ingredients to a large bowl and mix thoroughly. Fill the shell with this mixture; the filling should be flush with the top. Roll out the last piece of dough into a disk and use it for the top of the pie. Pinch it into place with your fingers. Cut a small vent in the top with a sharp knife. Brush egg wash on the top and sides. The pie can be further decorated by cutting or pressing patterns into the walls. Refrigerate the pie for at least 30 minutes. Meanwhile, preheat the oven to 325°F. Bake on the sheet pan until the crust is firm and golden, 1½ to 1¾ hours. Let the pie sit at room temperature for 15 minutes. Remove and discard the top of the pie and serve warm by scooping out the filling, leaving the crust behind.

ON PIES AND COFFINS

THE TUDORS loved spectacle. And pies. I'm sure you are familiar with the "four and twenty blackbirds baked in a pie" from the nursery rhyme (which probably originated in Tudor England). Those birds were just one of many items put in pies purely for effect, not for consumption. Live frogs were another popular choice, with the pie constructed so that when the pie was opened, the frogs would leap out and hop down the table, much to the guests' astonishment. Perhaps the most extreme case was Duke Philip of Burgundy, who, in 1454, presented twenty-eight musicians inside what must have been a truly enormous pie. But it is important to understand that these were not pies in the sense that we normally think of them. Instead, they were "coffins," cooking vessels made of flour and water that, once baked, preserved the food they contained. However, these thick, dense shells were not meant to be eaten. They were less like bread and more like pottery, which is why they lent themselves to practices closer to architecture than to cooking.

HENRY VIII: THE RENAISSANCE MAN, THE CHRISTIAN, AND THE KING

HENRY VIII WAS ACUTELY AWARE of England's image on the international stage and determined that the island nation should be on par with other European powers, not just militarily but culturally as well. He commissioned portraits in the Renaissance style, ones that used principles of the classical world to create realistic portrayals. He abandoned the royal portraits of the Middle Ages. He constructed and revitalized numerous palaces and monuments, like Greenwich Palace, Hampton Court, the Tower of London, and Windsor Castle. With Henry, the Renaissance came to England.

In the Middle Ages, books like Thomas Mallory's 1485 *Morte d'Arthur* were all about the knights of the round table: men occupied with fights, personal vendettas, and honor killings. They were men of a medieval society. With the Renaissance new modes of thought and conceptions of being were introduced. Renaissance works like Baldassare Castiglione's 1528 book *The Courtier* transformed ideas of how a person should behave. The Renaissance man was well-mannered and well-rounded. He was not only a skilled warrior but also had knowledge of the humanities, classics, and fine arts. And so we begin to see a shift from a warrior-like society to one that was governed by a set of legal codes and a centralized government.

As the Renaissance spread, the culture of Christian Europe was inevitably changed: the power and authority of the Catholic Church faced unprecedented challenges from monarchs. And it wasn't just monarchs who wanted to free themselves from the tight grip of Rome. In 1517 Martin Luther, a German monk, nailed his "95 Theses" (basically a list of his ninety-five problems with the Church) to the doors of the Wittenberg Cathedral, launching the Protestant Reformation and the division of the Christian Church into Protestant and Catholic sects. Religious upheaval exploded across the continent.

A few years later Henry VIII was stymied by Pope Clement VII, who would not grant him a divorce from his first wife, Catherine of Aragon. Catherine's parents were Isabella and Ferdinand of Castile and Aragon, two of the most powerful rulers in Europe (more on them and their power base in Spain in the next chapter) and Pope Clement VII wasn't about to enrage them by setting their daughter aside for Henry's new love interest. By 1534 Henry VIII had had enough. He broke ties with the Catholic Church and

Parliament passed the Act of Supremacy: meaning Henry was now not only the King but also the "supreme head on Earth" of the new Church of England. Now that is absolute power.

The calendar of the Catholic Church, its saints days, festivals, and rituals, had defined and structured people's lives for centuries. For many peasants these festivals were their main form of entertainment. Under the new Church of England these events were largely abandoned. Additionally, Henry had all of the 825 monasteries across England dissolved—and monastic life basically ceased to exist. England was no longer Catholic—it was forming its own Christian identity.

Henry is often assumed to have been a Protestant, because he broke ties with the pope in Rome and set up the Church of England. But Henry never saw himself as such. He saw himself as a Catholic attempting to wrestle power away from Rome and for himself, not as a monarch trying to make some kind of political-theological statement against Catholicism or for Protestantism.

Henry VIII was interested in far more than merely granting himself the divorce from Catherine of Aragon that the pope had denied him: he wanted to make the Church subject to the Crown. Yet when he died in 1547, the Church of England was still essentially a Catholic Church. After Henry VIII's death, as his children—Edward, Mary, and then Elizabeth—assumed the throne in quick succession, England swung back and forth between being officially Protestant or Catholic (depending on that successor's personal position). It wasn't until Elizabeth's reign that the Church of England became firmly Protestant. Her parents were Henry VIII and Anne Boleyn—and since the pope didn't recognize their marriage as valid, she had to adhere to Protestantism if she wanted to be regarded as the legitimate heir to the throne.

An incredible amount has been written about Henry VIII. Within the chronicles of his life, less savory aspects of his personality have become legend—mainly his fiery temper and penchant for executing those who had once been close to him. But something we might not know about him was his passion for hunting. In his youth he would often rise at dawn and spend the entire day hunting, only to return late at night. He loved the sport itself, as well as the venison brought home from the hunt.

While he had a reputation for being handsome and athletic and a generally dashing prince in his younger years, his health deteriorated quite significantly in his thirties and forties. Henry probably suffered a bout of smallpox at the age of twenty-three, and then seven years later he likely contracted malaria, which would have returned throughout his life (as malaria typically does).

Sporting injuries and open sores on his legs caused by restrictive garters he wore to show off his calf muscles did nothing to aid his general well-being.

The biggest injury Henry VIII suffered was during a jousting tournament when he was forty-four. He was thrown from his horse, and the horse actually fell on top of him. Anne Boleyn was told by doctors that Henry was going to die of his injuries—news that caused her to miscarry the boy she was pregnant with. Henry did recover, however, and once he was well enough he declared to Anne that the miscarriage was a clear sign they would never produce a male heir together (so far their union had only resulted in one child, a girl, future Queen Elizabeth I). He had her executed six months later. How did Henry go from being so in love with Anne that he moved heaven and earth to marry her, to wanting not just a divorce but her head to roll at the executioner's block as well?

Brain damage was not a neurological specialty of sixteenth-century doctors. But the reality that Henry probably suffered a brain injury during this jousting accident explains the shift in his personality and behavior. Sources before the 1536 tournament describe Henry in a positive light; he was strong, mentally sharp, even benevolent. After the accident, deep paranoia set in. He cycled through six wives, killing two of them. A moody, unpredictable, and vicious king emerged from that sickbed after the fated fall from his horse. Britain would be forever different because of it.

THE TUDOR TABLE

I BLAME HOLLYWOOD. I understand that it might be more entertaining to show Henry Tudor grabbing a great chicken leg from his plate, biting off a chunk to be noisily devoured, and tossing the spent remains over his shoulder, but it is wrong in almost every respect. Henry, who considered himself a refined gentleman, would have been utterly horrified. First, plates were not a thing. Food would be eaten from a trencher, a thick flat piece of bread. The table, often covered with three spotless tablecloths, would be kept immaculate, as would the diners, who carefully wiped their fingers on equally spotless napkins draped over their shoulders. Most diners would bring their own knives and spoons; the point of a knife was used in place of a fork. The many admonitions regarding table manners would be recognizable to most Americans today from their own childhoods, or at least from a persnickety great aunt: no elbows on the table, don't talk with your mouth full, chew your food, don't scratch yourself, and don't slurp your soup. Less entertaining but quite appropriate for a Tudor world that considered itself the acme of style and breeding.

Roasted Venison

SERVES 4 TO 6 *The following recipe for Henry VIII's favorite meat comes from the previously cited book* The Good Huswifes Jewell. *Venison is a notoriously difficult meat to cook, as it is extremely lean and has a tendency to go from perfectly cooked to dry as a box of Kleenex between the oven and the table. The steps in this Tudor recipe are a sophisticated solution. I highly recommend using an accurate instant-read thermometer for this recipe.*

FOR THE COURT BOUILLON:

2 medium yellow onions, roughly chopped

3 large carrots, roughly chopped

3 ribs celery, roughly chopped

2 bay leaves

10 whole black peppercorns

2 whole cloves

5 sprigs fresh thyme

1 sprig fresh rosemary

1 tablespoon kosher salt

FOR THE VENISON:

2 venison tenderloins (2 to 2½ pounds each)

Kosher salt

Freshly ground black pepper

8 ounces bacon or salt pork, thinly sliced

FOR THE SAUCE:

¼ cup red wine vinegar

½ teaspoon freshly ground black pepper

¼ teaspoon ground cloves

½ teaspoon ground mace

6 tablespoons unsalted butter

Kosher salt

PREHEAT the oven to 400°F.

TO make the court bouillon, add all ingredients to a stockpot with 6 cups water and bring to a boil on high heat. Reduce to a simmer and cook for 15 minutes. Prepare a large ice-water bath. Submerge the venison tenderloins in the simmering water and cook for 4 minutes—then start checking the internal temperature at 1-minute intervals. You are looking for 130°F. When it gets to that temperature, remove the venison and immediately shock it in the ice bath to stop the cooking. Let it cool in the ice bath for a few minutes and then remove it, dry it, and season it liberally with salt and pepper. Strain through a fine-mesh sieve into a bowl and reserve 2 cups court bouillon for the sauce.

WRAP the tenderloins in the bacon or salt pork and tie with butcher's twine. Place in a roasting pan. Roast in the preheated oven just long enough to cook the bacon. The meat is already perfectly cooked, so you don't want to take it any further. Remove the venison from the oven and let it rest for a few minutes.

WHILE the meat is resting, combine the vinegar, black pepper, cloves, and mace with the 2 cups court bouillon in a small saucepan. Simmer over low heat until reduced to ½ cup. Turn off the heat and whisk in the butter. Season to taste. Carve the meat and serve with the sauce.

Sugared Salad with Flower Petals

SALLET OF HERBS AND PETALS

This is another recipe from The Good Huswifes Jewell. *I've included it to illustrate both the similarities and differences between modern and medieval conceptions of salad. We recognize the basic dressing, but the period salad might have included more things that we consider herbs or spices, and the flower petals probably surprise anyone outside of (medium-pretentious) fine dining. The basic ingredients should be considered only as a suggestion or guide—feel free to include whichever herbs and veggies strike your fancy. Most shocking to a modern palate, this was finished with a handful of one of the rarest and most magical of spices—refined white sugar!*

2 bunches sorrel

1 bunch tarragon

1 head red oak lettuce

1 head lolla rossa lettuce or other red-leaf lettuce

4 English (seedless) cucumbers

1 Meyer lemon

4 large eggs or 12 quail eggs, hard-boiled and peeled

¾ cup extra-virgin olive oil

⅓ cup red wine vinegar

3 tablespoons granulated sugar

3 teaspoons Maldon sea salt

2 bunches pansies or other edible flowers

PLUCK the herb leaves from the stems and separate the lettuce leaves. Wash and dry thoroughly. Slice the cucumbers into rounds and make half-moons of the lemons. Carefully cut the eggs into slices or quarters.

TOSS the herbs and lettuces in a large bowl, then whisk together the oil and vinegar with 1 tablespoon of the sugar and 2 teaspoons of the salt salt and dress the herbs and

lettuces, reserving some of the dressing. Put the herbs and lettuces in the center of a dish and top with the flowers. Dress and arrange the cucumbers, lemons, and eggs around these and garnish with the remaining sugar and salt. The sugar can also be incorporated entirely into the dressing or served on the side. Presentation is key to this dish, so make the most of it!

The Cockenthrice

SERVES 8 TO 12 *I once nervously entered a sewing shop and, after looking over a number of products, finally asked the salesperson a series of awkward questions regarding large needles and very strong but natural cotton thread. Finally, and quite sweetly, she asked me, "What exactly are you trying to sew?"*

I didn't know exactly how to put it.

A cockenthrice is a mythical animal, composed of half a pig and half a chicken—sewn together. There are further variants involving which half goes in front and whether to paint it green or gold, but you get the point. References to and recipes for this admittedly insane concoction range from a 1380 manuscript to several Tudor cookbooks, and it was a favorite dish of Henry VIII. To me, along with a peacock clothed in its own feathers, it is the acme of Tudor cooking-as-theater. I have always believed that it is important to have "aspirational recipes"—dishes that are your next cooking goal or horizon, whether a perfect French omelet or a sculpture in sugar. My first goal was a humble apple pie, and for a long time, certainly from the first conversation with Victoria about Edible History, the cockenthrice represented my horrifying dream. The sizes of the pig and chicken should roughly match, at least around the midline circumference. Think of them as needing to have the same belt size. The only other limitation may be the size of your oven.

1 suckling pig

Kosher salt

1 turkey or chicken, preferably with feet on

2 cups Cinnamon Sauce (recipe follows)

FOR THE STUFFING
(FOR EACH 10 OUNCES OF PORK):

2 tablespoons beef suet or unsalted butter

1 tablespoon brown sugar

1 cup pitted prunes

1 cup pitted dates

¾ cup raisins or currants

Finely grated zest of 1 orange

¼ cup plus 2 tablespoons freshly squeezed orange juice (from 1 to 2 oranges)

Finely grated zest of 1 lemon

1 teaspoon freshly squeezed lemon Juice

1 teaspoon freshly grated nutmeg

1 teaspoon ground cloves

1 teaspoon freshly ground black pepper

1 teaspoon kosher salt

¼ teaspoon ground cinnamon

¼ cup plus 1 tablespoon sweet wine or sherry

2 teaspoons sherry vinegar or balsamic vinegar

SALT the pig liberally and refrigerate overnight. You can also brine the turkey if you like.

THE next morning, starting a few inches below the rib cage, cut through the skin and flesh of the pig up to the spine on both sides. Use a cleaver or a cleaver and mallet to separate the spine. Butcher all the meat off the lower half of the pig. It doesn't have to be pretty!

PREHEAT the oven to 350°F. I know you want to get down to the cool part, but first take the butchered meat from the suckling pig and weigh it. The amounts for the other ingredients given above are per 10 ounces of meat. Thus, if you end up with 1½ pounds (24 ounces) of suckling pig meat, then 24/10 = 2.4 or about 2½ times the given amounts. It doesn't have to be exact.

COMBINE the meat and the stuffing ingredients in a large bowl. Place in a casserole, cover, and roast in the preheated oven until the mixture reaches 165°F on an instant-read thermometer. Taste and adjust seasoning. Leave the oven on.

NOW, back to our mythical creature. Butcher under the wings and through the backbone of the turkey. Again, it doesn't have to be pretty. Next, do a fit test—the bird should insert into the bottom of the pig's rib cage with a few inches of overlapping skin.

YOU will need a big, strong needle of the type used for sewing canvas and heavy organic thread (made of cotton or something similar). A pair of pliers often helps. Suckling pigs can be quite greasy, which makes them difficult to handle. I have found that patting them down with cornstarch can make them much easier to control, and it can be rinsed off later. Pigskin is quite strong, so it is often easiest to drive the needle in with pliers to pierce the skin, and then pull it through from the other side. The bird is not as robust, so make sure to bring the needle from the inside up under the ribs to hold it. In through the pig, out through the bird! Start at the belly button and work your way around. When you reach your starting point, fill the body cavity of the cockenthrice with the stuffing. Now sew the pig together up its midline incision.

TRANSFER the creation to a very large roasting pan or sheet pan lined with parchment paper and roast until the deepest shoulder joint reaches 165°F on an instant-read thermometer, about 3 hours. Honestly, the white meat of the turkey is probably going to overcook. But is this recipe really about the turkey? Do you prefer turkey to suckling pig? Come on now. Let the cockenthrice rest before carving. The finished cockenthrice is best presented on a large cutting board with a channel to catch the juices. Make sure to bring to the table intact, so that your diners can take in your incredible creation! Serve with cinnamon sauce.

Cinnamon Sauce

SAUCE CAMELINE

MAKES ABOUT 2 CUPS *The medieval relationship to spices was deep and mystical and is often wildly misunderstood. The often-repeated notion that spices were used to conceal the taste of rotting meat is undercut by the simple fact that the extreme cost of the spices in any dish would almost certainly be vastly larger than the value of the meat cooked in them.* Sauce Cameline or Carmeline, *so called because of the reddish color imparted partly by the almost ridiculous amount of cinnamon in the recipe, is an excellent example; it was an all-purpose condiment for many dishes.*

4 to 5 slices sourdough bread
(about 3½ ounces)

About 3 cups burgundy wine to soak
the bread

½ cup raisins

1 cup red verjus

½ teaspoon kosher salt

½ teaspoon ground clove

½ teaspoon freshly grated nutmeg

1 tablespoon plus 1 teaspoon ground
cinnamon

Sugar or honey to taste

SOAK the bread in the wine. Remove the bread and discard any unabsorbed wine. Place the bread and remaining ingredients in a blender and blend, slowly increasing the speed of the blender to the maximum. Let it run for a good 3 to 5 minutes, occasionally scraping down the top, where larger particles can collect. Let the sauce sit and hydrate for 1 hour, and then reblend for another 3 to 5 minutes. If that seems like an absurd amount of time, it is. Now imagine grinding it by hand.

BREAD AND STATUS

BREAD WAS an absolute staple in Tudor England. Everyone ate it, but the precise type of bread they ate told you a great deal about who they were and where they were in the social hierarchy. In a way, it is very similar to the way accents designate class in Britain today. In only a few words, another Brit can almost instantly guess where you are from, your level of education, and your social background. Likewise, if you were biting into a manchet, a small round loaf of white bread made with finely milled flour, any Tudor would know you were anything but a peasant grinding your way through a rough slab of whole wheat, rye, and barley.

Bread was so important, in fact, that Henry VIII's retainers at Hampton Court palace had their bread and beer rations included in their salaries. While referring to the aristocracy as the "upper crust" is a fairly modern practice, that term's first usage came from a book of manners, food, and dress published in 1460, which specifically states to reserve the upper crust "for your sovereign."

FOOD AND PAGEANTRY
FOR THE PEOPLE

BOOKS BECAME CHEAPER and more widely available when the printing press was invented in Germany in 1440. In England, books began to be produced in English—which might seem obvious but Latin had been the universal written language up to that point. "Educated" men didn't write books in the common tongue. Now not only did more people have access to books, but they were written in a language most people could actually understand.

Books in circulation were often either religious in nature or almanacs, though there were a growing number of dietary manuals and culinary manuscripts being produced. Many of these fifteenth- and sixteenth-century culinary guides we have used in this very cookbook, like *Gentyll Manly Cokere* (1490), *The Good Huswifes Jewell* (1596), and *The Forme of Cury* (1490). These books functioned as a source for recipes but advised on health as well. In a time before "modern" medicine made in labs, food was medicine.

Tudor medicine was based on the ideas of our dear friend Galen and his Theory of the Humors from all the way back in Chapter One (talk about longevity!). A balance of the four humors (yellow bile, black bile, phlegm, and blood) was sought after by Tudors, just as it was by ancient Romans. While a harmony of yellow bile and phlegm might not be how we measure our health today, every time I'm in the cookbook section of a bookstore I can't help but chuckle at the diet books all espousing completely contradictory theories. One will tell you to cut out carbs and sugar, another to only eat meat and fat, while some extol the virtues of veganism and others praise the French attitude of "eating everything" but "in moderation." Centuries later, the jury is still out.

There is much discussion among food historians about how many fruits and vegetables were eaten in this period. Generally speaking, vegetables were considered poor man's food and meat was for the rich. Our modern-day notions of healthy eating were very different from the Tudors—but that doesn't mean they weren't concerned with health, a point proven by the many dietary manuals that were printed throughout the period. Vegetables and grains were more readily consumed by the poor. The rich still consumed fruits and vegetables, but tended to fill out their plates with more meat and fish.

Only the richest Tudors could afford to drink wine, as it had to be imported from the continent. Even in wine-producing countries, many winemakers could not afford to drink the beverage they made. Instead they made do with piquette, made by adding water to the leftover grape skins, seeds, and stems. Without modern additives and preservatives, Tudor-era wine had a much shorter shelf life (this young wine was also famously tough on the stomach). Henry VIII, in a creative display of his deep dislike of Catherine of Aragon, found a way to weaponize even wine against her, once he had discarded her for Anne Boleyn. In 1534 Catherine wrote to Chapuys, the ambassador of the Holy Roman Emperor as well as a personal friend, asking for some old Spanish wine. Henry refused to let the old wine be sent to her, insisting that the former queen only be served very young wine—causing her further discomfort just as her many health ailments set in.

Alcohol aside, one of the great debates about medieval drink in general is the question of water consumption. We know that people did not consume water in the quantities we do today. The question is how much water did they drink? The problem with water at the time was that it was often dangerous to ingest due to bacteria (this was before treated water). Fermented beverages were far safer to imbibe because fermentation kills bacteria. But just because alcohol was the libation of choice doesn't mean everyone was drunk all the time. Alcohol was not as strong as it is today, and a buzz would likely have been tempered by an impressive tolerance. Sometimes, though, drinking a lot was simply unavoidable; it was a vital part of social events and to refuse to drink during a toast was unthinkably bad manners. A toast, it should also be noted, was not a polite sip—you had to down the whole cup in one go.

Tudor banquet food was truly spectacular—and banquet dining in this period was far more sophisticated and well behaved than is generally believed. The modern image of medieval feasts where royals are throwing hunks of meat to their dogs and wiping their hands on their clothes would have shocked sixteenth-century diners. Table manners were strictly adhered to and were far more complicated than our modern dining etiquette.

Tudor meals were also a way to remind everyone of their place in the social hierarchy. Most meals were served in portions designed to feed four people, which was called "a mess." Seating at meals was arranged according to rank, so the most important person sharing the mess would help themselves first, followed by the next person in stature, and so on through the group of four.

A place setting would have consisted of a trencher—a large slice of stale bread that you did not eat but actually served as your plate. You brought your own silverware to the table—a knife. You used your knife not only to cut up your food, but also to pick it up. Some of the knives from the period had the tip of the blade divided into two little prongs—a bit of a precursor to the fork (forks were not common until the eighteenth century). A single cup was shared among a mess though it was shaped more like a bowl, and you drank from it using both hands.

Tudor monarchs used banquets to convey certain messages to their own subjects and to foreign rulers. Court entertainments essentially functioned as what we might now call "public relations." And foreign ambassadors seemed to have been pretty impressed by Henry VIII's court, as the papal nuncio wrote to Isabella D'Este of Mantua in 1515, "The wealth and civilization of the world are here." England was beginning to be seen as a sophisticated nation worthy of note—which was Henry's goal in everything he did.

One great example of this diplomatic showmanship was the Field of the Cloth of Gold, a meeting between Henry VIII and Francis I, King of France, that took place in Calais in 1520. It was a great tournament with lots of festivities and the general theme was goodwill after the treaty of "Perpetual Friendship" had been signed in 1518 between the two kingdoms. But Henry's behavior revealed that everything wasn't as amicable as it might have seemed on the surface.

When it came time to leave England, Henry didn't sail the English Channel until it had been cleared of all other ships. He was convinced he was going to be taken hostage by the French. Not a great start to a supposedly friendly diplomatic meeting. Once he arrived safely in Calais, Henry and Francis went to great lengths to impress one another—they were both Renaissance men and also quite close in age—contemporary competitors if you will. Henry built an incredible temporary palace, outside of which he had two fountains placed; one running with red wine and the other with white. Francis organized musical performances by some of the finest Renaissance composers. So much gold cloth was worn by both sides the entire spectacle was named for it. The amount of pageantry was as grand and imposing as they intended it to be.

Spiced Digestive

HIPPOCRAS

SERVES 8 TO 10 Hippocras *is a digestive, named for Hippocrates's sleeve, the bag used to filter the final product. Hippocrates was, of course, the ancient Greek often called the father of medicine for whom the Hippocratic oath, still taken by doctors today, is named. I find a coffee filter works better than the three to six bags and filtrations originally used, but the name is lovely and hints at the health benefits Tudors believed it conferred.*

1-inch-piece fresh ginger, peeled and sliced

4 whole white peppercorns

2 cinnamon sticks

2 cardamom pods

¼ cup sugar

1 bottle (750 ml) fine red wine

1 long pepper (see Note, page 111)

¼ cup brandy

BRUISE the ginger, peppercorns, cinnamon sticks, cardamom pods, and sugar in a mortar and pestle and mix with the wine and long pepper. Seal in a glass or plastic bottle with a tight-fitting lid and let rest at room temperature for 48 hours. Strain the mixture through a fine-mesh sieve into a pitcher, discard the solids, and stir in the brandy. (For a faster but ahistorical method, the spices can be mixed with a pint of wine and brought to a simmer, covered for 30 minutes, then chilled, filtered, and combined with the rest of the wine and the brandy.)

Decorated Marzipan

MARCHPANE

SERVES 4 TO 6 *Queen Elizabeth was famous for, among other things, her sweet tooth. She loved sugary desserts and sweetened wine and is said to have consumed so much sugar in her diet that by middle age her teeth were entirely black. The following recipe is the direct linear predecessor of our modern marzipan and lends itself particularly well to fanciful decoration. It comes from the 1594 cookbook* The Good Huswifes Handmaide for the Kitchin. *It is a bit of a pain to make in a modern food processor, a lesser but different kind of pain if you happen to have access to a wet grinder (most commonly used for Indian cuisine), and a fantastical nightmare if you want to try to make it the old-fashioned way with a mortar and pestle. This recipe can be scaled to any size, in batches, limited only by your final desired dimensions.*

¾ cup confectioners' sugar, plus more for pan

2 cups blanched slivered almonds

1 tablespoon plus 2 teaspoons rosewater

¼ teaspoon almond extract

Dried or candied fruit or nuts for decoration

FOR THE GLAZE:

1 cup confectioners' sugar

1 tablespoon rosewater

YOU will need a mold to shape the dough. A small tart pan with a removable bottom works well. Prepare the mold by dusting it liberally with confectioners' sugar from a sifter.

PLACE the almonds, the ¾ cup sugar, rosewater, and almond extract in the bowl of a food processor fitted with the metal blade. Add 2 tablespoons water. Process repeatedly for about 30 seconds at a time, assiduously scraping down the sides of the bowl in between. Keep going until it forms a smooth paste or dough. This may take 5 to 10 minutes.

PRESS the dough into the mold and chill it for 1 hour, then carefully remove it from the mold.

THE *marchpane* can be decorated with dried or candied fruit cut into fanciful shapes, nuts—really anything.

TO make the glaze, whisk together the confectioners' sugar, rosewater, and 1 tablespoon water in a medium bowl, then slowly add an additional tablespoon of water until you reach the consistency of thin Elmer's glue. Use this glaze to glue on the decorations.

MARRIED TO THE KINGDOM

WHEN HENRY VIII DIED IN 1547 he left behind three children, all from different mothers. There was Mary, whose mother had been Catherine of Aragon, Henry's first wife, whom he spent years trying to divorce. There was Edward, whose mother had been Jane Seymour, his third wife who died from complications after childbirth. She was also the only one of Henry's wives to receive a queen's funeral—it pays to birth boys. And then there was Elizabeth, born to Anne Boleyn, the second and perhaps most controversial of Henry's wives, who was ultimately sentenced to death when Elizabeth was still a baby—supposedly for having sex with her brother, among other things. (Accusations largely believed to be false today.)

As the only living male heir, Edward immediately became king after his father's death. King Edward VI's reign was short, just six years. He died at the age of sixteen having always been a somewhat sickly child. Next up was Queen Mary I, often referred to as "Bloody Mary"; a devout Catholic like her Spanish mother before her, she tried to pivot England back to Catholicism and sentenced quite a few Protestant "heretics" to death in the process. And then came Elizabeth, one of the longest reigning monarchs in British history, and certainly one of its most famous queens.

Queen Elizabeth I is often referred to as the Virgin Queen, an assumption about her sexual status deduced solely from her position as a woman without a husband (though rumors would abound throughout her life about a long-term affair with Sir Robert Dudley, First Earl of Leicester). But what so many stories and histories about her reign fail to recognize is that Elizabeth's refusal to marry was far more nuanced than just not wanting to share power with a man. On February 10, 1559, Elizabeth stood before Parliament and made an incredible speech. She was tired of the marriage proposals, her counselors constantly advising her to take a husband, the criticisms and accusations like "How could a woman not want to marry and bear children?!" She decided to speak plainly about her choice not to do so:

> I am already bound unto an husband, which is the kingdom of England, and that may suffice you . . . And reproach me no more . . . that I have no children: for every one of you, and as many as are English, are my children, and kinsfolk.

In her eyes she was married—to the kingdom of England—and she did have children—the people of England. She was twenty-five years old when she made this speech and had been queen for a little over a year. It was the middle of the sixteenth century and she was speaking to a room filled entirely with men. It was nothing short of revolutionary.

Her reign was marked by religious tolerance, victory over the Spanish Armada, and the flourishing of theater, literature, and the arts influenced by the Northern European Renaissance. William Shakespeare and Elizabeth were contemporaries. While she governed in a style never before seen, he dared to write plays for the common people, in the common tongue.

And perhaps this is at the crux of what makes the Tudors so interesting to us all these years later; maybe they remind us moderns of ourselves. They were boundary-breaking people, flipping the script on marriage, religion, and art, doing it their own way, establishing new traditions and norms.

When Elizabeth died at the age of sixty-nine in 1603, the reign of the Tudors came to an end. With no direct offspring of her own, the crown passed to her cousin, James VI of Scotland. When James assumed the throne, the Union of the Crown was decreed and he officially became King James I of England, Scotland, and Ireland. Essentially, Elizabeth's refusal to marry created modern Britain.

While the internal foundations were laid for an early modern nation-state outside the British Isles, events were occurring that would define Britain's role on the world stage in the centuries to come.

Men like Sir Walter Raleigh were granted royal charters from Queen Elizabeth herself to "explore and colonize" any lands not ruled or occupied by Christian people, resulting in the failed Roanoke Colony (in modern-day North Carolina) as well as a few voyages to parts of the Caribbean and what is now Newfoundland. During the final years of Elizabeth's rule, the seeds were sown for Britain's future as one of the most powerful empires in the world. An empire so vast, that the sun would never set upon it.

AL-ANDALUS
8TH to 15TH centuries

I N THE YEAR 755, a long lost and presumed dead Umayyad prince, Abd al-Rahman, re-enters our story to write his own magnificent tale—one that includes conquering foreign lands, building a new society, and creating new identities. After that murderous dinner party in 750 (which began in Chapter Two), when the recently victorious Abbasids slaughtered the Umayyad family, Prince Abd al-Rahman, grandson of the caliph Hisham, escaped.

Some sources say he managed to escape with one of his sons, his brother, and his servant Badr. They ran for their lives, trying to outpace the Abbasid soldiers on their tails, and swam across the Euphrates. It was there that his brother apparently drowned.

What happened to his four-year-old son during the chase, we do not know. All we know is that five years later, in 755, he and his faithful servant Badr emerge in North Africa. No longer in hiding, al-Rahman was ready to fight back. In the years to come he would sail north from Africa to the Iberian peninsula, today Portugal and Spain. He would conquer the peninsula and establish a European-based Umayyad caliphate. For over seven hundred years Spain would be ruled by Muslims. They called this land al-Andalus.

Al-Andalus was a country rich in jewels, a shining beacon of culture nestled at the edges of a rather gloomy Europe still recovering from the collapse of the Roman Empire. The largest libraries of the continent were in al-Andalus, filled with volumes by Arabs, Jews, Christians, and those ever-coveted ancient Greek and Roman manuscripts. The capital, Córdoba, had running water and paved streets that were lit up at night. Residents could enjoy any of the hundreds of public baths, mosques, and thousands of shops. There was a book market and paper factories to support the production of books. On the outskirts of the city, an eleventh-century Versailles-esque palatial complex was erected. Booming trade with the rest of the Mediterranean world and beyond kept the ports busy with goods, ideas, and people from every corner of the medieval world streaming in.

Why isn't al-Andalus a part of European history? When medieval European history is taught in schools, what is scarcely mentioned is the Muslim caliphate that existed in mainland Europe for seven hundred years alongside Christian kingdoms. If it is mentioned, it is an anomaly, some foreign aberration that took the real Europeans (i.e., the Christians) centuries to defeat and get rid of. In reality, Islam helped to shape European identity; not from afar, but on its very own shores.

The West's relationship with Islam is very, very old. In fact as soon as the Roman Empire collapsed, the battle between East and West began. And in many ways—it hasn't ended. It's just changed form. The legacy of Muslim rule in Europe is everywhere. We just have to look closer.

MEATBALLS AND EGGS

THE RECIPES in this chapter come from the remarkable thirteenth-century *Anonymous Andalusian Cookbook*. While composed in Europe, in its level of literacy and sophistication it shares more with cookbooks of the Islamic Middle East than with European cookbooks of the time, which were often no more than lists of ingredients and very basic techniques. A few items run throughout the well-organized chapters and specific cooking directions, chief among them meatballs and eggs.

Meatballs and eggs might be humble dishes to some, but to the chefs and diners of Moorish Spain, they were ubiquitous and often extraordinary. The practice in these recipes of covering a dish with eggs for its final cooking was a powerful way of gently cooking while retaining flavor and richness. Meatballs were made of every kind of meat and were frequently used as a garnish, even for dishes that featured a different protein, such as fish. For virtually every meat recipe, there is a more complex version, often titled "extraordinary," that invariably includes making meatballs of the same meat as the main roast. The roast itself was often stuffed with the meatballs, and the two were served together. While we see this type of "three ways" cooking in our most high-end restaurants today, this technique—a platform for showcasing the chef's skills—has a thoroughly ancient history.

Small Birds or Meatballs Made of Sheep's Meat

SIFAT ASAFEER MASNU'A MIN LAHM AL-GHANAM

6 TO 8 SMALL BIRDS OR 15 TO 20 MEATBALLS, SERVING 4 TO 6 *Ever since the first cookbooks, we have seen the almost perverse desire to make one food look like another. This dates as far back as ancient Rome, and it is repeated across cultures and regions, probably because human beings like surprise and delight in their food. The basic meatball recipe is incredibly ubiquitous in the cooking of Muslim Spain. Meatballs are used as an all-purpose garnish in multiple dishes, including fish dishes! Meatballs to be used as a garnish should simply be rolled into one-half-inch spheres.*

FOR THE MEATBALLS:

1 pound boneless leg of lamb, cut into ½-inch chunks

1 medium yellow onion, finely chopped

1 large egg, lightly beaten

2 tablespoons all-purpose flour

1½ teaspoons freshly ground black pepper

2 teaspoons ground cinnamon

1 teaspoon dried lavender

1½ teaspoons kosher salt

Canola oil for frying

FOR THE SAUCE:

¼ cup plus 2 tablespoons sherry vinegar

2 tablespoons Murri (page 51)

¼ cup extra-virgin olive oil

1 teaspoon freshly ground black pepper

2 teaspoons ground cumin

¼ teaspoon saffron

TO make the meatballs, place all the ingredients except the oil for frying in the bowl of a food processor fitted with the metal blade and process until quite smooth, scraping down the sides several times. Form a portion of the mixture into a ball 2 to 3 inches in diameter. Gently pinch one end to make a squat bowling pin shape. Push the small end up and back to form the head and neck of the bird, and pinch out a small beak at the front. Now pinch the other end to flatten and raise it to form the tail. Take a small portion of the meat and flatten it into a heart shape. (It is easiest to do this on a piece of wax paper.)

Split the pointed end to the middle of the heart and spread the two sections apart to make wings. Press them in place on the back of your bird. Repeat with remaining meat mixture. (Alternatively, roll into balls about 1 inch in diameter.) Chill for 30 minutes on a sheet pan lined with parchment paper.

LINE a sheet pan with paper towels. Heat ½ inch of canola oil in a cast-iron skillet over medium-high heat. Add the birds or meatballs and fry, turning occasionally, until well browned on all sides and cooked through, about 5 minutes. Drain on the paper towels.

FOR the sauce, combine all the ingredients with ¼ cup water in a saucepan large enough to hold the birds or meatballs and simmer over medium-low heat, whisking gently, for 3 minutes. Add the cooked birds or meatballs to the sauce and gently spoon the sauce over them. Transfer to a bowl and serve.

Chicken Soup
(That Regulates the Humors)

ZIRBAJA

SERVES 4 TO 6 *So, it turns out my grandmother was right, and that she was faithfully following at least a millennium of medical wisdom. This soup, which appears in virtually all medieval Arab cookbooks, is accompanied by several stories in the text and is described in one as "the apple of the kitchen, there is no harm in it at all." It is also sweet, warm, and comforting, which are lovely attributes in both soups and grandmothers.*

2 tablespoons extra-virgin olive oil

1 pound boneless, skinless chicken breast, cut into 1-inch cubes

1 to 1½ teaspoons kosher salt

1½ teaspoons freshly ground black pepper

2 teaspoons ground coriander

1 ½ teaspoons ground cinnamon

½ teaspoon saffron

2 tablespoons plus 1½ teaspoons sugar

4 cups low-sodium chicken stock

¼ cup sherry vinegar

¾ cup almond flour

1 tablespoon rosewater

HEAT the olive oil in a stockpot over medium heat. Add the chicken and season with most of the salt. Toss the chicken to brown, 2 to 3 minutes. Add the spices and sugar and cook for 30 seconds. Add the chicken stock and vinegar and whisk in the almond flour. Bring to a boil and reduce to a simmer. Cook until the chicken is just done, 10 to 12 minutes. Finish with the rosewater, then taste for seasoning and adjust.

Artichokes Stewed with Chickpeas

SUN'AT LAWN BI-HARSHAF

SERVES 4 TO 6 *In the original, this recipe begins, "Take the meat and cut it up." Virtually all of the dishes that primarily showcase vegetables in the* Anonymous Andalusian Cookbook *also include meat. The fact that they also very commonly do not specify the type of meat to be used underlines that the meat, while a constant, was not the focus of the dish. Regardless of the type of meat used—or even if you opt to leave it out entirely—this is a lush and hearty stew topped with crisped and roasted artichokes.*

1 tablespoon lemon juice

3 artichokes

1 teaspoon whole coriander seeds

1 tablespoon extra-virgin olive oil

1 medium yellow onion, finely chopped

1 teaspoon freshly ground black pepper

1 pound lamb, beef, or chicken, cut into ½-inch cubes or smaller (optional)

1 (29-ounce) can chickpeas, rinsed and drained (about 3 cups)

1½ to 2 cups low-sodium chicken or vegetable stock

2 tablespoons Murri (page 51)

3 tablespoons unsalted butter

3 large eggs, beaten

1 cup panko breadcrumbs

Kosher salt

PREHEAT the oven to 425°F.

WHEN preparing artichokes, it is best to wear gloves to prevent staining. Prepare a large bowl of cold water and add the lemon juice. Cut off the top of one artichoke with a serrated knife, leaving 1 to 1½ inches above the heart. Cut all but 1 inch of the stem. Tear off the small leaves around the base and then peel the stem with a vegetable peeler. Place the artichoke stem up and slice it in half. Using a small melon baller or other scoop, completely remove the fibrous choke at the center and discard. Transfer the artichoke to the lemon water. Repeat with the remaining artichokes.

PLACE the coriander seeds in a medium, oven-safe sauté pan with a tight-fitting lid over medium heat and toast until fragrant. Add the olive oil, then the chopped onion and the black pepper. Cook until the onion is translucent. Add the meat, if using, the chickpeas, stock, murri, and butter. Bring to a boil over high heat, reduce to a simmer, and cook for 10 minutes. Place the artichoke halves on top, cover, and continue to cook until the artichokes are tender and the meat is fully cooked, about 20 minutes.

POUR the beaten eggs over the top of the chickpeas and around the artichokes and sprinkle with the breadcrumbs. Season with a large pinch of salt, sprinkled over the whole dish. Bake, uncovered, until the eggs are set and the breadcrumbs are browned, 8 to 10 minutes.

THE ORNAMENT OF
THE WORLD

WHEN THE ROMAN EMPIRE fell, Hispania, like much of Europe, came under Visigothic rule. While the Visigoths (a Germanic tribe) might have been strong warriors, they were not bureaucrats. The infrastructure Rome had built, like roads and aqueducts, fell into disrepair with no central collective tax system to manage them. Buildings were picked apart for their materials. The big country villas of the elite became like little chiefdoms. The roads were dangerous. People stopped moving around as much. Trade didn't entirely dry up, but it certainly wasn't operating at the same levels as it had before.

In 711, when the Umayyad caliphate still ruled from Damascus, military invasions of the Iberian peninsula commenced. In the decades that followed, what the Romans and Visigoths had once called Hispania became part of the Islamic Empire under the new name al-Andalus. Sitting on the shores of the Atlantic Ocean, it was the westernmost edge of the Islamic world, and living so far away from the capital, for the most part the people of al-Andalus got away with doing as they pleased. When, after the Abbasid Revolution, a new caliphate was established in Baghdad, al-Andalus hardly noticed. Life on the frontiers went on largely unchanged.

Perhaps this is how al-Rahman managed to take al-Andalus so quickly. By May 756, just six years after his family was overthrown, he had established a new kingdom for himself. When the Abbasid caliph in Baghdad, al-Mansur, heard of what had happened he was furious but could not deny the brilliance of the entire saga, nicknaming al-Rahman "The Falcon." It was a name that would stick. Baghdad would make no move to reconquer the territory.

The former Visigothic capital of Córdoba became al-Rahman's new capital. At first the Muslims were a minority, but rapid conversion and intermarriage quickly changed that. Al-Andalus became a diverse melting pot of religions, races, and creeds, the meeting point between the old world of Rome, the new emerging European identities across the Pyrenees, and peoples of the Middle East and North Africa. Arabic became the official language. People became "Arabized." Conversion was not enforced; all peoples of "the book" (i.e., Christians, Jews, and Muslims) were guaranteed safety under Islamic rule. Though of course there were rules for Christians and

Jews—they were not allowed to proselytize or to criticize the Prophet and they had to pay a special tax.

Under al-Rahman's reign the construction of the Mosque of Córdoba began. For many decades the Christians and Muslims of Córdoba had prayed alongside one another in the Church of Saint Vincent, with only a partition down the middle. But in 785, al-Rahman bought the church and its grounds with the intention of building a grand mosque worthy of his new seat of power. Over a thousand years later, the mosque still stands. Its iconic red and white brick arches stretch out in seemingly endless rows; stand in one corner of the mosque and the other end is barely visible. Islamic architectural motifs define the space, but materials from old Roman buildings were used, as were subtle nods to the pre-Islamic culture of Hispania. When the Christian reconquest took place, the mosque was not torn down, instead a Baroque cathedral was built at the center of it, creating a space that today feels like something out of an architect's hallucinatory fusion fever dream. A mosque, built upon a church, with a cathedral at its center; each layer of sediment reveals a previous identity, a previous occupant. On one wall of the mosque al-Rahman had these words inscribed, "It embodied what came before. Illuminated what came after."

Al-Rahman brought more than just architecture with him to al-Andalus. In an attempt to re-create the full ambiance of his homeland, he had palm trees, lemons, limes, grapefruit, almonds, apricots, saffron, mulberry trees, oranges, rice, and sugarcane brought to the peninsula, where they began to grow and slowly became a part of both the local diet and the natural flora. The orange trees that line the streets of Córdoba and Seville today are all thanks to al-Rahman. The palm trees throughout southern Europe, from Nice to Majorca, are also thanks to him. In fact, it would be the Spanish who would bring the palm tree to the Americas in the 1490s. The palm trees that dot Caribbean beaches and line the streets of Los Angeles today are all thanks to one tenth-century Umayyad prince, homesick and in permanent exile.

Heartbreak leads humans to extraordinary places. I wonder what kind of heartbreak al-Rahman must have felt when he looked upon these relocated palm trees every day. They must have reminded him of home: of the son he lost. Presumably his wife or mother of his child too. Perhaps there were other children. Not to mention the loss of his entire family. Did he hold rage against the Abbasids? If he dreamt of revenge, he certainly never acted upon it. At least not in the traditional sense. He lost everything and instead of carving out a quiet life of refuge in some obscure corner, he built a new world.

Toward the end of his life he would write:

A palm tree stands in the middle of Rusafa,
Born in the West, far from the land of Palms.
I said to it: How like me you are, far away and in exile,
In long separation from family and friends.
You have sprung from soil in which you are a stranger;
And I, like you, am far from home.

—Abd al-Rahman

Abd al-Rahman never proclaimed himself caliph during his reign of al-Andalus; rather he held the title "emir." It was his grandson, Abd al-Rahman III, who in 929 proclaimed al-Andalus to be the true caliphate and center of Islam. This was, to put it mildly, a big move. It was a direct challenge to the Abbasid seat of power in Baghdad. However, the Abbasids were facing their own political issues in the Middle East, and again took no action against al-Andalus. Europe was another world away.

Abd al-Rahman III, who ruled from 912 to 961, was perhaps the Western equivalent of Harun al-Rashid. Under his reign al-Andalus flourished as a center of learning, art, trade, and cross-cultural communication. The caliphal library held over four hundred thousand volumes. A movement akin to the Baghdadi Translation Movement took hold. Intellectuals from all over Europe flocked to Muslim-ruled cities like Córdoba, a safe haven of intellectual progress amid the dark ages of the rest of the continent.

Abd al-Rahman III built a huge palace complex outside of Córdoba called Madinat al-Zahra (named for his favorite concubine), where a large royal court could flourish alongside palm trees and orchards of fruit from the east. Al-Rahman III's court was incredibly diverse. Muslims, Jews, and Christians were all enmeshed in palace life, from the Christian women in the caliph's harem who fathered his children, to his Jewish grand vizier, Hasadai ibn Shaprut (who famously helped negotiate an alliance between al-Andalus and the Byzantine emperor Constantine VII).

The multiculturalism of al-Andalus in this period contrasted sharply with the darkness that had set over much of the rest of Europe, so often referred to as "the Dark Ages." There were clear indicators of the cultural differences between al-Andalus and the rest of the Europe—but there were also more subtle contrasting characteristics, including language.

It didn't take long for Arabic to become the official language of al-Andalus. It was the language that was spoken commonly among the population (of all backgrounds), and also the language of state politics, academia, the language spoken in the mosques, and in which the Quran was written. Arabic was the language of every aspect of Islamic society.

Perhaps today we take for granted our twenty-first-century ability to read major religious texts in most languages. But over a thousand years ago, Christians, if they wanted to read the Bible, had to be fluent in Latin, a language only spoken by the highly educated elite, the one percent if you will. Even thirteen hundred years ago Latin was a dead language. This meant that most Christian Europeans could not understand the words that were spoken to them in Church. The majority of the population was isolated linguistically from their own religion. Perhaps this is why imagery became so crucial in churches; unable to read, write, or understand the words of their own holy books, most Christians took in biblical stories visually. As Christians sat in pews every Sunday, all those altarpieces, paintings, and stained-glass windows must have provided a lot more information than the man in the pulpit blathering on in some foreign tongue. Outside of church, the common people were speaking the beginning of modern European languages, as they emerged from local dialects: French, German, English, and Italian in their nascent stages.

In the year 955, a woman named Horswitha, who lived as a cannonness in a convent in Gandersheim, Germany, learned about Córdoba and the land of the Umayyads that lay to the south. A diplomatic delegation had been sent to the court of King Otto I by al-Rahman III, and Horswitha, highly educated and of noble blood, somehow landed herself in the king's inner circle and managed to converse with the diplomats. From one of them in particular, Racemundo, the bishop of Elvira, she learned of Córdoba, of its hundreds of public baths, its "tens of thousands of shops" (perhaps an exaggeration), the running water that supplied the city, and its "well-lit streets." When Horswitha later wrote her secondhand description of the Andalusian capital, she called it "the ornament of the world." The accounts must have seemed like something from another world away, perhaps more similar to the descriptions of ancient Rome she read, rather than her own contemporary time. It also must have made quite an impression that this Muslim caliph had a bishop as part of his inner circle, in addition to his Jewish grand vizier, Hasdai, who also played an integral role in diplomatic missions for the caliph.

A NEW ERA OF IBERIAN CUISINE would emerge from the fruits, vegetables, herbs, and spices brought to Spain by Abd al-Rahman I. Not just ingredients but cooking techniques and recipes found their way into the new food culture of al-Andalus.

It is true that spices from the East had been making their way west into Europe for centuries, and that many dishes of medieval Europe already incorporated these Asian spices, as well as that sweet and sour flavor profile that is today more commonly associated with Persian food. What the Muslim presence in mainland Europe did—especially in a cultural center that was visited by elites, who would subsequently bring what they had seen home with them—was elevate and refine.

We saw in Chapter Two how Al-Warrāq's cookbook *The Annals of the Caliphs' Kitchens* was complex, detailed in ways no European cookbook came close to achieving for many hundreds of years. In al-Andalus that same style of cookbook appeared on Western shores. The *Anonymous Andalusian Cookbook*, from which the recipes in this chapter are sourced, is the perfect example of this level of sophistication: its specific weights and measures, step-by-step cooking instructions, and intricate pastry techniques.

Murri, that fermented condiment we know so well from Baghdad, was introduced, as were many other foodstuffs that today are staples of Spanish cuisine: rice, saffron, almonds, oranges, and apricots. It would be hard to imagine Spain without these ingredients. There would be no paella: that gently stewed rice dish, colored with saffron, and filled with seafood and meats that is essentially a pilaf, a Middle Eastern dish that would be recognizable today or a thousand years ago.

After 1492, when Muslims and Jews were expelled from Spain, a society obsessed with the public consumption of pork emerged. Walk the streets of any Spanish city today and you will see cured legs of *jamon* hanging in a window. Iberico ham, sausages, grilled pork loins, small pieces eaten with a drink before dinner as a tapas, or incorporated into the main course—pork is everywhere in Spain. Could its popularity be traced back to people trying to prove their "Christian-ness" post expulsion? After all, if you're eating pork, especially in public, you couldn't possibly be Muslim or Jewish. For many deemed "heretical" by the Spanish state, the comfort and safety of conformity was to be found in the humble pig.

As Jews were accepted into Andalusian society, at all levels, their cuisine and culinary practices invariably fused their way into the culture as well. Because Jews were prohibited from cooking or working on Saturdays, the Sabbath in Judaism, dishes such as the following "buried" casserole from the *Anonymous Andalusian Cookbook*, would have been prepared on Friday nights. A hearty stew cooked the night before the Sabbath, it remained buried in the ashes of the fire until the following morning, soft glowing embers keeping the beef casserole warm, ready to be eaten the next day.

A TREASURE HOARD OF BREAD

THE GLORIOUS art of bread making is, sadly, beyond the scope of this book. However, the wealth and diversity of breads from this world are truly extraordinary. There were rich breads, flatbreads, sweet breads, loaves, and many, many more. They could be cooked in bread ovens, in buried *tannur* ovens, or even in hot coals.

The vital place of breads is not surprising when you consider that the majority of dishes were stews, best when sopped up with a hearty slice of bread.

The thirteenth-century *Anonymous Andalusian Cookbook* that preserves all of these recipes also brings a vision of the beautiful custom of "the kings of the East," in which such a king commands his bakers to serve a great variety of breads on a broad tray, in the center of which they present his favorites, but surrounded by many other options from which one "eats of that that pleases and attracts." I can only suggest that you do the same.

Jewish "Buried" Casserole

LAWN YAHOODI MAHSHU MADFOON

SERVES 6 TO 8   *This slow-cooked casserole is referred to as "buried" because it was pre-pared the day before the Sabbath and then buried in the coals and ashes of the fireplace to cook overnight—essential to respecting the Jewish prohibition against working or cooking on Saturday. This recipe will cook in a modern oven in the hour given, but will achieve the same rich, complex, and delicious result as if left in the ashes overnight. You will be unsur-prised to learn that meatballs can also be incorporated into this dish. Make one-half-inch meatballs following the recipe on page 188 and include them with the meat.*

FOR THE EGG LAYERS:

1 cup all-purpose flour

1 tablespoon ground cinnamon

1 tablespoon freshly ground black pepper

2 teaspoons kosher salt

9 large eggs, beaten

Oil for pan

FOR THE MEAT AND GARNISHES:

¼ cup extra-virgin olive oil

1 large yellow onion, minced

½ bunch cilantro, chopped (about ½ cup)

3 pounds boneless chuck steak, cut into slices and pounded thin

1 cup water or low-sodium beef stock

1 tablespoon Murri (page 51)

1 tablespoon ground coriander

2 teaspoons ground cinnamon

1 teaspoon freshly ground black pepper

1 teaspoon dried lavender

2 teaspoons kosher salt

2 tablespoons roughly chopped mint leaves

2 tablespoons toasted pine nuts

2 tablespoons toasted pistachios

PREHEAT the oven to 325°F.

FIRST make the egg layers, which are some-where between an omelet and a crepe. Whisk together the flour, cinnamon, black pepper, and salt. Slowly whisk in the eggs until smoothly and entirely incorporated.

SELECT a 2- to 3-quart casserole dish with straight sides. Add a thin layer of oil to the casserole and place over medium-high heat until just shimmering. Add about one-third of the egg mixture to the casserole, making sure it covers the bottom entirely. Cook until firm and bubbles appear on the surface, like a thick pancake, and flip over. Cook until

very firm; don't worry about overcooking. Reserve this egg pancake and repeat the procedure with another one-third of the egg mixture. Remove the casserole from the heat about halfway through the cooking process (after you have turned the second pancake) and let it finish cooking in the hot pan off the heat, then leave it in the pan. This will be the bottom layer.

ADD the ¼ cup olive oil to a medium sauce-pan and place over medium-high heat. Add the onion and cilantro and cook, stirring frequently, until well browned, about 10 minutes. Add the meat, water or stock, murri, coriander, cinnamon, pepper, lavender, and salt. Bring to a boil over high heat then reduce to a simmer and cook for 12 to 15 minutes.

TAKE the casserole with the egg layer in place in the bottom and add roughly half the meat on top of it in an even layer. Place the other pancake on top and flatten with your hands. Add the rest of the meat on top, along with any cooking liquid. Allow the meat and liquid to settle for about 1 minute, then cover the top with the remaining egg mixture, distributing it evenly.

BAKE in the preheated oven for 1 hour. Garnish with the mint leaves, pine nuts, and pistachios and serve.

Green Stew of Fish

TAFAYA KHADRA' MIN AL-HOOT

SERVES 4 TO 6 *This baked "stew" of fish is bright, powerful, and subtle all at the same time. The fish is cloaked in a rich and herbaceous mixture of herbs and spices and cooked in the oven, where fennel plays a supporting role perfectly.*

2 medium bulbs fennel

1 cup mint leaves, plus 1 tablespoon chopped

4 cups cilantro leaves and stems, plus 1 tablespoon chopped leaves

1 medium red onion, roughly chopped

1½ cups extra-virgin olive oil

2 teaspoons kosher salt

1 teaspoon freshly ground black pepper

2 teaspoons whole toasted coriander seeds

2 teaspoons ground ginger

2 teaspoons whole toasted caraway seeds

2 pounds halibut fillet, cut into 2- to 3-inch chunks

4 ounces ½-inch meatballs, precooked (page 188; optional)

PREHEAT the oven to 400°F.

CUT off the fennel stalks and reserve some fronds for garnish. Cut off the bases of the fennel and then cut each bulb in half. Remove the cores by making a V-shaped cut in each, and then cut the fennel vertically into narrow planks.

IN a blender combine the 1 cup mint leaves, 4 cups cilantro leaves and stems, and the onion with the olive oil and salt. Blend until smooth. (Traditionally this would have been even more liquid, the kind of results you'd

get with a juicer, so you can use a juicer for this if you have one, but increase the quantities by about half as the yield will be smaller.) Mix in the spices.

TOSS the fish with this sauce and then transfer the fish and sauce to a 12-inch round baking dish. Insert the fennel slices among the fish pieces. Scatter the meatballs on top, if using. Bake until the fish is opaque and flaky, 15 to 20 minutes.

GARNISH with the chopped mint and cilantro, and the reserved fennel fronds.

Roasted Duck with Nuts and Garlic

SIFAT SHIWA' ALWAN MIN IWAZZ AL-QURT LI-ABI SALIH AL-RAHBANI FI MATBAKHIHI

SERVES 4 TO 6 *A well-roasted duck can be the centerpiece to any dinner, whether a modern party or a gathering eight centuries in the past, and this one is a showstopper. The vibrant preparation combines a powerful marinade with a delicate roast infused with nuts, garlic, and ginger.*

FOR THE DUCK:

1 (4 ½- to 5 ½-pound) duck

¼ cup blanched almonds

½ teaspoon sugar

¼ cup walnut halves

¼ cup small cloves garlic

FOR THE MARINADE:

¼ cup roughly chopped yellow onion

¼ cup roughly chopped garlic

¼ cup chopped cilantro leaves and stems

½ cup Murri (page 51)

1 cup red wine vinegar

2 cups sherry vinegar

2 tablespoons extra-virgin olive oil

1 tablespoon plus 1 teaspoon ground coriander

1 tablespoon plus 1 teaspoon ground cinnamon

1 tablespoon plus 1 teaspoon ground ginger

1 tablespoon plus 1 teaspoon ground cumin

1 tablespoon plus 1 teaspoon dried thyme

PREPARE the duck by trimming the excess skin around the neck area and the cavity. Cut off the wing tips with a sharp knife or kitchen shears and discard, along with the giblets.

COMBINE all the marinade ingredients in a blender and blend until smooth. Place the duck in a large zip-lock bag and add the marinade, squeezing most of the air out to ensure that the duck is fully covered. Refrigerate overnight in the marinade.

PREHEAT the oven to 425°F.

REMOVE the duck from the marinade and pat dry. Place the almonds and sugar in a food processor fitted with the metal blade and process to a paste, scraping down the sides. Place the duck breast side up on a roasting rack or wire rack in a roasting pan. With a sharp paring knife, make a series of deep but narrow slits in the flesh, poking the knife in ½ to ¾ inch. Pinch off pieces of the almond paste the size of whole almonds and alternately push these and the walnuts and garlic into the slits (one item per slit). It is best to do this one at a time, first cutting the hole, enlarging it slightly with your fingertip, and then pushing in the paste, walnut, or garlic. You may have a bit of the walnuts, garlic, and/or almond paste left over, depending on the size and architecture of the duck.

ROAST in the preheated oven for 30 minutes. Reduce the oven temperature to 300°F and continue to roast until the deepest part of the thigh reaches 175°F on an instant-read thermometer, about 1 additional hour.

LET the duck rest for 10 minutes before carving and serving.

Nut-Stuffed Breast of Lamb

JANB MASHWI

SERVES 4 TO 6 *Lamb breast is a sadly underused cut. It combines the meat of the ribs and the belly, both succulent and flavorful. The stuffing in this version highlights the flavor of the meat without overshadowing it. The balance and sophistication of the cooks of this period is still to be marveled at today.*

½ teaspoon freshly ground black pepper, plus more to taste

½ teaspoon kosher salt, plus more to taste

1 cup toasted blanched almonds

1 cup toasted blanched hazelnuts

2 tablespoons breadcrumbs

1 teaspoon ground cinnamon

1 teaspoon dried lavender

¼ teaspoon ground clove

¼ teaspoon saffron

2 teaspoons extra-virgin olive oil

1 (2½- to 3-pound) lamb breast

PREHEAT the oven to 325°F.

PLACE the ½ teaspoon pepper, ½ teaspoon salt, and all the remaining ingredients except the lamb in a food processor fitted with the metal blade. Process until the mixture comes together but retains some texture—don't grind it to a smooth paste.

WITH a long, thin knife, make a cut between the ribs and the belly of the lamb. Fill this space with the stuffing mixture. Season the outside of the lamb generously with salt and pepper.

TRANSFER to a sheet pan and cover with foil. Bake until tender and easily pierced with a knife, 1½ to 2 hours. Remove from the oven and increase the oven temperature to 450°F. Remove the foil, return the lamb to the oven, and roast until the top is brown and crisp, about 15 additional minutes. Allow to rest for 10 minutes before carving and serving.

THE ALHAMBRA

IN 1009 INTERNAL WARS and disputes began to hit Alandalucia hard. Two hundred years into a pretty glorious rule, things got messy. And it wasn't because of any external rivalries or claims; it was due to internal politics, various players vying for power, wanting the "ornament of the world" for themselves.

By 1031, the Córdoban caliphate had fully collapsed. In the wake of its fall many little independent city-states known as *taifas* emerged, battling it out for control of the peninsula. The whole of Spain descended into a vicious power struggle, not so different from the Renaissance Italian city-states like Venice, Rome, and Naples constantly warring in the later Middle Ages. The taifas were generally Muslim ruled, but there were also a few small Christian kingdoms beginning to compete for power too.

Power shifted back and forth between various dynasties and groups, like sand shifting back and forth underneath crashing tidal waves. In 1085 Alfonso of Castile, a Christian ruler from the north, took over Muslim-controlled Toledo. The Muslim ruler of Seville, al-Mu'tamid Muhammad Ibn Abbad, fearing for the safety of his own city, decided to call upon the Moroccan Almoravids for help in fighting the Christians. At the time it seemed a logical move—call upon fellow Muslims for help—but the consequences ended up being far from what either side wanted. The Almoravids did help defeat the Castilians, but then they went on to conquer every other taifa as well, installing themselves as the rulers of al-Andalus for 150 years. A new caliphate had begun.

There was just one major problem. The Almoravids were Orthodox, and the religious tolerance that had defined Umayyad al-Andalus evaporated in an instant. Book burnings and the strict enforcement of religious laws ensued.

Ironically it was Christian-ruled Toledo that remained the bastion of tolerance and progressive ideals as the rest of Spain fell under the sway of Islamic fundamentalism. Intellectuals moved away from Córdoba as the torch was passed and Toledo became, for a moment, the intellectual capital of Europe.

The Jewish citizens of al-Andalus suffered the worst. Their past as a wandering people was once again made a reality as they were exiled from many taifas; their ability to call any place home was determined by the whim of whichever ruler held power. In some cities like Toledo, they were accepted. But in other places, Jewish communities were massacred.

In 1031 Samuel the Nagid (also known as Samuel ibn Naghrela) and his family decided Córdoba had become too dangerous for them. The Naghrelas were a wealthy and powerful Jewish family who had very old roots in al-Andalus that extended back to pre-Visigothic rule. They were merchants, rabbis, and political advisors. Samuel was highly educated and fluent in Arabic and Hebrew. He spent years on the road working in the spice trade, crisscrossing around the Mediterranean basin. Eventually he landed in Granada, a new city being built on the Darro River at the foothills of the Sierra Nevada Mountains.

Samuel found work as a scribe, but his brilliance quickly pushed him forward into the highest echelons of society, eventually working for the ruling Zirid family of Granada itself. He also became the nagid, the head of the Jewish community in the city. It was a position that held religious symbolism but also gave him huge political sway with the rulers of Granada, who needed his help to maintain the support of the city's large Jewish population. He wrote poetry. He commanded the Zirid army in battle. He was an incredibly dynamic character.

His son Joseph Ibn Nagrila continued the family legacy of exercising a lot of influence, and succeeded his father as the vizier of Granada as well as the nagid of the Jewish community. And while Joseph may have ruled successfully for a period, growing anti-Jewish sentiment that was rife throughout the peninsula finally reached Granada. Fearing the nagid was growing too powerful, in 1066 a Muslim mob took over the palace and crucified Joseph, along with many of the city's Jewish residents.

Joseph was crucified atop Sabika Hill, famous for its red clay, and the "Red Fort" or al-Qala al-Hamra that had once stood there. In years to come, the memory of this massacre and the structures that had once stood upon this hill would fade into the muddy history of the "warring years." Eventually, a new fortress, a palace rather, was constructed in its place: the Alhambra.

The last Muslim dynasty of Europe came to power in 1236. The fundamentalist rule of the North African Berber dynasties (first the Almoravids, then the Almohads) came to an end in the 1230s when Christians and Muslims joined forces to kick them out of al-Andalus once and for all. The campaign, led by King Ferdinand III of Castile, was a success. One prominent Muslim family that had helped Ferdinand take Córdoba (his personal prize) was the Nasrid family. As a token of appreciation for their help, Ferdinand gave the ruling Nasrid, Ibn al-Ahmar, the city of Granada in 1236.

Despite ruling for 256 years, the policies of the Nasrids remain murky in the pages of history. Mostly they are known as the last caliphs of al-Andalus. But they are also known for the incredible palatial complex they left behind, the Alhambra, which still stands today.

A modern-day tourist can take a similar route as that of a fourteenth-century person visiting the Alhambra, a long winding uphill journey from the city center to the palace. In bright mid-morning light one November, I made this hike, from the ancient Albaicín neighborhood to the top of the Sabika Hill. As I made my way down narrow cobblestone streets, lined with *carmens* (villas), I thought about the many others who had walked this path to the Alhambra over the centuries.

I imagined a young mother, some seven hundred years ago, emerging from around a corner I had just passed. Perhaps she was bringing her young son to the Alhambra to join his uncle as an apprentice in the gardens surrounding the sultan's palace. An entire city of workers who labored in all manner of fields to keep the sultan and his family fed, housed, and entertained lived atop the hill. I daydreamed about the mother and the boy who would join this city and leave his mother's home for good. I could almost see them walking in front of me.

They would have left the labyrinth of Albaicín and walked up to the edge of the Darro River, on the opposite side of the river stood the Sabika Hill, soaring straight up before them. As they crossed the same stone bridge I had, the river rushing beneath, the pathway through the forest of San Pedro would have unfurled before them. Up, up, up they would climb, zigzagging left and right toward the Gate of Arms, the entry point of the Alhambra.

Panting, small beads of sweat on my brow despite the cool breeze, I reached the gate, which was like an immovable stone drawbridge, extending out from smooth walls of redbrick, seemingly floating over the entire city. I imagined the boy turning around to look out as I did, to see the familiar Mirador of San Nicolas, where he and his friends used to play, and gaze out at the Alhambra, lit up at night, wondering what took place behind its secretive walls. It seemed so small, and so far away.

I smiled to myself, musing that, perhaps in the years to come the boy would become a master horticulturist. An expert in flowers, a savior of dying roses, a magician of lime trees. He would know the pathways through the cyprus tree groves surrounding the Generalife gardens so intimately, that he could walk them blindfolded. As I passed through the interior of the Nasrid palaces, I could almost see the shadow of the boy moving quietly through a hall or covered walkway to access an interior garden, where he would be filled with awe. Walls covered in arabesques, the holy words of the Quran interlaced with foliage, repeated over and over, from eye level, rising up toward the vaulted ceilings. Ordinary citizens of Granada might see similar architectural motifs in the mosques of the city. But not like this.

When I left the Alhambra that day, I walked slowly down the dirt path imagining how the mom must have felt as she left her son behind. It would have been the end of the day, maybe the call to prayer was ringing out. As I approached the Darro River, I could hear a voice. I wasn't sure where it was coming from at first, but it was a man singing—and his voice was beautiful. At the bottom of the path, next to the river, sat an old man on a rocky outcrop, singing his heart out, looking up to the sky. His voice reverberated off the slopes of red earth, off the walls of the palace, off the surface of the water. It was a sad song. A song about a time that doesn't exist anymore. I stopped and listened.

THE RECONQUISTA OR THE CHRISTIAN "RECONQUEST" of Spain, took many years. Centuries in fact. The first big push started in the thirteenth century, as Ferdinand III took many cities throughout southern Spain, crucially Córdoba in 1236. And while Granada remained a Muslim-ruled city, the last stronghold of al-Andalus, it slowly came to be completely encircled by a new Christian Spain, one that held none of the tolerance that had been a hallmark of Islamic rule in Iberia.

In 1474 a woman came to the throne of Castile, and she would change the world forever. Isabella I of Castile was of old royal blood. Her family had been fighting for centuries to rid Muslims from what they saw as their rightful homeland. When she married King Ferdinand II of Aragon in 1469, the unification of their kingdoms, coupled with their continuation of the Reconquista, sealed the fate of Spain.

In spring 1491 Castilian armies surrounded Granada. There were no large bloody battles, no legendary military confrontation; the plan was simply to cut off the supply lines to the city, to siege it from the outside and strangle it into submission. Half a year later the plan worked. The last Nasrid sultan Abu Abdallah Muhammad VII, more commonly known as Boabdil, surrendered the city on November 25, 1491. Isabella and Ferdinand promised Boabdil in their private meeting that no Muslims or Jews would be harmed in the handover, and that all the residents of Granada would be allowed to practice their own religion freely and without fear of persecution.

A few months later, only two days into that pivotal year of 1492, Isabella and Ferdinand arrived in Granada to claim their prize. They made the long, arduous climb to the Alhambra. They dressed in Islamic-style clothing for the occasion, as Boabdil handed over the keys to the city. Muslim rule in al-Andalus was over. A period spanning seven hundred years had come to its end.

It didn't take long for Isabella and Ferdinand to go back on their word. To betray Boabdil and the people of Granada. On March 31, 1492, they issued the Edict of Expulsion: the Jews of Granada—Jews living anywhere in their lands—were ordered to leave Spain by July 31, 1492.

A prominent Jewish Granadan, Isaac Abravanel, somehow managed to convince the Catholic monarchs to postpone the expulsion date to August 2. Just a few days, most likely under the guise of allowing for more time, but it was a symbolic move. The date August 2, 1492 in the Gregorian calendar correlates to the exact date in the Jewish calendar memorializing the anniversary of the destruction of the Temple in Jerusalem, the first official expulsion of Jewish people.

For the time being Muslims were allowed to stay, but eventually forced conversions would take place on a mass scale. Many Muslims left. Many converted in name but not practice. By the turn of the new century in 1500, one would be hard pressed to find a single practitioner of Islam living in Spain. At least openly so. If found guilty, the punishment was death.

Isabella and Ferdinand would continue their Christian cleansing of Spain, through the establishment of the Inquisition. For two hundred years, any person considered to be a heretic, whether that meant secretly a practicing Jew or Muslim, or even a wayward Christian, was subjected to brutal torture, and often death.

Today in Granada, every January 2 there are celebrations commemorating the day Isabella and Ferdinand took the Alhambra. Visit any museum in the city and guides will happily tell you, as they stand in halls built by the Nasrids, how successful the Catholics were against the "foreign, invading" Muslims. The Spanish rejection of seven hundred years of their own past is a chilling reminder of how history can be rewritten by the victors. Traces of the truth survive if you're willing to search. A faded star of David above an old doorframe. Delicate shavings of acorn-fed *jamón* with a drizzle of light green olive oil masking bigotry and violence.

I ONCE VISITED THE TOMB OF ISABELLA AND FERDINAND in the Royal Chapel of Granada. The ground level of the chapel is a baroque orgy of excess, but descend below to where their actual bodies lay and the mood is more somber. Fresh lilies were lying between their coffins, wrapped in ribbons in the colors of the Spanish flag and woven into a decorative bow. The coffins are small, wooden, not like their elaborate marble display coffins up above. As I stood in the crypt, I couldn't help but think how strange it was to be alone in the same room with these two monarchs. Isabella and Ferdinand fundamentally transformed the trajectory of human history and initiated torrents of human suffering on unimaginable scales. Two small wooden boxes holding the bodies of two people who died a very long time ago, but whose actions still affect us all today.

CANDY AND ALCHEMY

THE RECIPE for sugar nougat is transformative—perhaps not from lead to gold, but from simple egg to glossy confection through technical sophistication that might seem quite magical. In fact, there is a direct line from candy-making to the practice of alchemy— early "magical" chemistry seeking the transformational secrets of the universe. No, really. Consider that the initial ingredients, refined white sugar and rosewater, are products of chemical refinement and distillation, respectively. It is then the precise temperature control of the sugar as it is mixed with the beaten egg whites that creates the correct texture, much to the despair of first-time nougat makers and pastry students. Trust me, I have watched half a class produce either a gooey mess or a tooth-breaking horror. The thirteenth-century confectioners of Valencia may not have been transmuting lead into gold, but the delights they made are very much part of the same scientific tradition that we have the medieval Arab world to thank for.

Sugar Nougat Mousse

MU'QAD AL-SUKKAR

SERVES ABOUT 8 *This is closer to a nutty meringue or marshmallow fluff than a chewy nougat. Modern nougat is often made with honey and sugar, but when this recipe was first recorded sugar was a new and highly prized commodity, produced by a mixture of early food science and alchemical wizardry, and it was highlighted as a sign of sophistication and refinement. Granulated sugar also is very neutral in flavor, which lets the nuts remain the real stars of the dish. Don't skimp on the quality of your nuts or dig out an old bag of pistachios or almonds from the back of your cupboard. Buy the finest, freshest, and most aromatic nuts you can find. You'll need a candy thermometer to make this.*

Please remember: Hot sugar is dangerous. It is the napalm of the kitchen. I cannot overstate this. Because it is so much denser than water, it will hold its heat far longer, so if you splash some on yourself it will continue to burn you; it is also sticky. If you get some dangerously hot sugar on your finger and instinctively put it in your mouth, you will now have a burned finger and a burned tongue as well. Some people like to keep a small bowl of ice water next to their cooking sugar just in case they need to quickly cool a burn with a dunk in the water bowl.

½ cup rosewater

2 cups granulated sugar

5 egg whites

1 cup pistachios

1 cup marcona almonds

Confectioners' sugar, to finish

COMBINE the rosewater and the granulated sugar in a medium saucepan and place over medium-high heat with a candy thermometer clipped to the side. Rosewater tends to boil a great deal more than regular water so watch it carefully. Cook until the sugar reaches 266°F.

PLACE the egg whites in the bowl of a stand mixer fitted with the whisk attachment. Whip the egg whites until foamy. As soon as the sugar reaches 266°F, with the mixer running very carefully pour the hot sugar down the side of the bowl (avoid getting any on the whisk as it can splatter and burn you) and whip until the mixture is light and fluffy and has cooled to a manageable temperature, about 5 minutes. Switch from the whisk attachment to the paddle attachment and continue to beat until the meringue falls and flows like dense lava, about 5 additional minutes.

FOLD in the nuts and transfer to a serving bowl or individual glasses to serve; the dessert is meant to be eaten with a spoon. Sift additional powdered sugar over the top.

Almond Crepe Pudding

JUDHABA

SERVES 6 TO 8 *One of the most remarkable things about this elegant pastry dish is that it was very often cooked with a roasting chicken suspended above it. The savory chicken drippings would be incorporated into the dish and the two would be served together. On its own it is a thick, custardy cross between a mille crepe, a custard, and a bread pudding, delicately flavored with almonds and elegantly spiced.*

FOR THE CREPES:

Unsalted butter, plus melted butter for nonstick pan

2 cups all-purpose flour

1 teaspoon instant dry yeast

2 tablespoons sugar

1 large egg

2½ cups whole milk, warmed

¼ teaspoon kosher salt

FOR THE FILLING:

2 cups natural almonds, toasted

2 cups sugar

1 teaspoon ground cinnamon

½ teaspoon ground clove

1 teaspoon ground ginger

¼ teaspoon saffron

8 large eggs

¼ cup rosewater

¼ cup whole milk

½ teaspoon kosher salt

2 sticks (16 tablespoons) unsalted butter, melted

FOR THE SYRUP:

1 cup confectioners' sugar

2 tablespoons rosewater

A few drops of red food coloring

PREHEAT the oven to 325°F.

TO make the crepes, butter the bottom of a 9-inch cake pan.

IN a blender, combine the flour, yeast, sugar, egg, milk, and salt and blend until smooth. Let stand until small bubbles begin to form from the fermentation process, 30 to 40 minutes. Place a 9-inch nonstick pan over medium-high heat. Carefully wipe the bottom of the pan with a wadded up paper towel dipped in melted butter and add just enough crepe batter to cover the bottom of the pan, about ¼ cup, tilting and swirling the pan to ensure that it is completely covered. Cook until bubbles form and the top begins to set, about 2 to 3 minutes. Carefully flip with a spatula and cook through. It is fine to cook

these more thoroughly than you would ordinary crepes to make them easier to handle. Reserve the crepes (you can stack them) and repeat the process until all batter is used (it will yield about 10 crepes).

TO make the filling, combine the almonds, sugar, cinnamon, clove, ginger, and saffron in the bowl of a food processor fitted with the metal blade and pulse until the almond pieces are the size of grains of rice. Add the eggs, rosewater, milk, and salt to a blender and blend until smooth.

NOW assemble and bake the pudding. Place a crepe on the bottom of the prepared cake pan and heavily brush with melted butter. Be decadent and don't skimp! Cover the crepe with a layer of the almond mixture and pour over just enough of the egg mixture to cover it, about ¼ cup. Repeat the process until all the crepes are used. Top the last crepe with the butter and the sugar mixture but no egg mixture. Bake in the preheated oven for 55 minutes. Allow to cool completely in the pan on a rack.

TO make the syrup, whisk together the confectioners' sugar and rosewater until smooth. Add a few drops of food coloring for a pleasing rose color.

DRIZZLE slices with the rose syrup just before serving. It can be served warm or cold.

1492

WHEN BOABDIL RODE AWAY from Granada forever, he apparently wept. His mother, who rode with him (along with his one-thousand-person retinue), chastised him, "Why should you weep for a city you could not even be bothered to defend?" She must have understood what a momentous event this was. Not just for her family but for all Muslims in al-Andalus. Because it was truly unbelievable. Al-Andalus was over. The "ornament of the world" had been smashed under the Christian boot. Spain was beginning.

During the six-month siege of Granada, a large encampment had been established outside the city. Here the soldiers waited. That night in November that Boabdil finally agreed to put an end to it all, the night he admitted defeat and agreed to surrender the city, Isabella was at the encampment.

She must have been elated. In her mind, her ancestors had spent hundreds of years attempting to wrestle Iberia from Muslim control. This was a victory of epic proportions for Christians, generations of fighting were finally over, and it was time to celebrate.

There was someone else at the party that night, who we know well, celebrating with Isabella, a man named Christopher Columbus. For many years, Columbus had been circling the crown, popping in now and again to request an audience, to ask for money for a project he had in mind. During the Reconquista, Isabella had no time for this Italian with some mad idea of sailing west, not east, to reach India (remember how much those medieval Europeans loved their spices). She had dismissed him a few times. But tonight she was in a good mood. They'd just conquered Spain! Why not give the rest of the known world a go? Columbus was granted money for his mission.

On August 2, 1492, the day before Christopher Columbus and his crew boarded their ships, the *Pinta*, the *Niña*, and the *Santa Maria*, they spent a final night in Palos de la Frontera, Spain. There was chaos at the port and in the town that day, for the second of August was the day on which all Jews were expelled from Spain by royal decree. Those who had not already managed to leave, desperate and panicked, attempted to flee for safety aboard ships, as the minutes ticked down, persecution only hours away.

Expelled from their homeland, Spanish Jews and Muslims would go on to create diaspora communities across the globe. They hid their true identities to hitch a ride aboard a ship headed for a new world, a place the Inquisition had not yet reached. As Columbus set sail on August 3, from these turbulent ports of Iberia, an entire new world order began to emerge. All the continents of the Earth would come into contact with one another for the first time. Millions would die as a result. Hierarchical structures of unimaginable scale and reach would grow over entire societies, eclipsing the sun, decimating and consuming like a poisonous weed. The seeds of our modern identities planted into soil stained red with blood. The dawn of European colonialism had arrived.

THE GREAT
CI

RCULATION

THE GREAT CIRCULATION

15TH to 17TH centuries

TRY FOR A MOMENT to imagine Italian food without tomatoes. Sichuanese or Indian food without chilies. Britain without potatoes. Switzerland without chocolate. America without beef or pork. Mexico without limes. Any country anywhere without sugar, tea, or coffee.

In 1491 this was the lay of the land. Banana trees did not yet populate the tropical forests of South America. Horses did not gallop across the plains of the American West. That most classic northern European duo of meat and potatoes did not grace the Sunday table. Chopped peanuts did not yet thicken Malaysian and Indonesian stews, nor did roasted ones provide that delectable crunch to Thai or Vietnamese noodle dishes. There was no sugarcane in the Caribbean. Bees did not pollinate American flowers. No one in Europe, Africa, or Asia smoked tobacco.

We humans have a tendency to view our culinary heritage as a primordial component of our identity. Your grandmother's chicken soup recipe feels like part of the family's DNA. The spices you tenderly toast over low heat have always been in the pantry. The spit-roasted pig has surely been a centerpiece of gatherings as far back as anyone can remember. But the truth is, most of the cuisines we cherish so deeply and the dishes we associate with our personal histories are totally defined by foreign ingredients.

When people began to move across oceans in the fifteenth century (by choice or force) plants, foods, animals, and diseases moved with them. Tomatoes, potatoes, chili peppers, and chocolate, which all originate in the Americas, made their way to Europe, Asia, and Africa for the very first time. Introducing themselves slowly at first, then planting firm roots, enmeshing themselves into the culinary identities of their new homes with such strength we would hardly know they were recent arrivals to cuisines that feel so old. From the Middle East, Europe, and Asia, sugar, lemons, limes, bananas, coffee, and rice were introduced to the Americas, along with cows, horses, and pigs. To put it simply, the origin of every single modern culinary identity finds its roots in this period.

This movement of plants and animals around the world as a consequence of 1492, has traditionally been referred to as "the Columbian Exchange" named for, yes, Christopher Columbus. While he certainly helped to initiate this phenomenon, to continue to refer to one of the most momentous events in global history by the name of a genocidal monster feels wrong. It is outdated and not a terminology I am interested in perpetuating. The age of Columbus is over. A new name is needed for this period and its consequences for global food systems. I propose: the Great Circulation.

In the late fifteenth century, the European obsession with spices from the East reached a crescendo. No longer were Europeans content to consume spices imported via the Silk Road. They now wanted direct access to the lands from which nutmeg, cloves, and pepper originated; they wanted to cut out the middlemen and import the riches of the mythical East themselves. But first they had to figure out how to get there. Believing all spices came from a place called India, they set sail from the coasts of Spain and Portugal in search of this distant land.

After Christopher Columbus and his ships cast off from Palos de la Frontera, Spain, on August 3, 1492, they landed on the island of Hispaniola in the Caribbean two months later. He believed (or wanted to believe) that he was in India—hence he called it the "West Indies" and those who lived there "Indians." The period that followed Columbus's voyage is often referred to as "the Age of Exploration" or "the Age of Discovery," but I'm not so sure you can discover that which already exists. Did the Roman emperor Claudius discover Britain? Did the armies of the Islamic Empire discover the Iberian Peninsula? Did the Mongols discover Hungary? No. They just learned about these places for the first time.

As the Spanish and Portuguese sailed around the world, followed by the British and the Dutch (and eventually most European nations) they realized that they could not simply walk into Calcutta and demand control of the pepper trade. Entire kingdoms, empires, and societies had to be subordinated. Powerful people had to be overthrown—and often murdered. A desire for "trading opportunities" gave way to genocide and ultimately colonialism: forced European governance over previously independent peoples. The power structures established so many centuries ago between Europeans and everyone else, on the shores of Hispaniola, in the Andes mountains, the forests of Virginia, the port cities of India, and on the white sand beaches of Indonesia, are the foundations of our modern interconnected world. This "New World" was not discovered—it was made.

While the Great Circulation will take us to pretty much every corner of the world, let us begin in the misty mountains of the Andes in 1532. The Inca emperor Atahualpa was outside the town of Cajamarca with his massive army when 168 Spaniards appeared demanding an audience. He is curious but certainly not threatened. He is the most powerful man on the continent. How could he possibly have foreseen how this story would unfold?

Indigenous Ceviche

SERVES 4 TO 6 *Ceviche is a technique of preserving or "cooking" fish in an acid. But before the Spaniards arrived with their weird limes, lemons, and bitter oranges, Indigenous peoples had developed the technique using the fermented juice of one of the world's most delicious plants, the passion fruit. Another technique was to marinate the fish in* chicha de jora, *a mildly alcoholic drink that was often fermented with the expedient of using the enzymes in human saliva to transform starches into fermentable sugars. You got that right, spit-fermented booze! Fortunately, passion fruit vinegar is readily available, saving you the trouble of fermenting it yourself. The passion fruit itself is well named—intensely sweet and delicious with tart, edible seeds.*

1 pound freshly shucked cherrystone clams

½ cup passion fruit vinegar, plus more if needed

1 small red onion, very thinly sliced

1 jalapeño pepper, seeded and finely chopped

½ teaspoon kosher salt

2 ripe passion fruit

1 ripe avocado

½ cup multicolored cherry tomatoes, halved

2 tablespoons fresh cilantro or culantro leaves

Maldon sea salt or other sea salt

COMBINE the clams, vinegar, onion, jalapeño, and salt in a small bowl, making sure the clams are totally submerged. If necessary, add a little more vinegar. Refrigerate, covered, for 1 hour.

CUT the passion fruit in half, scoop out the flesh, and reserve. Prepare the avocado a few minutes before you are ready to serve. Cut into the avocado lengthwise, until your knife contacts the pit. Now rotate the avocado around the pit until the flesh and skin are completely cut. Twist the avocado into two separate halves. Tap your knife into the pit

and rotate it firmly to remove the pit from the flesh. Discard the pit by pushing it gently forward and away from the blade with your thumb. Score the flesh horizontally and vertically with the tip of your knife, cutting down to the skin but not through it. Scoop out the cubed flesh with a large spoon.

DRAIN the clams, onions, and pepper from the vinegar mixture and combine with the passion fruit, tomatoes, and avocado. Garnish with the cilantro leaves, season with a pinch of sea salt, and serve immediately.

Peruvian Ceviche

SERVES 4 TO 6 *Traditionally this is made with the juice of sour oranges, but if you cannot find those, fresh lime or orange juice makes a decent substitute, or try a combination of the two. There is a long history of Japanese influence in Peru, going back to the expatriate Japanese warriors used to guard Spanish silver, and that influence is felt in the different degrees to which the acid in the juice may be allowed to "cook" the fish in this dish. Marinate the fish for as little as 5 minutes or as long as 30 minutes.*

Kosher salt

1 ear fresh corn, shucked

½ cup (¼-inch cubes) peeled sweet potato

½ cup freshly squeezed sour orange juice (from 2 to 3 sour oranges)

3 cloves garlic

1 pound sushi-grade sea bass or sole, cut into bite-size slices

1 small red onion, very thinly sliced

1 habanero pepper, seeded and very thinly sliced

1 tablespoon fresh cilantro leaves

Maldon sea salt or other sea salt to taste

BRING a pot of generously salted water to a boil over high heat. Fill a large bowl with ice water. Cut the ear of corn into ½-inch rounds, and then cut these into quarters or wedges. Add the corn to the water and cook fully, 3 to 5 minutes, and immediately transfer to the ice water to stop cooking. Add the cut sweet potato to the boiling water and cook until tender, 7 to 10 minutes. Transfer to the ice water, drain, and reserve with the corn.

ADD the bitter orange juice, garlic, and ½ teaspoon salt to a blender and process until smooth. Start with the blender speed low and slowly raise it.

COMBINE the fish and the juice mixture in a small bowl, making sure the fish is entirely covered. Add the sliced red onions on top and a few slices of habanero. Habanero peppers have a lovely floral quality but are genuinely hot, so I like to add a few here and then garnish with more on the side. Remember, as with salt, you can always add more but you can never add less! Marinate the fish from 5 to 30 minutes in the refrigerator, depending on how well "cooked" you'd like the fish to be.

REMOVE the fish, onion, and pepper from the juice mixture and combine with the corn (you may not want to use all of the corn) and sweet potato. Add the additional habanero on the side, then garnish the ceviche with the cilantro leaves, season with sea salt, and serve.

Mole Mestizo with Turkey and Chorizo

MOLE MESTIZO

SERVES 6 TO 8 *This is a remarkable recipe because it catches a classic and beloved dish in the middle of a transition. Rich and fragrant moles, particularly those that, like this one, combine chilies and chocolate in a savory stew, are among the world's great sauces. Spanish conquistadors had their own tradition of fragrant stews that were heavily influenced by the long Arab rule over Iberia. Obviously, it was much easier to find indigenous hot peppers in Central America than to import black pepper from the actual Indian continent they had hoped to find. Thus, this is a mixed or Mestizo dish, combining Spanish pork sausage with local turkey and aromatic spices drawn from across the globe. To rehydrate the chilies, soak them for at least one hour in cold water. The most important thing when cooking this dish is to take your time, or rather, let the dish take its own sweet, complex, and savory time. Put on some music; enjoy your day.*

2 large yellow onions, chopped

3 cloves garlic, chopped

½ cup raisins

¼ cup rehydrated and seeded ancho chiles

¼ cup rehydrated and seeded negro chiles

8 ounces chorizo, cut into ¼-inch pieces

½ cup canola oil

1 pound turkey breast, cut into 1-inch cubes

1 tablespoon plus about 1 teaspoon kosher salt

2 teaspoons sesame oil

¼ cup toasted sesame seeds

¼ cup blanched sliced almonds, toasted dark

¾ cup canned crushed tomatoes

2 teaspoons dried marjoram

1 tablespoon fennel seeds

1 teaspoon ground cinnamon

¼ teaspoon ground clove

¼ cup cocoa powder

3 cups low-sodium chicken or turkey stock

PLACE the onions, garlic, raisins, and both types of chilies in a food processor fitted with a metal blade and pulse to form a chunky paste.

PLACE the chorizo in a cold medium saucepan and then cook over medium-low heat. Cook until well rendered and the edges are browned, 7 to 10 minutes, stirring

occasionally. Remove the chorizo and reserve. Add 1 tablespoon of the canola oil to the saucepan and increase the heat to medium-high. Cook until the oil is shimmering and add the turkey. Season with 1 teaspoon of the salt and let cook until well browned on the outside. Transfer to a bowl and reserve in the refrigerator while you prepare the mole.

ADD the remaining ¼ cup plus 3 tablespoons canola oil and the sesame oil to same saucepan and reduce the heat to medium-low. Add the onion mixture from the food processor and the remaining 1 tablespoon salt and cook, stirring occasionally, until the mixture is entirely cooked, about 30 minutes. Some caramelization is good, but if the mixture starts to really stick and burn before it is cooked, you can add a bit of the stock.

ADD the rest of the ingredients except for the stock and cook for another 10 minutes. Add the stock. At this point, you want to process this into a thick and rich stew. The easiest way to do this is with an immersion blender, but you can also transfer the mixture to a standard blender, process until smooth, and return to the pot. Cover and simmer for . . . ever. Or at least 40 minutes, stirring occasionally. It genuinely will only get better and better. Add the turkey and most of the chorizo, reserving some for garnish, and continue to cook until the turkey is fully cooked, about 15 minutes. Taste for seasoning, top with the reserved chorizo, and serve.

THE GREAT TURKEY CONSPIRACY

WHY ARE TURKEYS called "turkeys," anyway? And why, in France, are they called *d'inde*, meaning "from India"? Actually these names are different versions of the same lie. In an era when navigational knowledge truly was wealth and power, and when the act of divulging it was punished by agonizing and spectacular death, it is not surprising that there was a great deal of deception about who was going where and how they were getting there. Thus, there was equal deception about which products were imported from what lands—and this large and flightless bird somehow became both a holiday staple and the flagship for this kind of subterfuge. If you were going to name the bird after its original home, it would have been called an "America." But what if you didn't want someone to know where you had imported it from? Obviously, you would pick another famous and far-off place on the trade routes that people were not likely to question, such as India (if you were French), or Turkey, if you were English.

THE GREAT AMERICAN EMPIRES

IN THE EARLY FIFTEENTH CENTURY in the valley of Cusco, Cusi Yupanqui, the ambitious son of a local ruler, overthrew his father and began a series of successful territorial expansion campaigns. By the time his grandson, Huayna Capac, was sitting on the throne in 1493, the Inca Empire was the largest empire in the Americas. It stretched south from Columbia to central Chile, west from the Pacific Ocean, and east into the Amazon rainforest.

Life in the empire was, by medieval European standards, pretty good. Numerous cities were dotted across the empire, all large and architecturally complex, filled with temples plated with gold and silver from the rich mines of Peru. A centralized government kept citizens in check. Large-scale public works projects kept them employed. Rich and fertile land, shaped into terraced gardens and farms throughout the Andes, kept people fed.

The Andes Mountains are the birthplace of the potato. Over four thousand species are native to the region and were used by the Inca in a variety of dishes and preparations. One of them, *chuño*, was made by laying potatoes out in the cold night air, allowing them to freeze and then thaw with the sunrise. This process was repeated until the potato had shrunken down to a dark gray lump, moisture essentially squeezed out to create a non-perishable gnocchi-like-shaped food. Chuño could last for years and was often used as military rations; packed up by armies to be boiled for meals on the go.

In the 1520s, curious reports began to trickle down from the north of the empire. Reports of men with strange pale faces, riding extraordinary beasts, were coming ashore every now and then from floating wooden fortresses. But Huayna Capac would not live long enough to decide what to do about these curious invaders. He had already come down with an illness no one had ever seen before. Fever, vomiting, along with pockmarks covering his body. Within a week he was dead. His son and successor died shortly thereafter of the same disease. Smallpox had arrived in the Americas, moving faster than the Spanish who had brought it to the New World.

When Francisco Pizarro, an illiterate conquistador from Extremadura, the poorest region of Spain, disembarked from his ship in 1528 in northwest Peru, a civil war was raging amongst the Inca. With Huayna Capac and his successor dead, two of Huayna Capac's other sons—Huascar and

Atahualpa—were battling it out for control of the empire. On the battle-field, Atahualpa would ultimately prove victorious; Huascar, bloody and wounded, was marched to a town called Quicpai, where Atahualpa's forces made him watch as they executed his wives and his children before killing him. No love appears to have been lost between these two brothers.

It took four years for Pizarro and his group to finally catch up to the new Inca emperor in Cajamarca. At Pizarro's side were his half-brothers Hernando, Juan, Gonzalo, and Francisco Martin, along with Hernando de Soto (who would go on to conquer Florida), a number of enslaved Africans, twelve notaries (who provide us with most of the descriptions we have of these early years of conquest), a Dominican friar, a number of enslaved Morisca women (of Islamic descent, presumably brought over from Spain), more slaves from Nicaragua, and a handful of merchants. All in all there were 168 of them.

On November 15, 1532, Hernando de Soto was sent to meet the emperor at his encampment outside the city. As his horse plodded through the mud, de Soto saw tents stretched as far as his eye could see; Atahualpa's eighty-thousand-strong army had made their campsite on the hills surrounding Cajamarca. Though the Spanish had steel blades, armor, horses, and cannons, they were outnumbered four hundred to one. The first meeting didn't go particularly well. In his early thirties, with a deep voice and bloodshot eyes, Atahualpa seemed largely disinterested in the Spanish. He sat on a low stool and barely made eye contact. It was agreed Atahualpa and de Soto would meet again in the town's square the next day. Before nightfall both sides were already secretly planning their strategy: the Spanish to kidnap the emperor and Atahualpa to kill the Spanish.

The central square of Cajamarca was larger than any that existed in Spain in 1532. Six hundred feet wide, and six hundred feet long, the square was enclosed by a stone wall that had two gateways on either side, opening onto the streets of the town. The Spanish were early. They waited in silence in the square as hail began to pour down from the heavens. Hours later Atahualpa arrived, seated atop a litter, carried by a number of nobles and personal guards, as thousands of Inca poured through the square's two doors.

What ensued was the Battle of Cajamarca—and it was a bloodbath. The small Spanish band took down an estimated six thousand Inca soldiers and did not lose a single man in the fight. From atop their horses they slashed and cut and stabbed their way through the crowds, trampling soldiers and cutting through the soft cotton armor the Inca wore. Contemporaries write of the Inca nobles and personal guards continuing to hold Atahualpa up as they were chopped apart. Reinforcements would stream in to take their places only to have their own arms sliced off. Old World steel and animals of war decimated thousands in just a few hours. When the battle was over, Pizarro took Atahualpa prisoner and put him in the Temple of the Sun. So valuable was Atahualpa to Pizarro that he slept next to the emperor in the temple that night.

For eight months Atahualpa remained a prisoner of the Spanish, mainly kept in Cajamarca as the Spanish made their way around his empire, pillaging gold, slaughtering the natives, and dismantling the world of the Incas with their chaos. But on the night of July 2, as a few conquistadors sat around playing cards, word came that an Inca army loyal to Atahualpa was only a few miles away, coming to liberate him. In a collective panic the Spanish decided they had to kill Atahualpa. But this wouldn't be like shooting down an unknown enemy. They had come to know Atahualpa over the months. This was intimate and personal. Atahualpa cried and begged for his life. Pizarro wept. But fear and mistrust won out. The emperor was strangled to death—after he had converted to Christianity and asked Pizarro to watch over his sons.

When Inca royalty had been wiped out and Spanish rule was firmly in place, the foreign invaders' attention shifted from overthrowing monarchies to the mining of precious metals. The silver and gold that had drawn the Spanish deep into the Andes would spread across the trade networks of the world. Silver mined in Potosi (in modern-day Bolivia) became a global currency, famously called "pieces of eight" because it was worth eight *reales* (the Spanish coin at the time). It also became known as the *peso*, the main currency of the Portuguese, Dutch, and British empires— and one that is still used today in Mexico, where Pizarro's cousin, Hérnan Cortés, conquered another American empire.

OF ALL THE MANY CONSEQUENCES OF THE BATTLE OF CAJAMARCA in 1532, the introduction of a Peruvian root vegetable to Europe might not seem particularly important. But it was, in fact, revolutionary. It would transform the way people were able to feed themselves.

Potatoes were initially grown in monastery gardens, which were like the botanist test labs of their time. But Europeans remained skeptical of the potato for many decades. Was it poisonous? Did it cause leprosy?

Maybe it was an aphrodisiac? No one was quite sure what to make of it. It was much smaller than the russet potatoes baked in ovens or cut into french fries today—perhaps more akin to the baby reds that often go in potato salad. Eventually a combination of terrible weather and raw hunger forced Europe to change its attitude toward the spud.

From the fourteenth to mid-nineteenth centuries, Europe was in the grip of the Little Ice Age. Bitterly cold winters meant that harvests regularly failed and peasants were often one bad season away from starvation. Food riots regularly took place across the continent, as European peasants consumed fewer calories per day than their contemporaries living in hunter-gatherer societies of Africa or the Amazon. Ironically, the cool temperatures and abysmal harvests were only made worse by the genocide of Indigenous peoples in the Americas. The death of about 90 percent of the American Indigenous population as a result of European contact led to the abandonment of massive tracts of agricultural land. The trees and thick vegetation that grew in its place soaked up so much carbon dioxide from the atmosphere that the planet actually became cooler. European colonizers had no idea their American genocide was starving people back home.

The potato, acclimated to the freezing temperatures of the Andes, grew quite well in the northern climates of Europe. At first it was grown largely as hog feed or as food for prisoners. But when French scientist Antoine-Augustin Parmentier was captured by the Prussians during the Seven Years' War (1756–63), he was fed nothing but potatoes during his imprisonment. And much to his surprise he did not find his health deteriorating; in fact, he felt physically quite well.

When he was freed and returned to Paris in 1763, he realized he had a solution to Europe's long struggle with famine. Parmentier began to preach the gospel of the potato to anyone who would listen. He threw potato dinner parties for high-society guests and planted patches of potatoes around Paris with heavily armed guards standing watch over them at night. When people saw the potato being treated as an exclusive delicacy for the rich and famous, they wanted in. The potato-branding overhaul worked.

Without potatoes, what would a traditional British roast look like? Gnocchi would not feature on Italian menus. Crispy Spanish *patatas bravas*, slathered in spicy mayonnaise, would vanish from your tapas spread. Where would Hungarian food be without Mesoamerican ingredients? The traditional stew, *paprika krumpli*, made with potatoes, tomatoes, and paprika are all thanks to the farmers and cultivators of Indigenous America. And the potato didn't just transform European cuisine. Potatoes are just as ubiquitous in Middle Eastern, African, and Asian cuisines: found in curries, soups, and stews, and fried, sautéed, baked, and boiled in numerous culinary creations.

What was and is so unique about the effect of the potato on Europe was that it gave Europe a tool to feed the starving masses and improve the lives of the average people—not just the rich. A society that is well fed is also a society that tends to be politically stable. The potato was a colonial commodity; it gave European rulers enough security at home to go forth and conquer most of the world. The trophy extracted from one victory provided the power for the rest.

Potatoes became such a crucial staple that in the 1840s, when Ireland experienced the great potato famine, one million people starved to death. Another million immigrated to the United States, enmeshing Irish identity into the fabric of American culture. Sometimes I wonder what Saint Patrick's Day would look like in the United States if Pizarro had never set sail, if Parmentier had never gone to war, and if a small island in northern Europe had not become reliant on an American root vegetable so many centuries ago.

THERE WERE THE INCA, AND THEN THERE WERE THE AZTECS—the other great indigenous empire of the pre-Columbian Americas. The center of the Aztec empire was Tenochtitlán, a city built upon an island in the middle of a lake. Three causeways led from the dry land surrounding Lake Texcoco to the floating urban center, where pyramids soared high into the blue sky, colorful flowers spilled off the edges of rooftop gardens into the bustling streets below, where hundreds of thousands of Mexica moved about their city. Today we know this place as Mexico City.

On the eve of Spanish conquest five hundred years ago, the Aztec Empire, an alliance of three city-states—Tenochtitlán, Texcoco, and Tlacopan—was ruled by Montezuma. He assumed the throne in 1502 and successfully led the Aztecs to the apex of their power by establishing a strong centralized government with a highly organized bureaucracy, restricting the power of the noble class, and building a skilled military. Montezuma's Tenochtitlán was divided into different districts, each with its own local council, temple, and central market square. Tenochtitlán also had a library, a zoo, ball courts, magnificent palaces, and exquisite pyramids. When the sun went down behind the mountains surrounding Lake Texcoco, the pine torches that dotted the streets of downtown were lit up to illuminate the way.

The city's central market was located on the north end of the island. Women made up a large portion of the buyers and sellers in the marketplace; a number of them even became government-appointed officials who helped run the market, ensuring both the quality of the goods sold and fair prices. The marketplace was divided into different sections for each commodity, from foods to household wares to animals and cloth. A visitor to the market in the fifteenth century would have found heaping piles of cacao in one alley, large pots of sweet honey in the next, and birds' eggs carefully displayed in a stall around the corner, followed by tables covered in bars of green dried algae from the lake. Venison, rabbit, frogs, and ants were just some of the proteins available. The market's food stalls sold prepared foods for the home cook short on time: premade tortillas, squash already peeled and cut up, ready to be cooked, tomato sauces, fried onions, and ground cacao, ready to be made into delicious and frothy beverages. But the market also sold fully cooked dishes—like tortillas filled with beans, toasted corn, and cakes made with amaranth seeds—perhaps for those whose dwellings lacked cooking equipment, or simply for those who were out and about and needed a meal on the go.

In 1519 the Spanish conquistador Hernán Cortés arrived on the east coast of Mexico. The initial interactions between the Spanish and the locals were mixed. Hostilities broke out immediately between the Spanish and some groups, while other groups presented peace offerings, usually in the form of enslaved people from yet another group. One woman presented to the Spanish was the child of a Nahua nobleman, who had been captured years before and sold into slavery by the Mexica. We do not know the name she was born with, but the Spanish gave her the name Marina (though she is also known as Malintzin or La Malinche). She spent her initial weeks with the Spanish merely observing—unbeknownst to the Spanish, her fluency in Nahuatl and Yucatec Mayan (and eventually Spanish) allowed her to discern the complexity of the political situation at hand. In one awkward meeting between the Spanish and Nahuatl speakers, Cortés's translator, Jeronimo de Aguilar, proved inadequate at translating. Marina stepped in and translated the Nahuatl speaker's words. The Spanish were shocked; they did not expect this enslaved young woman to be the key to their communications on this conquest. She quickly became Cortés's primary translator, privy to and responsible for some of the most important political exchanges in American history. She also birthed two of his children, a daughter and a son, who formed the first generation of Mestizos.

The prevailing narrative for many hundreds of years has been that Montezuma was weak: outmatched by the horses and weapons of the Spanish, he simply crumbled and handed the city over. But we have forgotten that the Spanish made alliances with other Indigenous peoples, like the Tlaxcala, who were sworn enemies of the Aztecs. An Indigenous Republic, ruled by a council of elected officials, the Tlaxcala were Nahuatl speakers just like the Aztecs. Between this alliance, the knowledge of locals like Malintzin, and all the other violent factors, the scales were irrevocably tipped against the Aztecs.

When the Spanish "officially" conquered a people, they would read aloud *The Requirement* or *Requerimento*, a document like a medieval version of the Miranda rights. It stated that the pope had given them (the Spanish) authority to take these lands (insert location) for the king or queen of Spain, and that since the pope was the representative of God on Earth, his word was law. The Dominican friar Bartolomé de Las Casas, who was one of Pizarro's 168, famously remarked that he did not know "whether to laugh or cry at the absurdity" of the whole performance. European nations would take over Indigenous lands from East to West and North to South in this manner, implementing foreign systems of government on societies that had never asked for them. It wasn't just their brute force and weapons that allowed them to be successful; diseases, such as smallpox wreaked havoc, wiping out millions of people. It is estimated that 90 percent of the Mexican population died from Old World diseases. Societies simply broke down.

It's a common theme for successful conquerors: subjugating a population when they are at their lowest point. Just think about how the Visigoths were able to take Rome because the empire was falling apart; or how the Islamic Empire was able to fill the power vacuum left by the collapse of the Sassanian Empire; or how Abd al-Rahman targeted a disunited Hispania on the fringes of the Eurasian continent and took it by storm; and how Pizarro took the Inca Empire in the midst of a civil war, and on and on.

IN 1554, AN EXOTIC DECORATIVE PLANT recently arrived from across the Atlantic was described by the Swiss naturalist Konrad Gessner. The plant had tiny yellow globes hanging from its branches. Gessner named them *poma amoris* or "love apples." In Italy they would become known as *pomi d'oro* or "golden apple"; in France *pomme d'or*. The tomato had traversed from Mexico across the high seas and was beginning to introduce itself to a new audience.

The first known European recipe utilizing tomatoes comes from Antoni Latini's 1692 culinary treatise *Lo scalco alla moderna* ("The Modern Steward"). The tomato sauce "in the Spanish style" is entirely unlike the smooth tomato sauce traditionally served on pasta today, and much more like a chunky salsa. Latini worked as a chef for a Catholic cardinal in Rome and for the Spanish viceroy in Naples; the latter position was perhaps the avenue through which he became accustomed to cooking with tomatoes. During the seventeenth century, tomatoes would have been largely consumed by the elite; like spices, they were an exotic food from a faraway land.

This medieval tomato was much smaller than its modern counterpart. Today the behemoth heirloom varieties adorning the tables of farmers markets share little in appearance with the wild plant that was carefully domesticated and cultivated by the Mesoamericans so many centuries ago.

That tomatoes have become so inextricably linked to, say, Italian cuisine, is a perfect example of how the culinary identities created in the wake of 1492 are the ones we still associate with today. Because everything we consume is fusion food. One country's national dish that represents a culture and a heritage is often made from fragments of three or four others. Is *sum tum* (green papaya salad) really Thai? Or is it Thai-Mexican-via-the-Portuguese fusion? Perhaps the spicy potato dish *battata harra* is in fact a Lebanese-Peruvian mash-up? And maybe *mole* is a stew that is also sort of like a map: one that traces the long journeys spices have taken from Asia west to al-Andalus and eventually across the ocean with the Spanish to Mexico, where cinnamon and cloves would meet tomatoes, chilies, and cacao in the cooking pot to simmer together into a new dish, in a new world.

The Aztecs have not survived but a food they cooked with has. The tomato's journey onto the plates of Sicilian peasants speaks to pivotal historical moments in which the world order was flipped on its head and transformed forever. It also speaks to small moments, like the action of one curious man loading a small plant onto a wooden ship so that he might study it back at home.

Tomato Sauce in the Spanish Style with Rack of Lamb

SALSA DI POMODORO ALLA SPAGNOLA

SERVES 4 TO 6 *This derives from the earliest known tomato sauce recipe, written in 1692 by Antoni Latini in his* Lo scalco alla moderna, *where it is described as "a very tasty sauce, for boiled dishes and anything else." It is paired with simple racks of lamb, adapted from the same period, as it was meant to go with a meat dish. The classic pairing of tomato sauce with pasta would not appear until much later. This is one of those recipes where the quality of your ingredients is truly paramount. If you have a local farmers market, my advice is not just to shop there, but to haunt it. Make friends. Talk to the tomato guy or gal, the one who is proud of their product and wants you to taste it. Don't stop there: great olive oil and fabulous vinegar will take this dish where it needs to be.*

1 pound fresh ripe tomatoes, halved and cored

1 serrano chili, seeded

½ medium red onion, finely chopped

1 teaspoon minced fresh thyme leaves

¼ cup extra-virgin olive oil

1 tablespoon plus 2 teaspoons sherry vinegar

Kosher salt

4 cloves garlic, finely chopped

1 teaspoon freshly ground black pepper

1 tablespoon roughly chopped rosemary leaves

2 lamb racks, frenched

1 tablespoon canola oil

THE secret to this dish is the intense, smoky flavor of the tomatoes. They can be prepared on a grill or under a broiler. Place them cut side down on a grill or cut side up under a broiler. Let them properly char, 3 to 5 minutes. Char the serrano as well. Remove the skin from the pepper with a sharp knife and discard. Mince the tomatoes with the serrano and mix with the onion, thyme, 2 tablespoons of the olive oil, the vinegar, and 2 teaspoons salt in a medium bowl. Let the sauce marry for at least 30 minutes or overnight.

COMBINE the remaining 2 tablespoons olive oil, the garlic, black pepper, and rosemary in a small bowl. Rub this mixture over the lamb racks and marinate in a resealable bag or covered bowl, refrigerated, for at least 1 hour and up to 8 hours.

PREHEAT the oven to 400°F. During this period, lamb like this would have been spit-roasted over a fire, which is lovely but inconvenient, especially if you are the indentured youth spending days by a roaring fireplace turning a spit. Here, pan-searing takes the place of the open flame and the unfortunate spit-boy.

LIBERALLY salt the lamb. Heat a heavy pan over high heat with the canola oil and sear the racks one at a time, fat side down, for 3 minutes. Transfer the lamb to a foil-lined sheet pan and bake until the internal temperature reads 135°F to 140°F on an instant-read thermometer, 15 to 20 minutes.

LET the lamb rest for 5 minutes before carving, and top with the tomato sauce.

FOOD AS TECHNOLOGY

THROUGHOUT MOST of history, until perhaps the last century, the most technologically advanced object was the oceangoing vessel. This was true of the might of the Athenian navy, to Admiral Nelson's nine hundred–man flagship, to the shockingly small Portuguese carracks, some no more than sixty feet long, that accomplished an almost unthinkable journey to India. Larger ships could serve as floating towns, with livestock and ovens on board.

Food itself can also be technology. Navies created elaborate systems of preservation for foodstuffs, heavily salting meat and double-baking ships' biscuits into rock-hard discs. The lime that nicknamed the British "limey" sailor was discovered as a technical solution to the problem of scurvy. Most shocking to me was learning that one of the most important military innovations throughout history was the humble potato. Prior to the popularization of the energy-rich potato, armies had to haul flour and, more remarkably, ovens with them, and they paused daily to bake bread. With potatoes, a soldier could haul his ration on his back, throw a potato into the fire when he stopped marching, and save the entire unit hours that could be dedicated to travel and rest. It is said that an army travels on its belly; to travel with a belly full of potatoes was to go faster and farther.

The mighty four-masters and the simple potato may seem at opposite ends of the spectrum, but they are, in fact, two sides of the same technological coin.

Salt Cod Stew

BACCALÀ IN UMIDO

SERVES 4 TO 6 *While I generally prefer fresh ingredients, I imagine this recipe as one that could be enjoyed on board an ocean vessel, striving for the Cape of Good Hope. Thus it includes only dry or preserved ingredients, like the salt cod itself. I do suggest garnishing with fresh herbs.*

1 pound salt cod

1 cup dried onion flakes

¾ cup white verjus

6 prunes, roughly chopped

¼ cup dried cherries

¼ cup almond flour

2 teaspoons dried thyme

1 tablespoon dried parsley

1 tablespoon dried marjoram

2½ teaspoons freshly ground black pepper

¼ teaspoon ground cinnamon

½ teaspoon ground cloves

½ teaspoon kosher salt

1 tablespoon chopped fresh parsley

1 teaspoon chopped fresh marjoram

SALT cod is, obviously, extremely salty and it takes some preparation to make it palatable. Cookbooks from the period, and today, debate whether it is best to soak it in hot water, cold water, or milk, and also whether to tenderize it by hitting it with a hammer. I have found that it is best to soak it overnight in a bowl of water to cover, then change the water in the morning and soak a bit longer. The hammer is unnecessary.

AFTER soaking, remove the salt cod from the water and cut it into 1-inch pieces. It will break apart more during the cooking process.

ADD all ingredients except for the cod and fresh herbs to a pot with 4 cups of water and bring to a boil. Reduce the heat and simmer for 45 minutes. Add the cod and cook for another 15 minutes. Serve, garnished with the fresh herbs.

Fish in Banana Leaves with Indonesian Peanut Sauce

SAMBAL KACANG

SERVES 4 TO 6 *We are familiar with rich, spicy peanut sauces from Thai, Malaysian, and Indonesian food, but the combination of ground nuts with hot chilies brings together two foods that, again, come from the other side of the world (South and Central America) and are brought there, again, by the spice-trading Portuguese. This sauce can be served as a condiment, or paired with fish, meat, poultry, tofu, and probably your shoes, if you ever have to boil them and eat them to survive. Banana leaves can be purchased frozen in many markets. For a more rustic version, use whole fish in place of the fillet.*

2 cups canola oil	2 tablespoons shrimp paste
1 cup peanuts with skins	4 to 6 fresh Thai (bird's eye) chilies
6 cloves garlic	¼ cup tamarind paste
4 shallots	2 tablespoons turbinado sugar
2 stalks lemongrass, bruised and chopped	2 pounds red snapper or sea bass fillets, skin on (about 4 fillets)
2-inch-piece fresh ginger or galangal, peeled	1-pound-package banana leaves
2 teaspoons kosher salt	¼ cup chopped fresh cilantro leaves

HEAT the oil in a deep, heavy saucepan and add the peanuts. Fry the peanuts until golden and fragrant, about 10 minutes. Remove the peanuts with a skimmer and set aside. Reserve ½ cup of the oil. Add the garlic, shallots, lemongrass, ginger, salt, shrimp paste, and peanuts to a food processor fitted with the metal blade and pulse to form a thick paste.

HEAT the reserved oil in the saucepan over medium heat and add 3 to 4 chilies. Cook for 3 minutes, then add the peanut mixture. Continue to cook until the mixture softens and the oil begins to separate, 5 to 7 minutes. Add the tamarind paste and sugar and continue to cook for 2 to 3 minutes. Taste and adjust seasoning—it will be intense.

PREHEAT a grill or an oven to 400°F. Chop the remaining chilies and set aside.

PLACE each fillet skin side down on a banana leaf. Spread some of the paste completely over the fish and fully wrap each in its banana leaf. Secure with toothpicks or twine, if necessary. Place the wrapped fish on the grill or on a baking sheet in the oven and cook for 15 minutes.

UNWRAP the banana leaves and garnish the fish with the chopped chilies and cilantro.

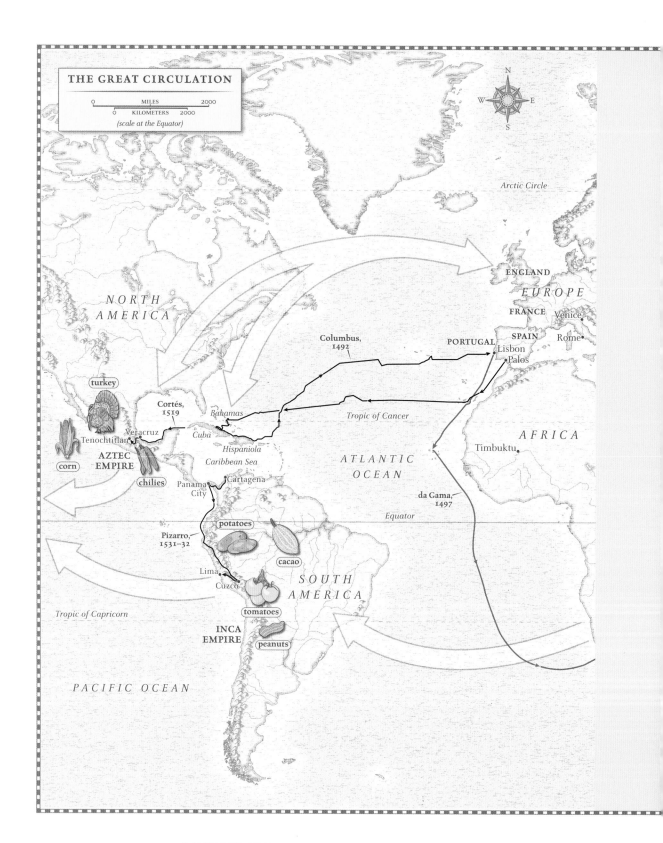

THE GREAT CIRCULATION

MILES 2000
0
KILOMETERS 2000
0
(scale at the Equator)

Arctic Circle

NORTH AMERICA

ENGLAND

EUROPE

FRANCE Venice

SPAIN Rome

PORTUGAL Lisbon
Palos

Columbus, 1492

Tropic of Cancer

turkey

Cortés, 1519

Veracruz
Tenochtitlan *Bahamas*
Cuba

corn

AFRICA

Timbuktu

AZTEC EMPIRE *Hispaniola*

chilies *Caribbean Sea*

Panama City *Cartagena*

ATLANTIC OCEAN

da Gama, 1497

Equator

potatoes

Pizarro, 1531–32

cacao

SOUTH AMERICA

Lima
Cuzco

tomatoes

Tropic of Capricorn

INCA EMPIRE peanuts

PACIFIC OCEAN

THE ANTHROPOCENE

The inception of our current ecological age was triggered by the events of 1492. As plants, foods, animals, and diseases crossed oceans and landed on new shores, they changed the climate and landscape of grounds they had never seen before.

This age, that we still live in today, is called the Anthropocene. The only ecological event of similar comparison is perhaps the separation of the supercontinent Pangea into two new continents one hundred and seventy-five million years ago.

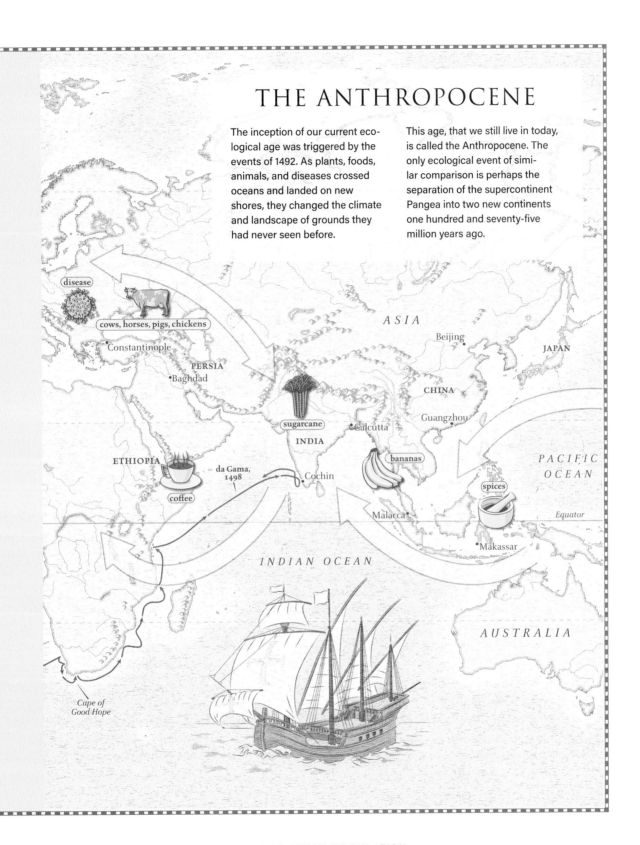

Sweet Potato Pudding

POTATO PUDING

SERVES 6 TO 8 *With all the intense flavors flooding suddenly back and forth across the Pacific Ocean and across the world, let's include two of the ultimate staple and comfort foods: the potato and its sweet cousin. In this recipe from a seventeenth-century English family collection, the type of potato is not specified, but in my opinion sweet potatoes work better, though you can substitute russet potatoes. (It's a sweet potato by the way, not a yam. Yams are a starchy tuber indigenous to Africa, not the Americas.)*

3 pounds sweet potatoes, peeled and cut into 1-inch pieces

Kosher salt

3 sticks (24 tablespoons) unsalted butter, softened, plus more for pan

4 large eggs

¼ cup sherry

1 tablespoon brown sugar

½ teaspoon ground cinnamon

PREHEAT the oven to 350°F.

BOIL the sweet potatoes in a large saucepan of salted water until very tender, about 15 minutes, and drain. Combine the sweet potatoes, 2 teaspoons salt, 3 sticks butter, and the remaining ingredients in the bowl of a stand mixer fitted with the paddle attachment and mix on low speed until fully combined. Generously butter a 9 x 12-inch baking dish and spread the mixture into it. Bake for 40 minutes until set and the top has browned.

THE SPICE ISLANDS

VALUE IS often directly related to scarcity and distance, and certain jewels of the spice trade—nutmeg, mace, and cloves—originally came solely from the Moluku Islands (in modern-day Indonesia), perched beyond the imagination of any medieval European cartographer and sparking folkloric tales across the West for centuries. A tale of Shakespearean power struggles emerged in the early 1600s when the Portuguese, English, and Dutch battled for control of the islands, while being played off one another by the local rulers. These were brutal sagas of piracy, starvation, disastrous bouts of scurvy, malaria, and cholera against a backdrop of stunning palaces and Buddhist temples, dense jungle and pristine shorelines.

Finally, the Dutch won control of the Spice Islands, a victory that would fund the Dutch golden age and turn Amsterdam into one of the world's leading commercial centers. The English, wanting a consolation prize after their defeat, made a swap with the Dutch. In exchange for a two-mile-long stretch of sand dotted with spice plants in the Banda Sea, the Dutch gave the British their colony, New Amsterdam, which became the British colony New York. The fate of the world was all twisted up in spice.

Frothed Chocolate

CACAHUATL

SERVES 4 TO 6 Cacahautl *was the original chocolate beverage drunk by the Mayan and Aztec elites. It was bitter, similar to black coffee, and was made frothy by repeatedly pouring it between two cups or bowls. This recipe represents one of its early European adaptations, from Henry Stubbe's 1662 treatise* The Indian Nectar. *If you want to experience something closer to the original, increase the chilies and omit the nuts, the cinnamon, and, of course, the sugar. It is not historically accurate, but a dollop of whipped cream is lovely as well.*

¼ cup cacao nibs

¼ cup cocoa powder

¼ cup toasted slivered almonds

¼ cup toasted hazelnuts

3 tablespoons cornmeal

¼ teaspoon red chile flakes

¼ teaspoon achiote

¼ teaspoon anise seeds

4 cinnamon sticks

½ cup sugar, plus more to taste

1 teaspoon vanilla paste

ADD all ingredients except the cinnamon sticks, vanilla, and sugar to a blender with 3 cups of water. Blend until smooth, about 2 minutes. Transfer this mixture to a small saucepan with the cinnamon sticks, bring to a boil, and reduce to a simmer. Simmer for 15 minutes. Add the ½ cup sugar and vanilla paste and whisk together.

FORCE through a fine-mesh sieve with a whisk or a spatula into a pitcher. Seventeenth-century Europeans often liked things very sweet, so serve with additional sugar on the side.

Goan Layered Custard

BEBINKA

SERVES 6 TO 8 *This delicious layered dessert is found in two places today: the Philippines and the Goan Coast in India, from which we can deduce that the connection must be the Portuguese. India, as the home of sugarcane, has the oldest tradition of confections and desserts in the world, but only in Goa do you see pastries involving eggs. The reason for this comes from, of all places, Catholic nunneries. Portuguese nuns traditionally wore habits with large headpieces that were stiffened with egg white. This left them, unsurprisingly, with huge amounts of egg yolks, and nunneries traditionally housed bakeries to make use of them and raise income, especially by selling the ubiquitous egg tarts pasteis de nata. The nuns brought their egg-laden dessert traditions with them when they went to the Philippines and India, where the treats were reinvented with local spices and coconut milk.*

1½ teaspoons freshly ground cardamom

1½ teaspoons freshly grated nutmeg

1¼ sticks (10 tablespoons) unsalted butter

1 (13.5-ounce) can coconut milk

2½ cups confectioners' sugar

1 cup all-purpose flour

12 egg yolks

1 teaspoon vanilla paste or pure vanilla extract

½ teaspoon kosher salt

PREHEAT the oven to 500°F or turn on the broiler.

WHISK together the cardamom and nutmeg in a small bowl and set aside. Butter a 5 by 10-inch loaf pan and cut a piece of parchment paper to place on the bottom to keep the cake from sticking.

ADD the coconut milk, sugar, flour, yolks, vanilla, and salt to a blender and blend until smooth, scraping the sides a few times. Pour a thin layer of batter into the bottom of the prepared loaf pan. Try to use just enough to cover the bottom—the more layers you can get, the better it will turn out. Bake in the preheated oven or place under the broiler until the top is well browned, 2 to 4 minutes. This is one of those times when slight variations from one oven to another will make a big difference.

REMOVE the pan from the oven or broiler and brush the browned top with melted butter. Sprinkle the buttered layer with a generous pinch of the spice mixture and pour on another thin layer of batter, distributing it evenly. Repeat this procedure until all of the batter, butter, and spices are used up.

REDUCE the oven temperature to 325°F. Let the *bebinka* rest for 5 minutes while the oven temperature reduces. Return the pastry to the oven and bake until a skewer or cake tester inserted in the pastry comes out clean, 25 to 30 minutes.

ALLOW to cool completely in the pan, then carefully unmold. Cut into cubes and serve.

INDIA, AT LAST

ON MAY 18, 1498, Vasco da Gama's ships creaked into the harbor of Calicut on the southwest coast of India. It had been a year since four ships set out from Lisbon to find a way around the southern tip of Africa and to the fabled land of India. Two of da Gama's sailors went ashore to check things out. The port was bustling with life. As traders from all over Asia, the Middle East, and parts of Africa moved about in a seemingly choreographed dance of loading and unloading goods, two dirty and weary Portuguese men looked about for someone to whom they could announce their arrival. Two Tunisian merchants recognized them as Portuguese, being familiar with their kind because of their home's proximity across the Mediterranean. Shocked to see white Portuguese men in India, a land that up to that moment had been devoid of white Europeans, they asked, "What the devil has brought you here?" To which the Portuguese sailors replied, "Christians and spices." (There was still a vague hope that the Christian kingdom of Prester John might be found here.)

The *zamorin*, the ruler of Calicut, invited the newcomers to meet him at his palace. A few days later, Vasco da Gama and some of his men were led from their ships to the audience hall of the zamorin. Along the way they made a pit stop at a local noble's house where they had lunch, a meal of fish and rice. After lunch they were taken to what they believed was a church but was actually a Hindu temple. As they made their way further into town, the Portuguese men were swarmed by curious people who wanted to see these strange bearded white men for themselves. They arrived at the palace an hour before sunset.

Da Gama was taken alone to see the zamorin. The doors to the reception hall opened slowly with all the pageantry of a royal household, to reveal the sovereign at the head of the room, reclining on a couch, chewing leaves and spitting them at regular intervals into a large golden cup placed beside him. Outside it was pouring rain. The pitter-patter of raindrops on the roof filled the silence of the room. Formalities were exchanged. Da Gama was impressed by the grandeur and wealth of the court. The zamorin gave the Portuguese permission to buy spices in India.

As da Gama left the audience hall he was brought out onto a veranda where his men had been told to wait for him. The sun had gone down and the heavy rain had stopped. Next to a large lamp, da Gama's men sat quietly, gazing out at the dark streets below, slushy with mud. The thick humidity was beginning to lift from the night air.

What did da Gama say to his men on that veranda in Calcutta in 1498? How did his crew react when they realized they had achieved their lofty goal? They had found a sea route to India. They had finally found the fabled land of spices. How long did it take the zamorin to realize he had made a dreadful mistake? One that would initiate the end of Indian independence. When he lay his head down that night to rest, what did he make of the day's events?

Often we cannot see the gravity of the situation while we are in it. Reactions and consequences are not always immediate. I can only think of Charles Mann's words, "We have been taught that history moves on great wheels, on world wars, on Napoleonic egos, on the revolutions of the masses, on vast economic upheavals and technological change. Yet small things, seemingly trivial details of everyday existence, can lead to convulsions in the world order."

ETHI

OPIA

ETHIOPIA
13TH to 19TH centuries

T HE YEAR WAS 1887 and Queen Taytu of Ethiopia was about to hold a spectacular feast high on a mountaintop, overlooking the country's new capital city, Addis Ababa. The September air was cool, and mist from the morning's rain still clung to the branches of the towering juniper trees. The breeze carried the steady scent of damp earth, upon which the aromas of berbere spices, turmeric stewed chicken, and pleasantly sour injera added their own perfumed layers.

Taytu lingered next to the dozens of large clay jars of *tej* (honey wine) that had been gathered to carry farther up the hill, where wooden troughs had been constructed so that wine would flow like rivers down into the tented banquet hall below. It was an extravagant addition that harked right back to descriptions of Eden and even royal Christian feasts of the medieval era.

In theory the meal was a celebration for the consecration of the new church of Entoto Maryam. But really this was a coming-out party. For Taytu, for Addis Ababa, and—for a new united Ethiopia. Nearly a century of political turmoil from the mid-eighteenth to the mid-nineteenth centuries, a period known as the *Zamana Masafent*, had broken down the power of the monarchy and divided the country into regional factions. Anarchy reigned, battles were fought, blood was spilled. Somehow the monarchy managed to survive the chaos, shut away in their capital Gondar, a medieval city of stone castles and brightly painted churches. But by the mid-nineteenth century, Queen Taytu's husband, Menilek II, had regained full control of the crown and he had grand plans for his homeland.

Menilek and Taytu began to unite a fractured Ethiopia and commenced a campaign to launch it into the modern world. By 1889 they would be emperor and empress of the Ethiopian Empire. But for this week of celebrations in Addis Ababa in 1887, they were still just king and queen.

For months Taytu meticulously planned every detail of the feast; ingredients were sourced from every corner of the country, each resultant dish representing the culinary traditions of the region from which it came. There was *talla*, a smoky beer made from malted and roasted highland barley, *awaze* pepper paste from Shawa, and pale hazelnut-colored honey from the kingdom of Jimma. In accordance with tradition, all the food served had to meet strict Christian Orthodox dietary requirements; so groups like the Muslim Harer in the East instead provided utensils for the tables, baskets for the injera, and decorations for the *das* (ceremonial tented banquet hall). At Taytu's table, every element of Ethiopian identity was represented.

The queen entered the cooking tent, circling around the all-female staff as they tended to large bubbling cauldrons. Taytu confidently gave a *shiro wet* (pea and lentil stew) that was looking too stodgy a good stir, before sampling a small piece of quwanta (beef jerky) declaring it not the right consistency. The chefs, familiar with Taytu's preferences and disposition, did not cower or tremble in her presence—there was simply too much to do. They absorbed her instructions and quickly returned to chopping, sautéing, and stirring.

In Europe and the Middle East, the kitchens of the elite were entirely staffed by men. In Ethiopia, cooking and especially the preparation of haute cuisine was very much a female role. Taytu herself oversaw the kitchens, ensuring that her signature mix of berbere spices—every household had their own recipe, but Taytu's was a state secret—adequately flavored each dish and that the best cattle and sheep were slaughtered for the feast's numerous meat-centric delicacies.

Over the course of five days, as the honey wine flowed, guests from all over Ethiopia dined in the great *das* overlooking Addis Ababa. And by all accounts it was a success. Guests were stunned by the sheer quantity of food and also by the cuisine's complexity. Oromo, Tigrayans, and Amhara broke bread together, dipping juicy morsels of lightly seared beef into glistening butter spiced with cardamom, nigella seeds, and shallots. Guests drank smoky barley beer and ripped off pieces of *injera*, large round flatbread dotted with hundreds of little pores, to scoop up mouthfuls of hearty chickpea stews laced with salted pieces of jerky. Taytu, seated with her husband at a grand table at the head of the tent, looked down over her subjects. A new Ethiopia was being woven together from all her various strands, a new quilt, representing a new national identity. Taytu raised a glass.

FASTS AND FEASTS

WE HAVE FOCUSED on the spectacular feast given by Empress Taytu in 1887, but in doing this, we have focused on precisely half of the cuisine. Ethiopia is the world's oldest explicitly Orthodox Christian nation and it is one that has preserved the tradition of celebrating Catholic Lent, with a division into lean days and meat days, as we have seen in other Christian cuisines, especially those of Europe in the Middle Ages through the Renaissance. While the Islamic inhabitants still celebrate the even more rigorous fasting of Ramadan, this is only done for a single month. Observant Ethiopian Christians abstain from eating meat for roughly half of the year, including every Wednesday and Friday. Members of religious orders may even practice this fasting for as many as 250 days out of the year! This inherent balance in the culinary life of Ethiopia, to me, makes the savoring of the rich and powerful meat dishes all the more delightful.

Berbere Spice Mix

BERBERE

MAKES ABOUT 1½ CUPS *Traditionally, berbere spice mix can be either a paste or a powder. Most families prepared their own, first sun-drying the peppers and herbs, then grinding them into a paste and re-drying it, and finally grinding the result into a fine powder. The successive stages of this process and the sun-drying add another depth of flavor to the final product. This fundamental ingredient is inherently unique to the cook or family preparing it. Most important is the final balance between fiery pepper and aromatic herbs.*

1 packed cup dried guajillo chilies

2 teaspoons toasted nigella seeds

½ teaspoon whole cloves

1 teaspoon ajowan seeds or
½ teaspoon each mild dried
oregano and thyme

2 tablespoons dried shallots

1 teaspoon garlic powder

2 teaspoons ground ginger

1 teaspoon ground cardamom

½ teaspoon ground cinnamon

½ teaspoon toasted grains of paradise
(see page 159)

¼ teaspoon dried basil

¼ teaspoon dried rue (see page 10)

USING kitchen shears, remove the tops of the dried chilies and then tear the chilies open to remove the seeds and internal membranes. They do not have to be perfectly cleaned of all seeds and membranes, and you can adjust the heat level by judiciously adding seeds back to the mix. Chop the chilies well with a sharp knife or kitchen shears to aid in the grinding process. Working in batches, grind all the spices together in a spice grinder until fine and thoroughly combined.

Spiced Clarified Butter

NITER KEBBEH

MAKES ABOUT 3½ CUPS *Niter kebbeh is vital to Ethiopian food. It is also great in eggs, curries, and sauces or spread on toast. Once you have this remarkably versatile ingredient in your arsenal, you will find a hundred more uses for it. Because the butter is clarified first, it also has a very long shelf life.*

- 8 sticks (2 pounds) unsalted butter
- 2 large shallots, roughly chopped
- 6 cloves garlic, sliced
- 2-inch-piece fresh ginger, peeled and sliced
- 2 teaspoons toasted nigella seeds
- 8 black cardamom pods, toasted
- 2 teaspoons coriander seeds, toasted
- 3 whole cloves
- 2 teaspoons dried oregano
- 2 teaspoons dried thyme

FIRST, clarify the butter. Melt the butter over low heat in a medium saucepan. Continue to cook, skimming off the foam that rises to the top. Try to skim off as much as possible, but a little residue will be removed in the final step. Continue to cook until there is no more foam and then add the remaining ingredients. Continue to cook for another 20 minutes and then strain through a cheesecloth into a jar with a tight-fitting lid.

FORGING A NEW NATION AND A NEW CUISINE

THE CUISINE celebrated and elevated by Empress Taytu should be recognized as the genesis of modern Ethiopian food. This was deliberate as well as creative. The empress intentionally drew tastes and aromas from across the diverse kingdom. This was more than creating a new national palate; this was intentionally creating a new national identity, no small task in an empire composed of diverse traditions of language, aesthetics, and religion. Teff for the injera came from Amhara and Oromia, fiery red peppers from Shawa and Yejju, honey from allied kingdoms of Jimma and Gera, and, of course, the diverse spices drawn from international trade all spoke to the reach and power of the new empire.

Pea and Lentil Stew

SHIRO WET

SERVES 4 TO 6 *Depending on the length and manner of cooking, this recipe can create different textures, from a thin sauce to a thick stew. Traditionally, texture is judged by ear, with the cook listening for the familiar "tik-tik" sound of the simmering pot. Whether thick or thin, it is rich, aromatic, and delicious. If you have yellow split pea and red lentil flour, you can use one-half cup of each and skip the first step.*

½ cup yellow split peas

½ cup red lentils

½ cup chickpea flour

3 tablespoons Spiced Clarified Butter (page 256)

3 shallots, finely chopped

3 cloves garlic, minced

2 teaspoons kosher salt

1½ teaspoons Berbere Spice Mix (page 254)

½ teaspoon ground ginger

½ teaspoon finely chopped Thai basil

½ teaspoon fenugreek

GRIND the split peas and the lentils in a spice grinder to make a flour. Whisk together with the chickpea flour in a medium bowl and reserve. Bring 5 cups water to a boil in a medium saucepan and hold at a simmer.

MELT the clarified butter in a heavy pot over medium heat. Add the shallots and cook until softened, about 5 minutes. Increase the heat to medium-high and cook until browned, about 10 additional minutes. Add the garlic and cook for 3 minutes, stirring constantly. Add the salt, berbere, ginger, basil, fenugreek, and the flour mixture and cook for 2 minutes, continuing to stir. Add the simmering water 1 cup at a time, whisking to combine between additions. Cover and simmer for 30 minutes, stirring occasionally and adding water in small amounts if the mixture is too thick for your liking.

BIBLICAL ORIGINS

MENILEK II WAS FROM the Solomonic Dynasty, a royal bloodline that was in power for a remarkable seven hundred years—from the ascendance of King Yekuno Amlak in 1270 to Emperor Haille Selassie's assassination in 1974. These royals traced their origin back to ancient times, to the reign of King Solomon and the Queen of Sheba and their fated meeting, a story that can be found in Christian, Islamic, and Jewish traditions. Every dynasty has an origin story, and Ethiopia's longest-ruling monarchy is no different. Mythic in nature, combining various elements and details from a number of different tales, origin stories legitimize and make legends out of otherwise seemingly ordinary people.

As the legend goes, many, many years ago the Queen of Sheba traveled across the Red Sea to King Solomon's kingdom in Arabia. She had heard of his power and his wisdom and wished to witness it for herself. While she was there, the queen became pregnant by King Solomon (sources vary on whether it was love, a trick, or a tryst) and gave birth to a son named Menilek. She raised her royal son in Ethiopia, but when Menilek was grown he went to Jerusalem to meet his father. The reunion must have gone well, as Solomon wished for his son to stay with him. But Menilek insisted he must return to his mother's land. Upon departing, Menilek, without his father's knowledge, took one rather extraordinary souvenir home with him—the Arc of the Covenant, the most important relic of the Israelites, a golden chest containing the Ten Commandments themselves. Menilek's capitol Aksum, in the north of Ethiopia, became the new home for the Ten Commandments (one of many theories about where they may have ended up) imbuing the Solomonic Dynasty with some very ancient and seriously holy roots.

From the capital at Aksum, Ethiopia's power grew, radiating out across the Horn of Africa. Its proximity to the Red Sea coast, to Arabia to the east and Egypt and the Holy Land to the north, turned the fabled kingdom into a major regional power player. Trade and commerce flourished. When looking at a map of this region, at first it might not seem like Ethiopia was well positioned to connect itself to the arteries of the Near East and even the Mediterranean world—but it was, and it did.

As the gospel of Jesus and a new religion called Christianity circulated throughout the Mediterranean basin in the first centuries of the

Common Era, word eventually reached Aksum. King Ezana converted around 330 CE and Christianity was adopted as the official state religion, making Ethiopia the second oldest Christian country in the entire world (after Armenia). In the same period in Rome, Christians were being martyred in the Colosseum. Europe was pagan. Ethiopia was Christian long before the West was.

A few centuries later another religion swept over the region: Islam. As the Islamic Empire rose to power in the seventh century, Ethiopia was toppled from its dominant position in the Red Sea region. Though the new religion enmeshed itself into numerous Swahili Coast cultures, Ethiopia stayed true to its Christian beginnings. Interestingly, no attempts were made by the Islamic Empire to bring Ethiopia into its realm. Some sources say this is because in 615 CE a group of Muslims facing persecution in Arabia, among them the Prophet Muhammad's son-in-law and successor Uthman, as well as his daughter Ruqqaya and two of his future wives, found safety in Ethiopia. King Armah protected them and treated them

THE SOUL OF A FOOD, OR,
AS CLOSE TO SPIRITUAL
AS I AM EVER GOING TO GET

EACH GREAT cuisine seems to have a "soul"—not in some mystical or magical sense but through a fundamental logic of flavors that underpins it and ties it together. Try to imagine Japanese food without soy sauce, or the umami-rich dashi of kombu kelp and bonito shavings. Indian food is cloaked in the warm spices of a masala, and Chinese food has its roots in ginger and garlic. I'm not sure what it says about us that much of American cuisine seems to be built around bland starchiness and the mild umami of seared meat.

Ethiopian food is one of the best examples of this prevailing tendency, an animating principle dominated by three elements. Most obvious is *injera*, a bread that is fiendishly difficult to make and whose sour taste and soft sponginess from fermented teff flour serve as both serving platter and utensils. The essential flavors rest on two pillars, the infused clarified butter *niter kebbeh* and the spice mix berbere. However, it is vital to remember that, whatever recipe I give, every cook and every family has their own variant, hotter or milder, more fragrant or less pungent, according to their taste and tradition. The soul of the cuisine is reinterpreted in the soul of everyone cooking it.

well and Muhammad never forgot this. Years later when King Armah died, Muhammad is said to have prayed for him and told his followers, "Leave the Abyssinians [Ethiopians] in peace." No attempts were made by any of Muhammad's successors—the Umayyads or the Abbasids—to conquer Ethiopia.

As the Islamic world grew around it, Ethiopia turned inward. Its own distinctive branch of Orthodox Christianity developed without the influence of neighboring Christian kingdoms. The ancient and medieval churches of Ethiopia are unlike anything else in the world. Many seem to emerge from the earth itself; birthed out of the soil from the bottom of a pit, rock-hewn majesties rising up toward the sun, only a smooth cross-shaped roof visible to the viewer standing at ground level. Other monasteries and shrines were carved into caves, high up cliff faces, accessible only by a system of rope pulleys.

The best examples of these uniquely Ethiopian churches are to be found in Lalibela, a northeastern city that became the capital under the rule of the eleventh-century Zagwe Dynasty (a short glitch in the long matrix of Solomonic rule). But Lalibela was also a king, apparently destined for greatness from birth because when he was born a swarm of bees encircled him. (His mother took this as a very good omen.) When Lalibela was a teenager, he visited Jerusalem, and upon his return he decided he wanted to create his own holy city, a pilgrimage site for Christian Ethiopians at home.

The result was eleven churches that stand to this day. Some are freestanding, chiseled and excavated out of rock; some are carved out of the mountains; and all are connected to one another by tunnels and passageways. The most famous church is Bete Giyorgis or the Church of Saint George, sometimes referred to as the "eighth wonder of the world." Standing on ground level, all visitors see is its cross-shaped roof, but peering down into the pit of volcanic tuff they see an entire church. Descending eighty-two feet via a spiraling set of stairs, visitors are met with a simple red facade, yellowing age crawling across its surface like timeworn vines. Inside is a shrine to Saint George, a venerated warrior, and a replica (or is it?) of the Ark of the Covenant.

But perhaps one of the most stunning holy houses of Ethiopia lies not in the ground, but in the sky. Abuna Yemata Guh, a church in the northern Tigray region, was carved into stone eight thousand feet up a cliff that stands alone in a desert, looking like something out of the American West. After a grueling three-hour hike and a stroll across a death-defying bridge, worshipers enter a tiny unmarked doorway into a cavernous room covered in beautiful bright paintings of Jesus, Mary, the apostles, and the saints.

I like to imagine that fifteen hundred years ago when Abuna Yemata Guh was first built, the artist who painted this otherworldly interior, neck aching from applying delicate brushstrokes to the ceiling, decided to take a break in the sun. Stepping out from the cool dark interior onto the narrow ledge, he saw sweeping views over great canyons dotted with small green shrubs. Perhaps he took a sip of his barley beer and a few mouthfuls of the bread he had carried up the mountain with him, as he thought about the next pattern he would draw from his perch in the clouds.

COFFEE AS COMMUNITY

WHILE THE earliest dates of coffee's cultivation are both unknown and shrouded in mythical stories of dancing goats, coffee unquestionably has its origin in Ethiopia. And although the Ethiopian church initially frowned on coffee, and even banned it, the beverage has become fundamental to the social culture of Ethiopia. In fact, to say one has "no one to drink coffee with" is an expression of loneliness and cultural isolation.

The ritual of coffee preparation and drinking can take up to several hours and is enjoyed for the process itself as much as the final results. It is performed primarily by women. A woman first decorates the room with grasses, flowers, and often aromatic incense. She then hand-roasts green coffee beans in a pan over a flame, crushes them in a mortar and pestle, and steeps them for her guests. Sugar is often added, and salt and butter are often used as well. But most important is the sense of ritual and social grace that pervades the setting, the guests sipping together and complimenting the preparer on the fineness of her coffee technique.

Beef Jerky

QUWANTA

MAKES ABOUT 20 PIECES *The Ethiopian climate lends itself to air-drying—thus the manufacture of Berbere (page 254) and this beef jerky. An oven at a low temperature approximates air-drying very effectively; a dehydrator will work as well.*

2 pounds top round or London broil, thinly sliced

¼ cup plus 2 tablespoons tej (see Note)

¼ cup plus 2 tablespoons Berbere Spice Mix (page 254)

Kosher salt

CUT the meat into long strips, about 1 inch wide. Whisk together the tej and berbere in a medium bowl. Toss the meat in this mixture to coat thoroughly, then refrigerate for 30 minutes. Preheat the oven to 175°F. Arrange the strips on a wire rack placed on a sheet pan and liberally salt both sides of the meat. Bake until dried and stiff, about 3 hours. Stored in a tightly sealed container, it should last for several weeks.

NOTE: True Ethiopian tej (honey wine) is deeply funky and can be hard to source outside of Ethiopia. If you cannot find it. Mead can be substituted for tej, but try to find the rawest one available. Another good substitute for tej is the rawest, funkiest orange wine you can find, with ½ teaspoon honey added per cup.

Pea and Lentil Stew
with Beef Jerky

BOZENA

SERVES 4 TO 6 *This preparation combines the two preceding recipes and elevates both.*

¾ cup Beef Jerky (page 263)

1 batch Pea and Lentil Stew (page 257)

BREAK up the beef jerky using your hands and add to the bowl of a food processor fitted with the metal blade. Pulse until the dried beef is well chopped but still has some texture. In a medium saucepan, combine ⅓ cup of the beef jerky, or more to taste, with the stew and ¼ cup water. Cook for 10 minutes. Serve garnished with the remaining chopped jerky.

THE RAW AND THE COOKED

THERE IS a strong tradition of eating raw meat in Ethiopian cuisine, and a number of stories and theories concerning its origin. The most popular of these is the idea that soldiers ate their meat raw to avoid revealing their positions with the smoke from cooking fires. This also dovetails with the fact that raw meat eating is commonly associated with manly camaraderie, including the tradition of demonstrating one's masculinity by selecting a larger chunk and then cutting it off very close to your lips with a sharp knife. In fact, the practice of eating meat raw almost certainly dates to antiquity and has as much to do with the sensual pleasures of eating the spicy, buttery, honey wine–accented morsels as anything else.

Meat, however, is virtually the only foodstuff eaten raw at meals. Vegetables are invariably cooked, and while you may be able to get a side salad today in Addis Ababa, this is a recent development and not at all part of traditional fare. Interestingly, Ethiopian food also had no tradition of desserts or sweets, except for a few snack items. But do not mourn for your salad and cheesecake, and remember, the idea of eating raw fish—sushi and sashimi, now gourmet staples—was until recently considered to be exotic and challenging. So select the most beautiful crimson cube, bathed in richness and spice, and enjoy.

Spiced Raw Beef with Dipping Sauce

GORED GORED AND AWAZE

SERVES 4 TO 6 *Needless to say, this dish will be as good as the meat you make it with. When buying meat for raw preparations, it is important to source a high-quality product from a reputable butcher, and let them know you will be serving it uncooked. A relatively lean cut like tenderloin is ideal—heavily marbled meats are wonderful when cooked but tend to have a greasy mouthfeel when consumed raw.*

FOR THE BEEF:

1 pound beef tenderloin, cut into ½-inch cubes

Kosher salt

2 tablespoons tej (see Note, page 263)

2 teaspoons Berbere Spice Mix (page 254)

2 tablespoons melted Spiced Clarified Butter (page 256)

FOR DIPPING:

¼ cup Berbere Spice Mix (page 254)

½ teaspoon cayenne pepper or more to taste

¼ cup tej (see Note, page 263)

½ teaspoon kosher salt

¼ cup melted Spiced Clarified Butter (page 256)

TO prepare the beef, season the tenderloin with salt. Just before serving, combine the beef with the tej, berbere, and melted clarified butter in a bowl. Toss with a silicone spatula to fully coat the tenderloin; taste for seasoning.

COMBINE the berbere, cayenne, tej, and salt for the dipping sauce. Serve the ¼ cup melted clarified butter on the side for dipping as well.

THE SOLOMONIC DYNASTY:
SEVEN HUNDRED YEARS OF POWER

WHEN YEKUNO AMLAK CAME TO POWER IN 1270, the Solomonic Dynasty was once again restored to power after two centuries' hiatus. Though the family could trace their ancestry back to the Bible, Yekuno Amlak's grandson, the fourteenth-century emperor Amda Seyon, wanted to further strengthen the legitimacy of his family's rule in the eyes of the people. Amda Seyon did so by commissioning the scholar Is'haq Neburä-Id to write the *Kebra Nagast*, the Ethiopian national epic: a retelling of the story of King Solomon and the Queen of Sheba, their son, Menilek, and the Ark of the Covenant. The *Kebra Nagast* also includes stories of the monarchy and tales of life in Ethiopia in the medieval period. It was the legitimization of a mythology into a national identity, one that would reign supreme until 1974.

Amda Seyon understood the importance of a tangible legacy. And so under his rule Ethiopia's first "history" was written, a royal chronicle in which the rulers are for the first time referred to as the "Kings of Ethiopia." The country's first legal code, the *Fetha Nagast,* or Law of Kings, was also composed, codifying ideas and legal concepts that would continue to be consulted by monarchs well into the twentieth century. Major religious works were translated from Arabic into Ge'ez (the ancient Semitic language of Ethiopia, within the same family as Arabic and Hebrew), works such as the *History of the Prophet*, the *Acts of the Apostles*, and the *Lives of Saints*. Their subject matter as well as the fact that they were translated from Arabic further demonstrates how intertwined this corner of the world was—in ideas and in language.

Ethiopia's status as the only Christian empire south of the equator and east of Europe turned it into a legendary place, tied into one of the biggest mysteries of the European medieval world: the myth of Prester John. Perhaps, dear reader, you might recall our introduction to this fabled character in Chapter Three when a letter supposedly authored by this Christian king found its way into the hands of the Byzantine emperor Manuel I Comnenus. The letter from 1165 describes an earthly paradise and requests military assistance for help against the Muslims. The European imagination was thoroughly piqued, inspiring a pope to send a mission to the East. And while we can be pretty sure that Prester John never existed, it would make a lot of sense that this faraway Christian land Europeans never were able to find in Asia was, in fact, Ethiopia: an ancient Christian country surrounded by the Islamic empire.

I often think of the medieval Old World as a game board upon which a series of tiles are in constant motion, each tile representing either a Christian or Muslim power. One tile, like Abd al-Rahman's Islamic caliphate in al-Andalus, clicks into place, eclipsing the Christian crowns surrounding it. Only a few centuries later, that tile will shuffle south down the board, as the Inquisition begins. A new tile moves east as the Christian crusading states establish themselves in Jerusalem only to slide back west at the hands of Saladin. The one constant in this game is that neither side can ever accept defeat, and they are continuously calling upon their fellow Christians or Muslims for help to fight against the other. The myth of Prester John is a manifestation of the European Christian desire to believe that they had allies beyond the West; in other words, they couldn't fathom being alone in a world surrounded by "heathens."

In a quest to make contact with other Christians, embassies of Ethiopians to Europe and Europeans to Ethiopia began in the fourteenth century. When Ethiopian emperor Wedem Ar'ad heard that Christians in Spain were struggling to overthrow the Muslim caliphate in Granada, he sent an envoy of thirty men to offer assistance to Ferdinand IV of Castile. Ar'ad's men never made it to Spain; they visited Rome to meet the pope, only to find that the Papal Schism (that time between 1378 and 1417 when no one could agree on who the legitimate pope was, so there was one in Rome and one in France) was in full swing, and made an additional trip to Avignon, where the one "true" pope had temporarily relocated. After traveling for a number of months they ended their European journey in Genoa, awaiting good winds to carry them back across the Mediterranean. What must this delegation have made of medieval Europe and its cities? Did they find their northern Christian brethren backward and barbaric? Potentially insane to live in such dirty crowded cities? What did they make of their churches and castles, with no trace of nature in any of their designs, but instead basilicas erected upon flat ground.

The Portuguese, ever the voyagers, were the most prolific European travelers to Ethiopia. The diaries, letters, and books they left behind give us valuable insight into everyday life in medieval Ethiopia. In the 1520s the Portuguese traveler Francisco Alvares arrived during Emperor Lebna Dengel's rule, and described in great detail the royal tent cities he saw.

No longer did the emperors reside in stationary capitals like Aksum or Lalibela. For a few centuries the monarchy became completely mobile, and by constantly being on the move, the emperor had the advantage of being directly involved in the daily happenings of his empire. He moved from region to region, inspecting his land, overseeing the collection of taxes, putting down a rebellious lord here and there. Whenever he and his court reached a location that had farms with enough cattle to supply them, as well as firewood and water, the entire massive retinue of thousands would come to a stop and set up camp for a while. However the court could never stay for long: living at the expense of the peasants and farmers of that area meant that entire orchards or a season's worth of crops would be wiped out in supplying the royal tent city and all its inhabitants.

Francisco Alvares wrote that the tent cities stretched for miles, thousands of tents and pavilions as far as the eye could see—the emperor, his family, and their inner circle, advisors, nobles, and high-ranking members of society, each with their own numerous attendants. The tents and pavilions were set up on large plains, any high ground reserved for the emperor and his five tents, which always faced west. A large red tent would be erected near the emperor's tents for banquets, ceremonies, and receptions—a great hall made of fabric, if you will. There were tents for religious ceremonies, which even had their own sacristy for vestments. There were tents for judges, courts, and prisons. There were tents for the *behtwaddads,* or favorite ministers of state. And of course there were tents for the masses—the many common people who cooked, cleaned, brewed beer, and made clothes. There was even a sub–tent city of bakeries, brothels, blacksmiths, and taverners. Yes, one could visit a tavern for dinner and wander home through the perfectly laid out streets between the tents, back to your own canvas dwelling.

The emperor's nomadic nature in no way diminished his authority or ability to wield power. In fact it strengthened it. By traveling in person to every corner of his empire, the emperor could keep abreast of the latest political developments and intrigues. The emperor was able to appoint and fire any official, and he needed no reason to do so other than because he wanted to. In fact it was so common for lords to get fired that if one was ever called to court, he would not leave home without his family and possessions, knowing there was a great likelihood he would never be returning.

Once a lord had been deposed, the emperor would force that lord to stay with the court for at least five years, if not more. In this way, a disgruntled noble couldn't run away to stir up a power base somewhere else in retaliation. They were made to stay local, loyal, and obedient. This is the kind of absolute power I imagine England's Henry VIII would have been incredibly jealous of.

Turmeric Stewed Chicken

ALICHA

SERVES 4 TO 6 *This mild and delicate dish was the favorite of King Menilek II and stands as a gentle counterpoint to the bold and fiery flavors of much of the rest of the feast's cuisine. Chicken is simmered in lamb stock, allowing the complex flavors to marry.*

1 tablespoon canola oil

1 pound lamb chops, fat trimmed completely

¼ cup Spiced Clarified Butter (page 256)

12 shallots, finely chopped (about 8 cups)

1-inch-piece fresh ginger, peeled and grated

1 teaspoon kosher salt

5 cloves garlic, finely chopped

1 cup tej (see Note, page 263)

3 black cardamom pods

2 tablespoons ground turmeric

1 teaspoon ground nigella seeds

½ teaspoon ground clove

½ teaspoon ground ajowan

¼ teaspoon ground cinnamon

4 skinless, bone-in chicken legs and thighs

6 large eggs, hard-boiled and peeled

1 to 2 Ethiopian Flatbreads (page 275), oven dried and crumbled

HEAT the oil in a deep pot over medium-high heat. Add the lamb and sear until deeply browned on both sides. Add 4 cups water, bring to a boil, then reduce the heat and simmer for 45 minutes, skimming any foam that rises to the surface. Turn off the burner and carefully skim any fat and remaining foam. Strain through a fine-mesh sieve into a bowl and reserve the broth. Discard the lamb.

MELT the clarified butter in a medium saucepan over medium heat. Add the shallots and ginger and cook until browned, 10 to 12 minutes, stirring often. Add the salt and garlic and cook until softened, continuing to stir. Add the tej and cook until well reduced. Add the spices and seeds and cook for 1 minute, stirring constantly. Add the lamb broth and bring to a boil, then reduce to a simmer. Add the chicken legs and thighs and cook, covered, until the chicken is fork tender, 30 to 35 minutes. Cut four to six lengthwise slits into each egg, just through the white, not cutting all the way through. Add the eggs to the chicken and cook for an additional 10 minutes. The chicken should be very tender and falling off the bone. Garnish with the injera crumbs and serve.

Whip-Cut Lamb Leg

ENFELE

SERVES 8 TO 12 *In this spectacular presentation, a bone-in leg of lamb is cut so that the meat stays attached to the bone but is butchered to make long strips, resembling a whip or, in my personal opinion, a giant jellyfish. The traditional cooking method was to suspend the lamb over a pot of boiling stew and cook it in stages by dipping it into the boiling stew and carving off just the cooked portions. It can, of course, be fully cooked at one time and presented less theatrically.*

1 (3- to 5-pound) bone-in leg of lamb

Kosher salt

¾ cup Spiced Clarified Butter (page 256)

About 3 pounds shallots, finely chopped to yield 9 cups (see Note)

3-inch-piece fresh ginger, peeled and minced

9 cloves garlic, finely chopped

¼ cup plus 2 tablespoons Berbere Spice Mix (page 254)

6 black cardamom pods

3 tablespoons toasted and ground ajowan seeds

3 cups tej (see Note, page 263)

8 cups low-sodium beef stock

Ground cayenne pepper to taste

A leg of lamb has two bones, and first we want to remove the smaller, upper one. Identify the knee joint and, using a very sharp knife, make a cut all the way down to the bone and up to the thick end of the leg. Extend this cut slightly past the knee joint (toward the thinner end) and spread the meat apart. Making small cuts with the tip of your knife, free the bone from the meat and cut through the knee joint. Remove and discard the smaller bone. Now, leaving a margin of a few inches where the meat attaches to the narrow end of the bone, make deep cuts, about 2 inches wide, all the way down to the bone and to the end of the leg, creating a series of flaps that are still attached to the bone. Working on one flap at a time, starting at the thick end, detach most of the flap from the bone, leaving it firmly attached at one end. Next, cut each of these flaps into a long single strip, starting just below the attachment and cutting in a spiral moving down toward the other end, as if you were unrolling a roll of thick ribbon. Repeat this process for each flap and season well with salt.

ADD the clarified butter to a medium stockpot over medium heat. Add the shallots, ginger, and 3 teaspoons salt and cook, stirring constantly, until the shallots are lightly browned, 15 to 20 minutes. Add the garlic and cook until softened, about 3 minutes, continuing to stir. Add the spices, seeds, and the tej and cook, stirring constantly, until the liquid is reduced by half. Add the beef stock and bring to a boil, then reduce to a simmer. Continue to simmer until reduced by about one-quarter. Season to taste with salt and cayenne. Make it as hot as you want! Remember, you are cooking the lamb for a relatively short time, so you want it to be boldly flavorful.

TO cook, dip a few inches of the lamb into the simmering pot for 3 to 5 minutes, depending on the desired doneness, and cut off just the cooked portions to serve. Of course, you can cook the entire leg or as much as you want at once, making sure to stir and agitate the lamb through the cooking liquid to ensure even cooking.

NOTE: A food processor can also be used for the shallots, garlic, and ginger, but be sure to rough chop them first and scrape down the sides once or twice while pulsing to keep the size relatively uniform.

INJERA

I MUST CONFESS that I am a bread guy. To me, no other staple food attains a comparable level of variety and sophistication across cultures, from the crust of a French baguette to the chew of naan cooked in a real tandoor, to the alternate joy of pizza crust perfected in a wood-fired oven. There are dense ryes and pumpernickels and pillowy bao, and I could go on forever with this list. High in this carbohydrate constellation is soft and delicately sour Ethiopian injera, which serves not only to accompany the meal but as both utensil and serving dish as well. Meals, so often stews, are ladled directly onto the delicate, lacy, crepelike bread, with more offered on the side, either folded like napkins or rolled tightly. Bits of food are picked up with torn pieces of injera to be eaten together. The bread also can be dipped, and at the end of the meal you are left with the sauce-soaked serving injera, often considered the best part.

But in all foods, there is a trade-off between art and science, of accurate measurement and pure technique. And perhaps nowhere is this more true than with the magic of injera. Of course, the women (it is usually women) who make it well also make it look devilishly easy. It isn't. But it is one of those rare and almost transcendent foods where time, temperature, and technique come together seamlessly in a food that is genuinely at the very heart of a cuisine. An Ethiopian meal without injera is almost not a meal at all.

Ethiopian Flatbreads

INJERA

MAKES ABOUT 8 *This method uses a commercial sourdough starter to produce a true fermented injera in two days. Using a standardized commercial starter will yield relatively consistent and reliable results—you can use your own homemade starter, but be ready to adjust on the fly, as there are numerous variables that can cause starters, and therefore batters, to behave differently. And keep in mind that the recipe for injera is very different from most other bread recipes, even flatbread recipes, primarily because teff is extremely low in protein and extremely high in starch. I'll be honest: This recipe is tricky. For a more controllable batter, replace ½ cup of the second addition of teff flour with ½ cup cake flour. The result will be less historically accurate but more manageable.*

½ cup sourdough starter

2 cups plus 2 tablespoons ivory teff flour

THE day before you plan to serve the injera, make a sponge: In a medium bowl, mix the sourdough starter, 1 cup teff flour, and 1 cup room-temperature water until combined. Cover, and allow to rise at room temperature 1½ to 2 hours, until bubbles form. Stir in 1 cup of the teff flour. Cover and allow to ferment until the dough doubles in size, about 2 hours. The dough will crack as it rises. When it has doubled in size, pat the dough down in the bowl and cover with 1 inch water. Cover and let ferment overnight at room temperature.

THE next day, pour off and reserve the water on top. Mix the remaining 2 tablespoons teff flour with 1 cup water in a small saucepan and cook over low heat, stirring constantly to prevent lumps, until thickened to the consistency of loose yogurt, about 2 minutes. Allow the mixture to cool slightly, then mix it into the fermented dough until it is perfectly smooth with no lumps. Stir in the reserved liquid in small amounts as needed to produce a thin batter, similar to a crepe batter. (If you run out of the reserved liquid and the batter is still too thick, use additional water.) It is best to keep the batter slightly thicker for your first flatbread—you can thin it out further as you get the hang of the cooking process.

TRANSFER the batter to a measuring cup or small pitcher. Heat an 8-inch nonstick skillet with a tight-fitting lid over medium-low heat. Pour the batter in a spiral motion from the outside of the pan toward the center to cover the surface. Allow to cook, uncovered, until small bubbles form and the top begins to set, then cover the pan. Continue to cook, covered, for another 2 minutes, steaming the flatbread. After 2 minutes, lift the lid and check the surface of the bread. You want the final bread to be lacy and spongy but not wet to the touch. If it still looks wet, cover the pan with the lid and check after 1 additional minute. Breads can take 2 to 4 minutes to cook, depending on the pan, the heat of your stove, the fit of the lid, and the density of the batter. If the batter seems too dense, thin it by stirring in small amounts of the reserved liquid or water. After you have made one or two breads, you should have a feel for how long they are taking.

SERVE one injera per person unrolled as a "plate" with additional injera folded or rolled like napkins passed on the side.

THE CASTLES OF GONDAR

BY 1636, THE EMPERORS had grown tired of moving. Emperor Fasiladas decided to establish a new capital in Gondar, which would remain the seat of the Ethiopian monarchy until Queen Taytu and King Menilek II established Addis Ababa in 1886.

In a pretty remarkable shift from the tent cities of centuries past, Emperor Fasiladas built a new sturdier home—a castle—as would many of his descendents. The castles of Gondar are architecturally fascinating and bewildering in their uniqueness. One would be hard pressed to find similar structures anywhere in Africa. At first glance they look like a castle one might find somewhere in medieval Europe, with the towers, a keep, arrow slits, a portcullis, flanking towers, and crenelated battlements. But closer inspection reveals surprising influences: rooftop battlements appear to have been transported from India; decorative motifs surrounding the windows look as though they come from the Islamic Alhambra palace complex. One can only imagine Ethiopian embassies to Europe must have picked up some architectural styles along the way.

The oldest and grandest of these castles in Gondar is the Fasil Ghebbi, the one built by Emperor Fasiladas. Today it is part of a complex surrounded by the castles and palaces of his successors, as well as a banqueting hall, three churches, a royal library, and bathing palaces. In its own time there was a large marketplace nearby, open every day except Sunday. The merchants of Gondar traded in salt from the Danakil Depression, fabric, iron, ivory, and gold. Gondar sat at the convergence of a number of trade routes, bringing in luxury goods from North Africa, Arabia, and beyond.

In 1752 an unexpected visitor from the West appeared in the city of castles, a man named Remedius Prutky, who hailed from Bohemia in Eastern Europe. Prutky was a Franciscan missionary tasked with traveling to the great kingdom of Prester John. Of course he didn't find Prester John, though he was fortunate enough to meet Emperor Iyasu II and spend a number of months at his court. From Prutky's diaries we begin to see the isolation that came with royal life in Gondar, as opposed to its previous open and nomadic form.

The emperor, unless he was eating with his mother, always dined alone. One particularly common meal for Iyasu II was a thick soup-like sauce into which injera was dipped. But Iyasu II was not expected to perform the grueling work of feeding himself. He had an attendant for that.

The servant would dip the pieces of injera into the sauce, delicately placing it in the emperor's mouth. Two to three large mouthfuls of bread and sauce were consumed before six mouthfuls of raw meat, swallowed whole, never chewed, were eaten by the emperor. No side dishes, no dessert. No guests.

On Sundays, however, once the emperor had eaten his fill, the second portion of the evening began. Reclining on a couch at the head of the room, the emperor watched as servants began to set out a fantastic feast for the ministers, courtiers, and other people of importance at court. As everyone took their seat at the table, a female servant, naked from the waist up, would make her way around the room and begin to feed the guests. Pieces of bread dipped in stews and juicy chunks of raw meat were fed to guests as the emperor reclined, watching, observing, taking in the scene. Only on special occasions would the emperor reveal his face—a gift to his subjects.

While the emperors certainly enjoyed power, good food, nice accommodations, and a host of servants to attend to their every need, I never get the impression that they were enjoying all the perks that come with, well, being very, very rich and powerful. Where were the parties? The dancing? The bon vivant good times of being king?

As the emperors continued their quiet lives of isolation tucked away in Gondar, cracks began to appear in the crown. The Zamana Masafent, the era of princes, commenced. From the mid-eighteenth to the mid-nineteenth centuries, regional warlords and local princes, unchecked by the secluded emperors, came to the fore of the political landscape and attempted to carve out power for themselves. A united Ethiopia was torn apart into warring states. It wasn't until Menilek II inherited the crown that Ethiopia began to come together again.

There's something about this image of a monarch eating alone and in silence that I can't seem to get out of my head. Imagine being so detached from society by tradition and law and custom that you cease to be a human allowed to put food into your own mouth, instead forced to eat alone—aside from the servant feeding you, I suppose. It seems like a deep kind of loneliness, that is cruelly matched by an utter lack of privacy. It is an existence robbed of one of the greatest pleasures of life: to sit around a table with others and to share food, drink, and conversation.

As we turn to seventeenth-century France and the utter opulence of the Palace of Versailles, we will find another monarch living this kind of surreal life. Louis XIV, the Sun King. Every desire, whim, and bodily function he had was attended to by an army of servants. But like the sun, Louis was ultimately alone, at the center of his solar system, a universe of his own design.

VERSA

ILLES

VERSAILLES
17TH to 18TH centuries

ON A SUNNY JULY AFTERNOON, the Hall of Mirrors in the palace of Versailles is packed with people. Visitors from every corner of the globe have descended on this legendary palace to see the hallowed halls for themselves. Hushed voices whisper to each other upon entering the room filled with light; views of the gardens through the windows are reflected back into the room by the seventeen enormous mirrors on the opposite wall.

Light hits each gilded surface and precious crystal prism dangling from a chandelier, further illuminating a room that is already bathed in glorious sunlight. A woman points to the frescoes adorning the ceiling, nudging her husband who is still taking in the gold statues, the columns of porphyry marble. A visitor's sneaker squeaks on the shiny parquet floor. A middle-aged man with a camera *clicks clicks clicks*. Sweaty children with streaks of sunscreen on their faces dash around outside the windows.

Since its construction in the early seventeenth century, Versailles has drawn crowds like moths to a very gilded flame. Once these guests wore corsets, mantuas, doublets, and breeches. Now they wear tee-shirts, jeans, and comfortable walking shoes. In recent decades the annual visitor list sits in the millions; it is one of the most visited historic sites in the world. But the diversity and breadth of individuals who visited the palace in its heyday was equally impressive. Kings and queens, those of noble blood and those of no rank at all, moved through its halls and across its grounds. Foreign ambassadors and dignitaries from Thailand, India, and the Ottoman Empire traveled thousands of miles to meet the French king. It might have been home to the one percent, but anyone was welcome to visit—as long as they were "dressed."

What is it about Versailles? Its grandeur and sheer opulence make an impressive architectural site. But the lure of Versailles goes deeper than an appreciation for brilliant engineering and the legendary figures who lived within its walls. Royals like Louis XIV and Marie Antoinette fascinate us moderns. It's the kind of infatuation that lands the Duke and Duchess of Cornwall on the covers of American tabloid magazines to this day. But royals also stir an indignation in others who cannot fathom the incredible wealth bestowed upon some by sheer chance of birth. The curiosity, obsession, and resentment royals invoke today are the same emotions that once put Versailles on a lofty pedestal from which it took a spectacular fall.

IN 1623 KING LOUIS XIII OF FRANCE built a small hunting lodge twelve miles outside of Paris. He named it Versailles, a word of mixed Latin and medieval French origins meaning to "turn over," mainly in reference to soil and earth that has been plowed and, therefore, "turned." It is a name that would come to suit it well considering its many iterations and how many times it would be turned over from ruler to ruler, from government to new government, from palace to museum.

His son, King Louis XIV, turned Versailles from hunting lodge to magnificent palace. Louis XIV was an absolute monarch. He ruled France with an iron grip, extracting enormous taxes from the populace to fund his extravagant building projects, his many wars (he became known as the "neighbor from hell" to most other European monarchs), his colonies in the Americas, and a lavish lifestyle that has become legend.

Louis is known as the Sun King. It is a title he bestowed upon himself when he adopted the sun as his emblem, because he believed that France and the universe revolved around him. (If readers hold any doubts about the size of his ego, they may relinquish them now.) Louis believed that he was ordained by God to rule France and that he was rather god-like himself. He depicted himself as a Caesar—another successor to Rome! Perhaps Louis's stratospheric self-confidence can be better understood considering the dynasty he came from and the history of the French crown.

The monarchy of France is an ancient institution, stretching back to the period in which Rome fell. In the fifth century, a man named Clovis, who belonged to one of the barbarian tribes that invaded Rome, ruled over northern France and parts of Germany. In 497 King Clovis of the Franks converted to Christianity and was baptized in Reims. The adoption of Christianity is crucial here—for with the conversion of Clovis, the French crown derived its legitimacy from God and the two institutions would remain intertwined. Over a thousand years later, in 1653, Louis XIV would also be crowned in the Cathedral of Reims. Tradition, eh?

But the seventeenth century was an unstable time for monarchs in Europe. In England, Louis's uncle, King Charles I, was overthrown and executed in 1649 during that country's own civil war. (England has the unique distinction of being the only country in the history of the world to have a revolution to overthrow their monarchy, and then another one to bring it back again.) The Enlightenment, a philosophical movement that promoted ideas of reason, progress, constitutional government, and a separation of church and state, was gaining ground across Europe. During the seventeenth and eighteenth centuries the movement gave rise to intellectuals like Isaac Newton, Immanuel Kant, Voltaire, John Locke, Jean-Jacques Rousseau, Adam Smith, and David Hume. The ideas that would come out of this movement would shape the American Revolution and the French Revolution. For Louis and his Bourbon dynasty, the writing was already on the wall.

But for a time the Sun King and his descendents would wield their power with impunity. And Versailles became the ultimate symbol of this power. When construction began on Versailles in 1661, Louis's end goal was not clear. However, as rivers were diverted from miles away, as lakes were carved out of dry earth, as the marble was laid out, room after room, people surely realized that Louis was building more than just a supremely beautiful home. He was after something bigger. Like so many rulers before him, Louis understood that the historian's record is subject to change and impossible to control. But stone is less malleable than words on a page. He was building a legacy to stand for generations after he was gone.

Pottage of Green Peas or Frogs' Legs

POTAGE DE PURÉE DE POIS VERTS

SERVES 4 TO 6 *A pottage (as opposed to a* potage, *French for soup) is a thick slice of bread soaked in soup or broth, then garnished heavily with other ingredients. This is a perfect example of a dish in transition from medieval to modern. In earlier times, a dish like this was served on a trencher of bread that acted as a plate and soaked up the liquid; eventually the bread would be discarded, leaving only the soup. To make the plank of brioche bread, slice about one-quarter of a loaf horizontally, about 1 inch thick, remove all crusts, and use this "plank."*

FOR THE PURÉE:

1 packed cup chopped sorrel

1 packed cup chopped butter lettuce

1 packed cup chopped chicory

1 packed cup chopped chard

6 tablespoons unsalted butter

Leaves of 3 sprigs fresh thyme

3 cups fresh green peas

¾ teaspoon kosher salt

3 tablespoons finely chopped fresh chives

2 tablespoons finely chopped fresh parsley leaves

FOR THE GARNISH AND BREAD:

1 tablespoon unsalted butter

2 cups fresh green peas

½ teaspoon kosher salt

¼ teaspoon freshly ground black pepper

1 thick, lengthwise plank brioche

3 or 4 butter lettuce leaves

3 or 4 chicory leaves

⅛ seedless cucumber (about 2 inches), sliced into half-moons

TO make the puree, combine the sorrel, lettuce, chicory, and chard in a medium saucepan with 1 quart water. Bring to a boil, reduce to a simmer, and cook, covered, for 30 minutes. Strain through a fine-mesh sieve into a bowl and reserve the broth, discarding the cooked leaves. Melt the butter in a medium saucepan over low heat and add the thyme, peas, and salt. Add the reserved broth, increase the heat to medium-high, and cook until the peas are just tender, 8 to 10 minutes. Transfer to a blender with the chives and parsley and blend until smooth. Taste and adjust seasoning.

TO prepare the garnish and bread, melt the butter in a small saucepan over medium heat and add the peas, salt, and pepper. Cook until just tender, 3 to 5 minutes. Place the brioche plank in a wide, shallow serving bowl. If the pea puree has cooled, reheat it gently, then thoroughly soak the bread with the pea puree, turning it once or twice. Top with the peas for garnish and arrange the lettuce, chicory leaves, and cucumber slices around them.

PORTION into 4 to 6 individual bowls, adding more puree as desired.

Frogs' Legs Version

POTAGE DE GRENOUILLES

SERVES 4 TO 6 *While peas remain the secret star of the dish, a particularly elegant way to set them off is with these bright and citrusy frogs' legs.*

2 sprigs thyme

1 bay leaf

3 sprigs fresh parsley

8 frogs' legs

Kosher salt

Freshly ground black pepper

3 tablespoons unsalted butter

1 scallion, chopped

¼ cup white verjus

1 cup freshly squeezed orange juice (from about 3 oranges)

2 tablespoons freshly squeezed lemon juice

1 thick, lengthwise plank brioche

Pea purée (see previous recipe)

FOR GARNISH:

½ cup pomegranate seeds

Lemon slices

MAKE a bouquet of the thyme, bay leaf, and parsley and tie with kitchen twine. Cut the frogs' legs in half and season with salt and a little pepper. Melt the butter in a sauté pan over medium heat and cook the frogs' legs until golden on both sides, about 3 minutes. Remove the frogs' legs and reserve. Add the chopped scallion and bouquet of herbs to the pan and cook until the scallion is softened, 1 to 2 minutes. Add the verjus, orange juice, and lemon juice, increase the heat to high, and cook until reduced by one-third, about 5 minutes. Reduce the heat to a simmer and return the frogs' legs to the pan until cooked through, about 2 minutes.

SOAK the bread with the pea puree as described in the previous recipe, top with the frogs' legs, and garnish with the pomegranate seeds and lemon slices.

PORTION into 4 to 6 individual bowls, adding more puree as desired.

Braised Partridge

PERDRIX À L'ESTOUFFADE

SERVES 4 *Game birds remain a staple of this cuisine of conspicuous consumption, and here they are "barded" with thin sheets of fat or cured ham to add another layer of flavor and refinement to the cooking process. The mushroom liaison was a general thickening ingredient chefs kept on hand and can be used to thicken all sorts of sauces, adding a graceful umami in the process. The pistachios and foraged mushrooms in the garnish were upscale ingredients, and even today, few things match a morel's uncanny deliciousness.*

FOR THE BRAISE:

4 partridges

Kosher salt

8 ounces pork fat or cured ham, thinly sliced into sheets

3 to 4 tablespoons unsalted butter

About 1 quart low-sodium chicken stock

FOR THE GARNISH:

2 tablespoons unsalted butter

1 bunch asparagus, trimmed

Kosher salt

¼ pound morel mushrooms, trimmed and halved

1 lemon, sliced into thin rounds

½ cup shelled pistachios

FOR THE THICKENER:

2 tablespoons lard or unsalted butter

2 tablespoons all-purpose flour

¼ cup finely minced yellow onion

¼ cup finely minced cremini mushrooms

1 teaspoon sherry vinegar

⅔ cup low-sodium chicken stock

¼ teaspoon kosher salt, plus more to taste

PREHEAT the oven to 325°F.

SEASON the partridges with salt and then cover each bird with a few thin sheets of fat or ham and tie it carefully into place with butcher's twine, as you would truss a bird. Melt the butter in a heavy saucepan that has a tight-fitting lid over medium-high heat and then sauté the barded (fat-covered) partridges until well browned on all sides. Add just enough of the stock to barely cover the partridges and bring to a simmer. Cover the pot, bring to a brisk simmer, and then transfer to the oven. Braise, covered, for 2 hours.

TO prepare the garnish, melt the butter in a sauté pan over medium heat. Add the asparagus, season with salt, and cook until just tender, about 3 minutes. Remove the asparagus and set aside and cook the morels in the same pan until just tender, about 3 minutes. Reserve both.

IN a separate small saucepan, melt the lard for the thickener over low heat. When melted, add the flour, onion, and mushroom. Cook until the onion is transparent, about 5 minutes. Remove from the heat and add the vinegar, stock, and salt. Whisk to combine thoroughly.

REMOVE the cooked partridges from the liquid and set aside. Measure 2 cups of the braising liquid and transfer to a small saucepan. Place the liquid over low heat and add the thickener in small amounts, whisking frequently and also whisking to combine between additions, letting it simmer and thicken until it coats the back of a spoon. You probably will not need all of the thickener. Taste and adjust for salt. To serve, place the partridges in a shallow bowl with some of the sauce and garnish with the asparagus, morels, lemon slices, and pistachios. Feel free to serve the remaining sauce on the side.

A ROYAL GARDEN OF DELIGHTS

ONE OF the greatest culinary changes of this period was the constellation of vegetables that appear on the French table. Newfound delights like asparagus and hothouse-grown oranges were the latest trends, while fresh peas were the height of culinary fashion, with prices to prove it.

The newfound popularity of fresh vegetables was driven, as always, by the passions of the king himself. The king's gardens were extensive, religiously cared for, and continually stocked with new and diverse plantings brought from around the world by his head gardeners. Orange, lemon, and pomegranate trees traveled to France from places like Spain, where they had been previously transplanted from the Middle East by the Moors.

But the greatest change was the simplest: humble greens that had once been thought too tough and unrefined for the delicate stomachs of the upper classes and fit only for peasants and beasts were given pride of place alongside delicate game birds and rich pies.

Oyster-Stuffed Capon

CHAPON AUX HUITRES

SERVES 6 TO 8 *A capon is a castrated rooster and at one time was quite a common ingre-dient, as it was considered more flavorful than a hen and more tender than an aggressive rooster. A regular chicken can be used as well.*

1 (3- to 4-pound) capon or chicken

Freshly ground black pepper

Kosher salt

8 ounces pork fat or bacon, sliced into thin sheets

3 sprigs fresh thyme

3 sprigs fresh parsley

1 bay leaf

¼ cup roughly chopped yellow onion

1 whole clove

1 cup sliced cremini or chanterelle mushrooms

12 to 24 oysters, shucked

1 quart low-sodium chicken stock

1 tablespoon capers

PREHEAT the oven to 400°F.

SEASON the bird inside and out with salt and pepper and place on a rack in a roasting pan or in a heavy skillet. Cover the outside of the bird with the thin sheets of pork fat or bacon, trussing them into place with kitchen twine. Roast for 1½ hours, or until the deepest part of the thigh reaches 165°F on an instant-read thermometer. Remove the bird and rack from the pan, or remove the bird from the skillet, reserving the drippings. Now, either use the pan to continue cooking or transfer the drippings to saucepan (if a skillet was used, continue cooking in it).

Place over medium-high heat. Make a bou-quet of herbs with the thyme, parsley, and bay leaf by tying them in a small piece of cheesecloth. Add the onion, the clove, and the bouquet of herbs to the pan and cook until the onion is softened, stirring occasion-ally. Add the mushrooms and continue to cook until softened, 3 to 5 minutes. Add the oysters and sauté for 5 minutes. Discard the herb bouquet and clove and remove the pan from the heat. Stuff the mixture into the cav-ity of the bird. Add the stock and the capers to the pan and return the stuffed bird to the pan. Bring the stock to a boil over medium heat, simmer for a few minutes, then serve.

THE SUN KING AND HIS FAMILY

WHEN LOUIS XIV CAME to the throne in 1643 at the age of five, the royal family lived in Paris in the Louvre (then a palace, today the famous museum). Because five-year-olds generally aren't qualified to run a country, the longtime political advisor, Cardinal Mazarin, and Louis's mother, Queen Anne, were appointed as his regents. Mazarin, also Louis's godfather and the man responsible for the king's education, was like a father to Louis, while Anne watched over her son with meticulous devotion. Anne and Louis were extremely close; they ate all their meals together and she was even said to mend his clothes herself. Louis was, after all, Anne's first child, her miracle born twenty-three years into her marriage with Louis XIII—a late-in-life arrival that had more to do with the fact that Louis XIII and Anne couldn't stand each other than any fertility issues. But the birth of Louis XIV was joyous enough for Anne and Louis XIII to spend one more night together, welcoming Louis's little brother Philippe in 1640.

But in 1648 the Fronde—a series of civil wars stemming from anger over France's involvement in numerous other wars across the continent, rising taxes, and high costs of food—began. The nobles and parliament sought to check the power of the crown peacefully, and then violently. In the middle of one tense January night in 1649, as fighting in the capital grew more fierce, Queen Anne, fearing for her sons' lives, fled with Louis, Philippe, and Mazarin to the Château de Saint-Germain. The memory of that night—the panic and the escape—left an indelible mark on Louis and instilled in him a strong dislike of Paris. Ultimately the Fronde failed, but it marked the beginning of a battle between the people and the elites that would not be resolved until the Revolution burned the entire political system to the ground in 1789.

By 1666 Mazarin and Louis's mother had both passed away. Louis was twenty-eight and in full control of his kingdom. After Mazarin's death he made it clear to those around him that he would not be accepting applications for the post as right-hand man to the king. He was the absolute monarch and he would rule absolutely.

Around this time he began renovations on his father's old hunting lodge. Perhaps it was his love of hunting that initially drew him to the royal residence (he adored the sport maybe even more than Henry VIII) or his dislike of Paris. Either way he began to expand it and in 1682 he abandoned the Louvre and Paris altogether, moving the entire royal family and court to Versailles. He would only visit the capital city eight times throughout the rest of his life.

Construction on such a mammoth project takes time. For all of Louis's life at Versailles, and really for the entirety of Versailles's golden age, the palace was a construction site. (Work was finally completed in 1715, the year he died.) It took thousands of workers, many of whom were ex-soldiers from the recently ended Thirty Years' War, to build the palace. Louis's visions were grand and his architects were similarly mad (or more likely terrified of saying no). The work was demanding, there were no safety precautions, and the pay was terrible. Thousands of workers died; corpses were driven away at night by the cartload. The mother of a deceased builder confronted Louis at a public audience at Saint-Germain. She hurled insults at him, calling him a "whore monger," a "tyrant," and "*roi machiniste*." Louis, not used to being spoken to in such a manner, was so shocked he actually asked if she was speaking to him. She was, and subsequently met her fate at an insane asylum.

The final result is one of the largest palaces in the world—a dizzying 679,000 square feet of gilt, glass, frescoes, and marble. Paintings by the great Renaissance masters decorated the walls, like Leonardo da Vinci's *Mona Lisa*, which hung in Louis's private apartments. The exact cost of Versailles's construction has been debated for years, but a solid estimate from court financial documents puts the total at 91.7 million livres. One livre was worth one pound of silver—so a lot of silver, a lot of money. Funds for the construction all came from the taille, a tax on the people of France and the royal family's main source of income. Nobles and the elite were exempt from paying it.

Along with the royal family, there were fifty main noble families, most of whom would have lived at Versailles. When Louis moved the entire court to the palace outside the city in 1682 he didn't just relocate his family; everyone, from court officials to ministers to nobles, was expected to make the move as well and not everyone was happy about it. (Louis found ways to make court life appealing. More on that later.)

Chief among palace occupants was Louis's wife, Queen Marie-Thérèse. To modern people it might seem obvious that the queen would live with her husband, however this was by no means a normal living arrangement at the time. But what Louis wanted he got. His marriage to the Spanish Marie-Thérèse could best be described as one of duty. The main purpose of this union was to produce heirs, and Marie-Thérèse dutifully gave birth to six children, only one of whom survived into adulthood. Some sources claim she loved the king and was heartbroken by his affairs. Whatever the queen felt, Louis was unbothered and began one of his long-term relationships a few years into their marriage.

Louise de la Vallière was young, beautiful, and crushingly naive. The king first set eyes on La Vallière when she was working for Henrietta, the Duchess of Orleans, who was the wife of Philippe, Duke of Orleans, aka Louis's brother. Louis was already very familiar with his sister-in-law Henrietta, as their affair had started years before. (Yes, he was sleeping with his brother's wife and everyone knew it.) But in an attempt to be more subtle about it, Henrietta and Louis decided he would pretend he was having an affair with one of her ladies, Louise de La Vallière. The pretense would give him all the reason to come to her apartments. What Henrietta did not expect was for the fake affair to become real. Soon Louis and La Vallière were very much an item and Henrietta was no longer the apple of his eye.

Louis repeated this pattern with all of his most important mistresses: in the social circle of one lover, he would find his next. Through La Vallière, Louis met Madame de Montespan, who would become the king's most influential mistress. Through Madame de Montespan, Louis met Madame de Maintenon, his next love and secret second wife after Marie-Thérèse died.

With Louis's women, another pattern emerged: escape to the nunnery. Heartbroken and desperate to escape court, La Vallière made several attempts to flee to a convent and become a nun. Cruelly, Louis forced her to stay at court for a maddening nine years after their affair ended, largely so he could use her as a cover for his affair with Montespan. Eventually he relented and La Vallière was granted her wish for a quiet life devoted to God at the Couvent des Carmélites Déchaussées. She lived out the rest of her years in an incredibly austere and brutal religious setting; she beat herself and refused water for days on end to experience the thirst Christ did on the cross. For her, all of this was better than life at Versailles. When Louis ditched Madame de Montespan, she too joined a convent.

Like Lucrezia Borgia, who used to run away to the San Sisto convent on the Appian Way when the brutal political games of her father and brother became too much, many royal and high-born women found peace from the viciousness of court life in these sacred spaces devoid of men.

ONE OF THE MOST ENTHRALLING CHARACTERS to live in Versailles in this period was Philippe, the brother of the king. There's a famous portrait of Louis and Philippe when they were small children. Louis is dressed up like a little king and Philippe is dressed as a girl. Queen Anne, who adored her sons, called Philippe "my little girl," nurtured his feminine side, and encouraged him to wear female clothes. As an adult, Philippe, the Duke of Orleans, brother of the king of France, was openly gay. He often wore dresses around the palace. His love for his longtime boyfriend, the Chevalier of Lorraine, was no secret: the court knew, his mother knew, and both of his wives knew. (Perhaps this made the affair between Louis and his first wife, Henrietta, a bit more palatable.)

Being gay in seventeenth century France was complicated. Officially it was a crime that could be punishable by death—and many were killed. However, treatment was usually determined by rank. For the elite of Versailles, same-sex relationships were tolerated if they were not flaunted; for an average Parisian of no status, it would have been a life of persecution. For Philippe, as long as he performed his royal duties (i.e., procreate with other royals to create more royals) he was free to live his life as he pleased. He had children with his first wife, the English princess, Henriette, and then after she died, with his second wife, the German princess Elisabeth Charlotte. They were convivial marriages that in the grand scheme of arranged royal marriages of the time perhaps weren't too bad: no one was murdered or imprisoned and all parties involved seem to have cared for one another.

Something the two Bourbon brothers shared in common was a love of war. Philippe was lieutenant general of the French army, second in command after Louis himself, and a brilliant military commander; his victory against long-term foe William III, Prince of Holland, at the Battle of Cassel was massive for France. *Monsieur*, as he became known, was very popular among soldiers, among the common people, and at court. He was smart, charming, and seemingly quite good at everything he set his mind to. While royals like his brother Louis come off the pages of the history books as controlled, regulated, and serious figures, Philippe is a breath of fresh air: a man who was brave enough to be himself, a man who lived.

Pepper Sauce (for Larded Saddle of Hare)

SAUCE POIVRADE

MAKES ABOUT 1½ CUPS

4 tablespoons unsalted butter

2 scallions, thinly sliced

Kosher salt

Peels from 4 oranges, most pith removed and finely chopped

Peel from 1 lemon, most pith removed and finely chopped

2 teaspoons freshly ground black pepper

⅔ cup white wine vinegar

1⅓ cups freshly squeezed orange juice (from about 4 or 5 oranges)

MELT the butter in a small saucepan over medium heat. Add the scallions and sauté, stirring occasionally, until softened, about 4 minutes. Season with a large pinch of salt. Add the orange and lemon peels and black pepper and reduce the heat to low. Cook for 2 minutes. Add the vinegar and orange juice and reduce by one-third over medium heat, 10 to 15 minutes. Taste and adjust seasoning.

THE BIRTH OF THE COOL

THESE RECIPES all come from La Varenne's majestic trio of cookbooks, *The French Cook*, *The French Pastry Chef*, and *The French Confectioner*, first printed in 1651. By now we have certainly seen that elaborate, over-the-top, and technically demanding preparations are hardly a new invention, but what most fascinates me about this moment in culinary history is that it is where we see the beginnings of many "classical" dishes that we might recognize from today (or at least in the last century, when classical French cooking was still the height of fashion).

The cuisine of the Sun King, going forward, represented a break between the food of the Middle Ages, dominated by spice and sourness, and the more rich and delicate palate we now think of as European. Some of these dishes—the following saddle of hare, for instance—will be recognizable in the nineteenth-century recipes of chef Georges Auguste Escoffier, considered the father of modern French cookery and the codifier of sauces and techniques taught in every Western culinary school.

Larded Saddle of Hare

RÂBLE DE LIÈVRE

SERVES 4 TO 6 *Larding is the process of introducing thin pieces of fat into holes made in an otherwise very lean meat with a thin hollow needle called a larding needle; these needles can be purchased in most specialty cookware stores. If you do not have a larding needle, you can approximate this process by piercing the rabbit with a pointed chopstick or knitting needle, fastening the fat strips to your instrument of choice with a bit of twine, and drawing the fat strips through the holes. This is more laborious but yields similar results to using a larding needle. This recipe is also a good example of how the definitions of meats can evolve. Today, a saddle of hare is just the center of the animal's back, legs and ribs removed. In this period, only the front legs were removed, and the back legs were trussed tightly.*

1 whole rabbit (about 3 pounds)

8 ounces salt pork or fatback

Kosher salt

Freshly ground black pepper

Pepper Sauce (recipe precedes on page 295)

PREHEAT the oven to 450°F.

REMOVE the front legs of the rabbit by cutting through the joints with a sharp knife. Fold the rear legs up against the body and tie them in place with butcher's twine. Cut the fat into strips about ¼ inch wide and about 4 inches long (long enough to pass completely through the rabbit at an angle). Place the strips in ice water. When the fat is thoroughly chilled, fit one end of one strip through the hollow end of a larding needle and force the needle through the flesh of the rabbit at a long, low angle. Repeat this process at 1-inch intervals along both sides of the rabbit and through the legs. You should be able to insert 10 to 12 pieces.

SEASON the rabbit with salt and pepper and roast on a rack in a roasting pan until well colored, about 15 minutes. Reduce the oven temperature to 300°F, cover the pan with foil, and bake until cooked through, 40 to 60 additional minutes. Wild rabbits should be cooked to 160°F at the deepest part of the thigh, but farmed rabbits are safe at 151°F.

Squab Torte

TOURTE DE PIGEONNEAUX

MAKES ONE 12-INCH PIE, SERVING 6 TO 8 *This is another spectacular presentation that provides a fantastic space for you to exercise your artistic flair. The visual appeal of the pie should match the pomp and circumstance of the diners!*

FOR THE DOUGH:

3 cups all-purpose flour, plus more for work surface

2 teaspoons kosher salt

2 sticks (16 tablespoons) cold unsalted butter, cubed

FOR THE MINCED VEAL:

2 pounds ground veal

¼ cup lard

1 cup finely chopped scallion

1 cup chopped fresh parsley leaves

1½ teaspoons freshly ground black pepper

2 teaspoons freshly grated nutmeg

2 teaspoons fresh thyme leaves

1 tablespoon plus 1 teaspoon dried marjoram

1 tablespoon plus 1 teaspoon dried savory

1 teaspoon dried lavender

1 tablespoon white verjus

1 tablespoon kosher salt

¼ cup dried red currants

FOR THE FILLING:

2 semi-boneless squab, or 1 large bone-in squab, halved

Kosher salt

Freshly ground black pepper

8 jumbo asparagus stalks, trimmed

4 chard ribs, leaves removed

2 hard-boiled egg yolks, halved

8 cremini mushrooms

4 canned artichoke hearts, halved and blotted dry

TO make the dough, add the 3 cups of flour and the salt to the bowl of a food processor fitted with the metal blade and pulse a few times to combine. Add the butter and pulse until fully combined. This is not a flaky dough like a modern pie, so don't leave small pieces of butter. Add a scant ½ cup cold water while pulsing intermittently until the dough comes together smoothly. Form into a disk, wrap tightly, and refrigerate for at least 30 minutes. Clean the food processor and metal blade.

ADD all ingredients for the minced veal except the currants to the bowl of the food processor fitted with the metal blade and process until completely incorporated. Add the currants and pulse a few more times to combine.

PREHEAT the oven to 350°F.

ON a well-floured surface, roll out the dough to a circle about 14 inches in diameter and line a 12-inch cake pan or pie dish with it. Spread the veal mixture on top of the dough. Season the squab halves with salt and pepper and place them at evenly spaced intervals around the edge of the pie. Arrange the asparagus stalks, chard ribs, egg yolks, mushrooms, and artichoke hearts between them. Show your flair! Bake in the preheated oven until the veal mixture reaches at least 160°F on an instant-read thermometer, 40 to 50 minutes.

Stuffed Carp in Puff Pastry

CARPES FARCIES EN PATE FEUILLETÉE

SERVES 6 TO 8 *This elegant dish combines one of the earliest puff pastry recipes with a decadent stuffed fish. It is truly elegant and worth the substantial effort. Of course, store-bought puff pastry sheets can be used.*

FOR THE PUFF PASTRY:

4 cups all-purpose flour, plus more for work surface

1½ teaspoons kosher salt

4 sticks (1 pound) unsalted butter, softened

FOR THE STUFFING:

12 ounces skinless carp fillets

1 stick (8 tablespoons) unsalted butter, cubed

3 tablespoons chopped fresh parsley

3 tablespoons chopped fresh chives

Leaves of 5 sprigs fresh thyme

1 tablespoon fresh marjoram leaves

1 tablespoon chopped fresh tarragon

1 large egg, plus additional for egg wash

Kosher salt

½ cup chopped cooked mussels (see Note)

¼ cup chopped cooked chanterelle or cremini mushrooms

¼ cup chopped cooked artichoke hearts from can or jar

2 teaspoons chopped capers

1 large carp, skinned and gourmet butterflied (see Note, page 95)

Freshly ground black pepper

FIRST, make the puff pastry. It is important to take your time with this process. Combine the 4 cups flour and salt in the bowl of a stand mixer fitted with the paddle attachment and slowly add 1½ cups cold water with the mixer on low speed. Wrap the dough tightly and allow it to rest for 30 minutes. On a well-floured surface, roll the dough into a square ¼ to ½ inch thick. Now, roll 1 inch of the edges on all four sides thinner so that they taper to ⅛ inch. With an offset spatula, gently spread the softened butter in an even layer in the center of this square, leaving a 2-inch margin on all sides. Fold the corners inward so they overlap in the center, sealing the butter inside. Wrap and chill for 30 minutes, then roll out the square to its original size and repeat the process of folding the corners in to meet in the center. Repeat this folding process three more times, for a total of four times, chilling the dough for at least 30 minutes in between. Wrap and refrigerate.

TO prepare the stuffing, roughly chop the carp fillets into 1-inch cubes and add to the bowl of a food processor fitted with the metal blade. Add the butter, herbs, 1 egg, and 1 teaspoon salt and pulse until smooth, scraping down the sides of the bowl. Transfer this mixture to a metal bowl and fold in the cooked mussels, cooked mushrooms, cooked artichoke hearts, and capers. Fill the body cavity of the fish with the mixture and season the outside with salt and pepper.

PREHEAT the oven to 350°F and line a sheet pan with parchment paper.

ROLL the puff pastry out so it will be large enough to completely enclose the fish. Place the fish on the puff pastry and draw up the edges around it, pinching the dough closed where the edges meet. Invert the pastry, sealed side down, onto the prepared pan. Brush egg wash on the dough. Fancifully decorate the outside with shallow cuts to resemble scales. Bake in the preheated oven until the internal temperature of the stuffing reaches 150°F, 50 to 60 minutes.

NOTE: To cook mussels, melt 2 tablespoons butter in a medium saucepan with a tight-fitting lid over medium heat. You can add some chopped scallion or shallot as well. Add the mussels, stir briefly, and add ¼ cup white wine or water. Cover and cook for 6 to 8 minutes, until the mussels have opened. Discard any that do not open. Remove the meat from the shells with a fork.

TO LIVE AT THE PALACE

LIFE AT VERSAILLES WAS FILLED WITH STRICT SOCIAL CODES and elaborate rules of etiquette. There were formalities and protocols for everything from how people filed into a room, to where they sat, how they dressed, conversed, ate, and slept. Ceremony structured the day and every morning at eight sharp one of the most bizarre rituals of life at Versailles commenced: the Grand Lever, or the waking of the king.

As the curtains of his four-poster bed were parted by his valet, Alexandre Bontemps, the most important nobles and princes would file into Louis's bedchamber, along with his nurse, physician, and surgeon. His nurse would kiss his forehead (the same nurse who had attended to him since he was a child), and another individual would help him into a clean shirt. His physician would examine his chamber pot. There was a brief pause for Louis's morning prayers—and then back to the dance. One man would hold a mirror while Louis washed his face, another would hand him a towel. The king was helped into each article of clothing by an individual dedicated to that one task alone: a master of the right stocking, a master of the left, a lord of the neckties.

These positions, though they seem absurd, were highly coveted. Those precious moments helping the king adjust his cufflinks might be your chance to ask for a favor, address some injustice done to your family, or simply make a joke to further your position in the king's good graces. It was a frivolous dance, a choreographed worship at the altar of power. And the entire ceremony, observed by up to one hundred nobles, would be repeated for the *Coucher,* when Louis went to bed.

Twenty household departments ran the palace, each a cog in a vast machine. These included the King's Cabinet, Buildings, Lodgings, the Commons Chapel, Entertainments, Ceremonies, as well as the King's Wardrobe, the King's Music, the King's Bedchamber, the Grand Stables, and the Small Stables. (In 1715, the rivalry between the Grand Stables and the Small Stables culminated in a full-scale battle in the courtyards. Coachmen from either side brawled in an outrageous display of office warfare.) And there was the King's Mouth—a five-hundred-person department dedicated to feeding the king. There were entire worlds at play among the many thousands who worked at Versailles.

Positions were often passed down from father to son, mother to daughter. They were hereditary jobs. One single family swept the chimneys of

Versailles for three hundred years. With their lives so centered on this household, colleagues became family, marriages took place, children were born—the downstairs of Versailles surely had many soap operas of its own.

Upstairs, however, was the center stage of life at the palace. After forcing the cosmopolitan elite to abandon their Parisian mansions and move to a hunting lodge in the woods (one that was also a construction site, no less) Louis had to make life at Versailles appealing. And so he created a packed social calendar of events, parties, plays, dances, and banquets that would give birth to a vibrant and colorful court life.

Every Monday, Wednesday, and Friday from six to ten p.m. the king hosted "Apartment," essentially a cocktail hour (or rather, hours) in the Hall of Mirrors and the king's apartments (hence the name), with music and dancing and lots and lots to drink. Every Tuesday and Thursday evening Louis had actors from Paris perform in the Comedy Room. The likes of Molière and Racine wrote plays especially for the court, which Louis himself sometimes acted in. (He was also said to be a great dancer, as comfortable performing the latest dance in front of his court as he was commanding it.) Gambling and card games were popular pastimes for the courtiers, as were strolls in the gardens or shopping for the latest fashions at one of the licensed merchants' stalls, set up in a room that is today the museum's gift shop. If none of these appealed, the bored *duchesse* could always find friends to gossip and hang out with in Louis's wardrobe master's apartments, where the doors were always open, all were welcome, and the table was filled with food and drink.

Everyone who lived at Versailles had their own apartments. These varied in size and condition according to a person's rank. Louis's main mistress of the moment would have very luxurious living quarters, while a lower-ranking young noble couple might have a more modest apartment. The palace became its own little city. There were thoroughfares and high streets in the form of hallways and galleries; each artery led to a different part of the palace where specific groups or families lived. The Noailles family, one of the oldest and most powerful noble families, lived in the attic of the north wing for so long the corridor that ran through it became known as "Noailles Street."

While the Grand Lever was a privileged ceremony only the most elite could observe and take part in, watching the king eat was open to all. The Grand Supper Setting (or *souper au grand couvert*) took place most evenings at 10 p.m., after the evenings scheduled entertainments. Louis loved food; he was a gourmand who took great pleasure in eating the choicest game birds, the freshest vegetables from his garden, and exotic fruits from his orchards. However, the royal family didn't necessarily all dine together every night, which often led courtiers into a mad dance rushing around the palace to watch the king enjoy his rabbit, the queen a soup down the hall, a prince a stew a floor below.

It was not a daily occurrence for the people of Paris to visit Versailles to take in a spectacle, but it was not completely foreign either. Upon a straight road from Paris to Versailles Louis had public transportation installed. The people of Paris could come and watch the festivals, walk in the gardens, and view the processions on special occasions. During Louis's reign Versailles was separate from Paris, but it was not inaccessible. Four-seater carriages made multiple trips a day along the main road, as did the cheaper horse-drawn omnibus, which could seat up to twenty and left twice a day from the Tuileries Palace.

The parties of Versailles were indeed as over the top as the stories and legends have made them out to be. In May 1664, Louis hosted a six-day festival in his new gardens for six hundred guests called "The Pleasures of the Enchanted Isle." The gardens were transformed into something out of a fairy tale; thousands of candles lit up the night as a ballet of the seasons was performed, featuring an elephant, a camel, and a bear. There were plays and dances, and copious amounts of food from dawn to dusk. Firework shows lit up the night with fleurs-de-lis and big cursive *L's* for Louis. Masked servants kept a steady flow of champagne circulating as bacchanalia reigned over the Sun King's grounds.

FRENCH CUISINE AS WE KNOW IT TODAY finds its origins in Louis's Versailles, as an enormous shift in taste took place. The Asian spices that had dominated the flavor profiles of medieval dishes—nutmeg, cinnamon, ginger, cloves, and pepper—began to fall out of favor. The flavors of the ingredients themselves became the focus of each dish. In 1654 the horticulturalist Nicolas de Bonnefans wrote about how food should maintain its "natural taste," setting the tone for generations of French chefs when he wrote, "Let cabbage soup taste entirely of cabbage; leek of leek; turnip of turnip" and so on and so on.

In his book *Le Cuisinier françois,* the legendary chef François Pierre de la Varenne wrote an entire section about vegetables. Considering how absent vegetables had previously been from the tables of the European elite, this was quite a departure. Gone were the days of heady and heavy spice mixtures; this new era of French cuisine was about the ingredients themselves. Varenne also introduced bisques, béchamel sauce, stocks, bouquet garnis, reductions, and an early hollandaise sauce. Delicate flavoring and precision methods made dishes of the former era feel *dépasser* or gauche. Like Trimalchio's ridiculous nouveau riche tastes back in ancient Rome, a dish with lots of spices was no longer in vogue.

It's hard to pinpoint the origin of a trend. Taste and fashion are defined by events and influential people but there is also the zeitgeist to consider. The period from which early modern French cuisine emerged was in many ways a more inward-looking France.

During his reign, Louis brought the finest craftsmen from all over the world to his court. He didn't want to import Persian carpets—he wanted them made in France—and better. If Venice made the finest glass, he would create a glass industry to match. The best furniture, cloth, lace— every craft, trade, and industry—would be in France. Foreign goods were subject to heavy taxation as part of the effort to shift the French consumer away from old specialty markets. Spices, the iconic exotic product, were similarly heavily taxed.

While Louis's neighbors (see Holland, Britain, Spain) poured money and resources into their colonies abroad, development of French territories in North America and the Caribbean grew slowly. Louis had little interest in diverting huge sums of money to wars in far-off places. He wanted dominance closer to home. He focused his energies on constructing *la France*—a culture to be universally envied and emulated. Thus the seedlings of a nation-state began to grow.

Nationalism is about identity, and French identity became defined in part by its cuisine as well as art and fashion. The first fashion magazine, *Le Mercure Galant*, began its publication in 1672, showcasing the works of designers and their lines of clothing that would morph into celebrated fashion houses. (Something France is still known for to this day.) Fables by Jean de la Fontaine and fairy tales like Charles Perrault's *Little Red Riding Hood*, *The Sleeping Beauty*, and *Cinderella* flowed from French pens and entered the cultural lexicon. A few generations on, this period would be immortalized in stories like *The Three Musketeers* and *The Man in the Iron Mask* by Alexandre Dumas.

France's identity did not emanate solely from Louis XIV's reign, but much of its image as we know it today stemmed from this period. Even the Revolution in 1789, which would come to define the political spirit of the nation, was in part due to him.

Glazed Whore's Farts

PETS DE PUTAIN

MAKES 15 TO 20 PIECES *Not to be confused with nun's farts and donkey's farts, other popular pastries of the period, these are delightful meringues regardless of their less-than-appetizing name.*

FOR THE MERINGUES:

5 egg whites

1 tablespoon orange blossom water

Pinch kosher salt

3 cups confectioners' sugar

FOR THE GLAZE AND FINISHING:

2 egg whites

Confectioners' sugar for dusting

PREHEAT the oven to 250°F. Line a baking sheet with parchment paper.

IN the bowl of a stand mixer with whisk attachment, whip the 5 egg whites, orange blossom water, and salt to stiff peaks. In three or four additions, sift the 3 cups sugar over the whipped egg whites and fold with a silicone spatula to combine. Scoop walnut-size portions of the meringue onto the prepared pan. (Are donkey's farts bigger? What about the nun's farts?) Gently mix the egg whites for the glaze with a pastry brush and brush the tops, then sift sugar over the meringues. Bake until the meringues are set and the tops are browned, about 30 minutes. Allow them to cool on the pan.

Frangipane Tourte

TOURTE DE FRANCHIPANE

SERVES 4 TO 6 *This is another version of an early puff pastry, in this case enclosing a pastry-cream filling. This is a direct precursor to modern patisserie.*

FOR THE DOUGH:

3 cups all-purpose flour, plus more for work surface

9 egg whites

1 teaspoon white vinegar

2 teaspoons kosher salt

Canola oil for the bowls

2 sticks (16 tablespoons) unsalted butter, softened

Egg wash for brushing

Orange blossom water for brushing

Confectioners' sugar for dusting

FOR THE FILLING:

½ cup shelled pistachios

½ cup slivered almonds, toasted

6 egg yolks

¼ cup all-purpose flour

½ cup confectioners' sugar

½ teaspoon ground cinnamon

¼ teaspoon kosher salt

2 cups whole milk

¼ cup currants

1 tablespoon chopped candied lemon peel

TO make the dough, in the bowl of a stand mixer fitted with the dough hook, combine the 3 cups flour, egg whites, vinegar, and salt and mix on medium speed until it forms a smooth ball, 10 to 12 minutes (increase the speed to medium-high halfway through). It should be elastic but barely sticky. If the dough is too soft or sticky, add a little more flour, a tablespoon at a time, mixing for 1 minute between each addition. Divide into two equal pieces, place each in an oiled bowl, cover with plastic wrap, and allow to rest at room temperature for 1 hour.

MEANWHILE, to prepare the filling, combine the pistachios and almonds in the bowl of a food processor fitted with the metal blade and pulse until finely ground. Reserve. In a medium bowl, combine the egg yolks, flour, ½ cup sugar, cinnamon, and salt and whisk vigorously to combine. Heat the milk in a medium saucepan over medium heat until just beginning to bubble around the edges, then carefully add to the egg mixture in

a thin stream while whisking vigorously. Whisk to mix completely and then return the mixture to the saucepan over medium heat and cook, whisking constantly, until the mixture starts to thicken. It will go from thin to thick somewhat suddenly—continue to cook for 1 minute. (Be careful not to let the eggs overcook—if the mixture looks lumpy, force it through a sieve.) Transfer the mixture to a clean bowl. Fold in the ground nuts, the currants, and candied lemon peel.

PREHEAT the oven to 375°F.

IT is important that you roll and stretch the dough to four times the diameter of the pie pan you are using. Use a 7-inch pie pan and stretch the final dough to about 9 x 28 inches. I find a good way to do this is to put a piece of tape this length on my work surface before beginning. You will also be making it slightly wider than the pie pan, a size that can also be marked with tape. Flour the work surface generously and roll one piece of dough out as thin as possible. To finish stretching the dough, slip the back of your hands under the edges of the dough and stretch it gently. Take your time. This is a delicate process, but using this method, you should be able to make it so thin you can read a newspaper headline through it. It is also very important for your butter to be the correct consistency, like mayonnaise. With a pastry brush, butter the entire surface of the dough. Now fold the dough in half, butter the exposed surface, and fold it again, to make a square just large enough to cover your pie pan. Line the pan with this dough and add the filling. Repeat the dough rolling, stretching, and buttering process to make the top layer. Brush the egg wash on the interior rim of the dough on the bottom, cover with the top layer, and crimp the edges to seal. Brush the top with orange blossom water and sprinkle with additional confectioners' sugar. Make a few decorative slits through the top crust without piercing the filling. Bake until the top has browned and risen, 40 to 50 minutes. It will puff significantly, although not as much as true puff pastry.

TWO BIG LIES ABOUT FRENCH PASTRY

"LET THEM eat cake!" is the vicious line widely attributed to Marie Antionette and also one of the many things she probably never said. The suggestion is that while people were demanding bread in the streets, she was surrounded by delicate filled macarons, elaborate layer cakes, cream puffs, and the like—so why didn't the starving peasants just eat these delightful treats? The second lie, however, is that despite what you may have seen in movies, this level of glorious patisserie was not invented until the era of later masters such as Antonin Carême, who is also credited with inventing the cool chef's hat that nobody wears anymore. Certainly no one wore that type of headgear in the kitchens of Louis XIV, XV, or XVI.

They did have cakes, though, and waffles, and macarons. But the cakes were heavy, thick, and well sugared, and so were the waffles, which were made with cheese. Macarons were more like almond cookies than the buttercream-sandwiched delights of today. High-rising puff pastry was just making its appearance, but the choux pastry for cream puffs and the aforementioned buttercream were still far in the future. However, history would prove that they were well worth the wait.

VIVE LA RÉVOLUTION

IN 1709, EIGHTY YEARS before the French Revolution began, tensions in the capital were high. In the final days of Versailles, Louis XVI took to sitting on the roof. Sitting in an armchair with a telescope, the last king of Versailles would watch the grounds below, the courtiers gossiping, the carriages arriving, from his perch up above. He spent many afternoons like this, always completely alone. It's a pretty wonderful metaphor for how distant the king had become from his people. Gone were the days of an open court—Louis XVI and Marie Antoinette only held court on Sundays. Completely isolated, the monarchy ceased to understand the French people.

Anti-royalist literature and propaganda were spreading like wildfire; obscene cartoons of the king circulated and posters offering up a new Lord's Prayer were plastered across Paris:

> Our father who art in Versailles
> Your name is not hallowed
> Your kingdom is no longer great
> Nor is thy will done by land or sea
> Give us this day, our daily bread for
> We cannot buy it.

We know how this story ends. King Louis XVI and Marie Antoinette would both lose their heads to the guillotine. The French Revolution burned the existing political system to the ground. The halls of Versailles grew silent. The art and furniture were auctioned off. The political center of France moved back to Paris. Versailles turned over again—to an abandoned royal residence in the woods.

Perhaps not surprisingly, large extravagant banquets fell out of fashion for a period. Chefs who had once found employment in royal or aristocratic houses suddenly found themselves out of a job. Some of these out-of-work chefs would be among the many millions of Europeans to emigrate to America in the late eighteenth and nineteenth centuries. In a young metropolis called New York City, these French chefs would introduce a new concept: the restaurant. Gotham's most favorite institution had arrived.

VERSAILLES

311

RK CITY

NEW YORK CITY
19th century

CHAPTER TEN

"SILVER SHELL" OYSTERS

STEWED CUCUMBERS

MOCK TURTLE SOUP

STEWED AND FRIED RUMP STEAKS

BAKED TURBOT
MUSHROOM CATSUP

CANAPÉS: ANCHOVY, WINDSOR,
CAVIAR, AND SMOKED SALMON

ATTEREAUX OF FAT LIVERS
VILLEROI SAUCE

BALLOTINES OF SQUAB OR QUAIL
À LA MADISON

POUSSE L'AMOUR AND PINEAPPLE PUNCH

CHOCOLATE SOUFFLÉ

ALASKA FLORIDA

I N 1800, THE ENTIRE CITY of New York fit neatly into what is now downtown Manhattan. Beyond Fourteenth Street were farms, woods, and the Wickquasgeck Trail, an old Lenape path that stretched along the middle of the island. (Today we call it Broadway.)

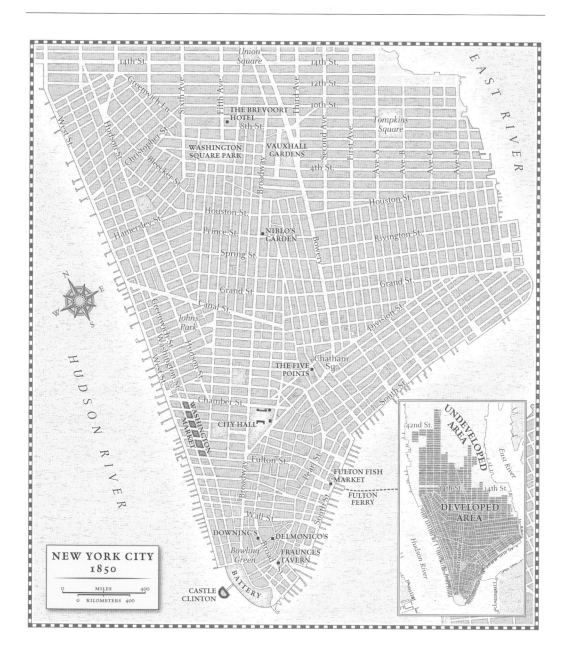

NEW YORK CITY
1850

MILES 0 — 400
0 KILOMETERS 400

This story of how New York evolved into what it is today is one I believe best told through food—and specifically that institution so bound to the city's identity: the restaurant.

The restaurant is an utterly unique public space. It is centered on a commercial exchange (food for money) but a rich and complex world of social interactions and cultural exchanges takes place beneath the surface. Restaurants are where we go to find comfort in our favorite dishes, try the latest food trend, or experience the cuisine of a country we have never been to. We go to restaurants to talk, to lament, to laugh, to read, to people watch, to be seen. We celebrate marriages at restaurants; we mourn the dead at restaurants. We remember these restaurants.

From antiquity and through the Middle Ages, there have been many different iterations of public eateries, from the countertops in ancient Rome where porridge and stews were sold to the stalls in the fifteenth-century Tenochtitlán marketplace selling amaranth cakes, to the oyster carts of early nineteenth-century New York City where briny mollusks were hawked for a penny a piece.

From Dutch New Amsterdam's—and then British colonial New York's—early years as a trading post and stopover between the Caribbean colonies and Europe, the city was filled with traders, merchants, and travelers passing through. Initially there were only taverns to cater to this group, but during the early decades of the nineteenth century a new crop of eateries emerged: chophouses, coffee houses, cafes, cafeterias, refectories, and oyster cellars, each with its own set of social codes, culinary culture, and categories of clientele. These spaces catered to a growing population whose daily lives and living situations demanded more types of places to eat.

The Swiss immigrant brothers Peter and John Delmonico introduced an entirely new concept when the legendary Delmonico's opened its doors in 1827: the menu. Eateries of colonial and early nineteenth-century New York didn't have menus in the way we think of them today, a selection of dishes formally written out course-by-course. Instead a chalkboard, placard, or waiter (through spoken word) conveyed what was on offer to customers. Previously eateries served meals at set times. A diner at Delmonico's now had the power of choosing which dishes he wanted to consume at an hour of his choosing. This was revolutionary. Their cafe with a serious kitchen quickly became a pillar of the New York City dining scene.

While the Delmonico brothers were Swiss, what they introduced to New York City was inherently French. The concept of the restaurant started in Paris, and not as a place but rather a thing, a restorative broth called *restaurer* (literally "to restore") or *restaurant*. These broths were made by cooking down some amalgam of meats, whether pork, beef, or poultry, for hours in a closed pot or *bain marie*. The result was a luscious, rich, meaty broth, believed to be nourishing, soulful, and especially good for those with weak constitutions.

The very first mention of this broth as a physical space is found in a 1769 edition of the *Almanah général* under the list of "Caterers, Innkeepers, and Hoteliers." Part of the way through this mammoth list of Parisian establishments a dedicated reader finds "Le Restaurateur," a place serving soul-nourishing bouillons and soups. These restaurants were different from the existing *table d'hôtes,* where ordinary French citizens, usually workers and artisans, had been able to find midday meals at fixed prices at set times. The ways in which the Parisian restaurateur evolved into the restaurant is a story that, while unique to France, is related to the New York City restaurant because the two are connected on an embryonic level. The experience of the Parisian restaurant traveled with European immigrants to America—and subsequently found a unique articulation on the shores of Manhattan, where it became an institution that evolved in tandem with the city. The evolution of the New York City restaurant mirrors the evolution of New York City.

MANY PROFESSIONALLY TRAINED CHEFS made their way to New York to find work after the French Revolution, as did the next groups of French immigrants who came after the upheavals of 1848 and then the 1870s. Some of these immigrants with restaurant dreams moved to present-day SoHo, where they opened restaurants and cafes serving "soul-satisfying food—*cuisine grand-mere*—at rock bottom prices." As French dishes were introduced into New York's standard culinary repertoire, the lines between what was French and what was American began to blur as French preparations and sauces seeped into preparations of new dishes with American ingredients. The style of French food codified by the legendary chefs La Varenne and later La Carême entered a larger Western culinary lexicon; their techniques are still taught in culinary schools today and their creations became a standard for a global haute cuisine. And New York City's gastronomic melting pot continued to simmer.

"Silver Shell" Oysters

SERVES 4 TO 6 *While both we and the New Yorkers of this period had an embarrassment of savory oyster recipes, this one stands out because of the rich pairing of hearty beef stock umami with seafood. In his 1884 cookbook* Handbook of Practical Cookery, *Pierre Blot recommends baking the oysters on silver shells specially designed for this purpose. If you've got a set of those, use them, of course, but below I provide instructions for using the oysters' own shells. Ramekins or scallop shells can also be used.*

1 dozen large East Coast oysters, such as Blue Points

4 tablespoons unsalted butter

½ teaspoon all-purpose flour

¼ cup low-sodium beef or veal stock

Kosher salt

Freshly ground black pepper

About ¼ cup breadcrumbs

Chopped fresh parsley for garnish

PREHEAT the oven to 375°F.

CAREFULLY shuck the oysters, being careful to reserve all of their liquor. Reserve 4 to 6 of the largest shells.

MELT 2 tablespoons of the butter in a small saucepan over medium-low heat. Add the flour and cook, stirring, until dark blond, about 3 minutes. While whisking constantly, add the beef stock in a thin stream. Increase heat to medium-high and continue to cook, still whisking, for a few minutes, until it has thickened and reduced somewhat. Add the oyster liquor and continue to cook, stirring constantly. Season with salt and pepper. Place 2 or 3 oysters on each shell (depending on the number of servings) and pour the sauce over them. Top with breadcrumbs to cover the surface and dot with the remaining butter, then bake until golden brown, about 15 minutes. Garnish with parsley and serve.

Stewed Cucumbers

SERVES 4 TO 6 *This slippery stew of an unsung cooked vegetable is another recipe that appears in both Rundell and Glasse's cookbooks in slight variations. While cucumbers do have a higher water content than, say, zucchini or eggplant, in this recipe, surprisingly, they have the texture of those vegetables in a perfect ratatouille. This calls for shallow frying in clarified butter, but oil can be substituted.*

2 seedless cucumbers

Kosher salt

1½ cups clarified butter or oil for frying

1 cup plus 1 tablespoon all-purpose flour

½ cup strong red wine, such as Bordeaux

1 teaspoon ground mace

¾ teaspoon freshly ground black pepper

¼ teaspoon ground clove

2 cups low-sodium beef stock

1 tablespoon unsalted butter

SLICE the cucumbers about ⅛ inch thick, season with salt, and spread out on paper towels to dry for 1 hour. Heat the clarified butter to 350°F in a heavy skillet over medium-high heat. Whisk together the 1 cup flour and 1 teaspoon salt. Dredge the cucumber slices in the seasoned flour and, working in batches, fry until golden brown. Pour off any excess butter and return the fried cucumbers to the pan. Add the wine, spices, and beef stock and bring to a boil. Reduce the heat to a very rapid simmer and cook for 5 minutes. Roll the butter in the remaining 1 tablespoon flour, add to the pan, and cook until further thickened, 2 to 3 minutes. Taste for seasoning and serve.

WHAT THE HECK IS A MOCK TURTLE
(AND WHY DOES IT HAVE A CALF'S HEAD)?

SHORT ANSWER: A mock turtle is a fake turtle (and that's what it was made out of). Long answer: Turtle soup was a true delicacy of the era and as large sea turtles were fished out and became scarce, the dish grew ever pricier. Shops would often hang large turtle shells outside their doors to demonstrate that they had the real thing. In this age of aspirational food, where the growing middle classes were able to enjoy more of the foods that were once reserved for the wealthy, there was a clever workaround. To turtle soup aficionados, the most delectable portion was the gooey and fatty collar. To approximate this gelatinous mass, a calf's head would be boiled for hours and the meat and skin stripped away in a rich broth. Whether this sounds appealing to you is simply a matter of taste, time, and turtle connoisseurship.

Mock Turtle Soup

SERVES 6 TO 8 *This recipe is drawn from Hannah Glasse's* The Art of Cookery Made Plain and Easy, *published in 1747—the most influential cookbook of this period. But wait, you ask, "Isn't that an English cookbook?" It was, just as in 1747 the city of New York was in a colony of England. That is hardly the point: this was an absolute bestseller and vital reference well into the nineteenth century, regardless of which side of the Atlantic you happened to be on. Similar versions appeared in the first major American published cookbook, Maria Rundell's 1806 compendium,* A New System of Domestic Cookery.

FOR THE CALF'S HEAD VERSION:

1 calf's head

4 cloves

1 teaspoon whole black peppercorns

6 bay leaves

1 yellow onion, halved

6 tablespoons unsalted butter

6 medium to large yellow onions, roughly chopped

12 whole cloves

1 teaspoon ground mace

1 teaspoon freshly grated nutmeg

15 sprigs fresh thyme

6 sprigs fresh rosemary

1 bunch tarragon

½ bunch parsley

8 anchovy fillets

½ teaspoon kosher salt

2 quarts veal stock

2 tablespoons all-purpose flour

1 pound cooked beef tongue, cut into ½-inch cubes

1 pound pork or beef head cheese, cut into 1-inch cubes

¼ teaspoon freshly ground black pepper

¼ teaspoon cayenne pepper

¼ cup plus 2 tablespoons Madeira wine

1 tablespoon freshly squeezed lemon juice

IF using the calf's head, place in salted water with the cloves, peppercorns, bay leaves, and onion halves in a large (large enough for a calf's head) pot and bring to a simmer, skimming off any foam that surfaces. Continue to cook for 2 to 3 hours, until the meat is very soft and easily peeled from the bones. Scrape off the meat, paying special attention to the gooiest bits. Remove the outer membrane from the tongue and shred or cut it into small cubes.

MELT 2 tablespoons of the butter in a large saucepan over medium heat. Add the onions, spices, herbs, anchovies, and salt and cook,

stirring occasionally, until the onion is softened, about 4 minutes. Add the veal stock and bring to a rapid simmer and cook for 40 to 60 minutes. Strain through a fine-mesh sieve into a bowl and discard the solids. Melt the remaining 4 tablespoons butter in another large saucepan over medium heat, add the flour, and cook, stirring, until blond. Add the strained stock in a thin stream, whisking constantly to avoid lumps. Bring briefly to a boil and return to a simmer. Add the calf's head meat or the tongue and head cheese, pepper, cayenne, Madeira, and lemon juice and continue to cook for 5 minutes. Taste and adjust seasoning.

Stewed and Fried Rump Steaks

SERVES 2 TO 4 *Another pub classic from Hannah Glasse, this is an excellent way to transform a tough steak into a tender and satisfying meal.*

1 pound rump or sirloin steaks

Kosher salt

Freshly ground black pepper

1 medium yellow onion, roughly chopped

¼ teaspoon ground mace

2 to 3 whole cloves

3 sprigs fresh parsley

3 sprigs fresh thyme

1 sprig fresh rosemary

1 anchovy fillet

½ cup white wine

6 tablespoons unsalted butter

1½ cups all-purpose flour

½ cup chopped raw oysters (about 8; optional)

Sliced pickles to garnish

SEASON the steaks with salt and pepper. Combine the onion, spices, herbs, anchovy, white wine, and 1 cup water in a medium saucepan with a tight-fitting lid and place over high heat. Roll 2 tablespoons of the butter in the flour just to coat and add the flour-coated butter to the pan. Add the steaks to the saucepan with a little more water, if necessary, to make sure they are covered by the liquid, bring to a boil, reduce to a simmer, and cover. Stew for 1 hour. Season the remaining flour with salt and pepper. Remove the steaks from the liquid, setting aside the saucepan with liquid, and dredge the steaks in flour. Melt the remaining 4 tablespoons butter in a sauté pan over medium-high heat and fry the steaks until golden brown, working in batches if necessary to keep from crowding the pan. Reserve the steaks. Pour off any excess butter in the sauté pan and strain the reserved cooking liquid into the sauté pan. Add the oysters, if using. Bring to a boil and reduce until thickened, whisking gently. Taste for seasoning and pour this gravy over the steaks. Garnish with pickles.

THE EVOLUTION OF THE
NEW YORK CITY RESTAURANT

EARLY EUROPEAN SETTLERS WROTE a great detail about the sea life in the waters surrounding the shores of New Amsterdam and colonial New York: oysters that grew up to a foot long, six-foot lobsters, whales, dolphins, and porpoises. The woods of Manhattan, the settlers observed, were filled with wild birds, foxes, wolves, bears, and mountain lions. It is difficult to envision today, but New York was once a bountiful natural paradise. In fact, New York City's harbor once contained more than half of the world's oysters, with billions of them carpeting the seabed and shores of the five boroughs.

First it was the Lenape, the people indigenous to the land on which New York was built, who relied on oysters as a staple food. Evidence of their oyster consumption is found in oyster middens—piles of discarded oyster shells—that occasionally resurface at modern-day construction sites. These once dotted the land of lower Manhattan.

When the Dutch arrived, the abundance of oysters in the waters surrounding New Amsterdam made them an obvious source of sustenance. Mollusks remained a central element of the diet as the island switched to British control in 1664 and remained a staple food well into the nineteenth century. (Eventually overfishing and pollution ruined the once-steady supply.) Oysters were plentiful, they were nutritious, and, most importantly, they were cheap. As one observer wrote in 1770, "Very many poor families have no other substitute than oysters and bread." Oysters were also an ideal food to consume on the go as they could be eaten raw on the half shell, requiring little work in terms of preparation—a bonus for the street cart vendor as well as his impatient customers. But New Yorkers didn't just consume their oysters raw; they also boiled them, baked them in pies, roasted them over the fire, and made stews out of them.

New Yorkers' enthusiastic consumption of oysters led to the creation of one of the city's first types of eateries: the oyster cellar. Oyster cellars (initially named so because they were located in basement floors) ran the gamut from grungy to luxurious and were often marked by a red balloon, the traditional sign of a brothel. (While some spots were highly respectable, others embraced the ancient link between oysters and sex.) Canal Street, once an actual canal that ran the width of Manhattan, was by the beginning of the nineteenth century home to a huge number of the city's oyster cellars, which famously offered the Canal Street plan: "all you can eat" oysters for six cents.

The most famous oyster cellar of the nineteenth century was Downing's, owned by Thomas Downing, whom Mayor Philip Hone in 1842 referred to as "the great man of oysters." Born to a free Black family in 1791, near the Chesapeake Bay, Downing was already an experienced oysterman when he moved to New York in 1815. At this time many of the city's oysters came from Sandy Ground on Staten Island, one of the richest oyster beds surrounding New York and the oldest continuously inhabited African American community in the United States, settled by free Blacks around 1799.

Downing did not live on Staten Island but rather at 33 Pell Street, in what is now Chinatown. In a small skiff, he rowed across the Hudson River every day to pick oysters and then sell them back in Manhattan. Over time his clientele grew, and in 1825 he opened his eponymous oyster cellar, Downing's, at 5 Broad Street. Downing's quickly became a hub for New York businessmen to slurp oysters and talk shop. Downing himself had an almost mythic reputation as the man who knew all the secrets of City Hall and Wall Street. And, as the most celebrated oyster cellar, Downing's was the caterer of official city events, catering such spectacles as the 1842 Boz Ball, given in honor of the author Charles Dickens during his first American tour.

Downing's success is illustrative of larger trends at play; in New York, entrepreneurship was accessible to minorities and immigrants—when they opened businesses in "appropriate" fields. While laws and social boundaries made access to higher education and many trades near impossible, the doors to the food industry were open. Already fluent in the universal language of food, minority and immigrant groups had a unique cultural purview to present in terms of culinary products—specialties from their homelands, recipes and cooking methods particular to their communities—giving their businesses an added edge.

Downing differentiated his oyster cellar from others by decorating his space with luxurious trappings, like rich carpets, curtains, and chandeliers. In doing so he attracted patrons of a certain class who felt comfortable and safe within these interiors. Downing succeeded in making oyster cellars respectable; it was the one oyster cellar where women could go—if their husbands accompanied them. And though his clientele was mainly white, the subterranean world of Downing's was a beacon of activism within the African American community. While the rich white elite of New York dined upstairs, Downing maintained a safe haven for the persecuted below. The basement of his oyster cellar served as a stop on the Underground Railroad, housing enslaved people who were on the run and refugees needing shelter. When New York abolished slavery in 1827, Downing helped to found the Committee of Thirteen, which worked to prevent free people from being kidnapped and returned to slavery in the South.

Downing was able to attract so many businessmen to his oyster cellar because, not unlike today, most business was conducted downtown in the financial district. However, as the city's wealthy businessmen began to move their homes farther uptown to get away from overcrowding and slums, it became harder for them to commute home for lunch; instead of a short carriage ride, the trip now took an hour in each direction. Demand soared for places to eat downtown during the week—which is why so many of the city's first restaurants and oyster cellars opened in the financial district.

Laborers and the working class also increasingly found their jobs too far from home for a midday meal. Places like Clark and Brown's, at the Franklin Coffee House, were among these early lunchtime eateries. The owners of Clark and Brown's were British, and their establishment can be categorized as a chophouse, a type of eatery that had a bar, some booths for dining, and a meat-forward service. They introduced New Yorkers to the shilling plate: roast beef or beefsteak with plum pudding, bread, a pickled walnut or mushroom catsup for zest, and a tankard of either ale or brandy.

For centuries New Yorkers have maintained a reputation for the speed at which they move—always on the go, driven by the pace of the city itself. As the city expanded and more eateries appeared across the urban landscape, the emphasis on swift, convenient service became even more apparent. The "business lunch" or "work lunch," as it came to be called, was eaten with famed rapidity. One visitor to the city in 1865 noted that New Yorkers consume their food "with a strange, savage earnestness, and in silence."

Manhattan's northward expansion also changed the way families ate at home. The "business lunch" or "work lunch" redefined mealtimes. No longer was it possible for families to gather at home for the midday meal, which had traditionally been the biggest meal of the day. Instead the family would now convene at the end of the day for dinner. Lunch shifted to a quick meal, often consumed on the go, in the midst of a busy day.

The growth of New York, especially during the first half of the nineteenth century, was unparalleled. Never before had a concrete jungle emerged so quickly from the earth. When the Erie Canal opened in 1825 it connected New York to the Great Lakes and hence the Midwest, which was becoming a huge center of production. As America expanded its empire west across the continent, New York remained connected to every new sprouting tendril, reaping the benefits as goods flowed in—and out—solidifying its position as the commercial and trade capital of the United States.

No facet of existence on the island was safe from the city's relentless growth. Much of the natural geography of the city was cleared to make space for more buildings, more homes, more factories, more roads. The Collect Pond, once a twenty-acre body of water that was idyllically situated between rolling hills in what is now Chinatown, was filled in 1801. Woods were chopped down, ponds filled in, hills leveled, wooden frame houses were torn down. In 1845 Mayor Philip Hone lamented, "Overturn, overturn, overturn is the maxim of New York. The very bones of our ancestors are not permitted to lie quiet a quarter of a century, and one generation of men seems studious to remove all relics of those who precede them."

The very land that had enabled Gotham to flourish in the first place—its abundance of food, its rich and well-connected waterways—was devastated by the very success it had wrought. By the turn of the twentieth century, the city's oyster beds were depleted. Drowned in sewage and runoff from factories, any remaining oysters were deemed unsafe to eat.

A DISH SERVED COLD

IN THE NINETEENTH century, the absolute test-piece of a high-end chef was not a perfectly cooked roast or a wonderfully poached fish. In fact, elaborate cold dishes were the pinnacle of skill, and the more elaborate the final result and the less it looked like food, the better. A century before,

Antonin Carême had stated that the art of cooking was closest to the art of architecture, and taught himself technical drafting to prove it. And when we look at similar food illustrations from Charles Ranhofer's encyclopedic *The Epicurean*, we see elaborate cathedrals and fantastic palaces of culinary delights.

At a glance they seem closest to an overwrought and multitiered wedding cake—but peer in more closely and, surprisingly, often you'll learn the dish is constructed from game birds or sliced meats dressed in dense sauces with battlements of colored gelatin or spiraling towers of truffles and crustaceans.

Baked Turbot

SERVES 4 TO 6 *Turbot is a meaty flatfish that is often cooked or poached quite delicately today. This is a more robust version from Glasse, with a sauce that makes use of mushroom catsup, a staple condiment of the time, and which can be elegantly elevated with the addition of shrimp and mushrooms.*

FOR THE TURBOT:

1 stick (8 tablespoons) unsalted butter, softened

1½ pounds skinless turbot fillet

Kosher salt

Freshly ground black pepper

Freshly grated nutmeg

2 tablespoons chopped parsley leaves

1 tablespoon all-purpose flour

¼ cup breadcrumbs

1 cup white wine

FOR THE SAUCE:

½ teaspoon all-purpose flour

3 tablespoons Mushroom Catsup (recipe follows)

½ cup cooked chopped shrimp (optional)

¼ cup cooked chopped cremini or button mushrooms (optional)

4 tablespoons unsalted butter

Lemon slices, for garnish

PREHEAT the oven to 425°F.

GENEROUSLY grease a baking dish with some of the butter. Place the turbot fillet in the prepared dish and coat with the remaining softened butter. Season well with salt and pepper and then grate liberally with fresh nutmeg. Sprinkle with the fresh parsley, dust with the flour, and top with the breadcrumbs. Add the wine to the bottom of the baking dish. Bake for about 20 minutes, until the top is golden brown and the fish is flaky and reads at least 145°F on an instant-read thermometer. The fish can be finished under a broiler for deeper color.

RESERVE the fish on a warm serving dish and strain the liquid through a fine-mesh strainer into a small saucepan. To finish the sauce, make a slurry with the flour and the mushroom catsup. Combine with the strained liquid in the saucepan and bring to a boil over medium heat, whisking constantly. Add the shrimp and mushrooms, if using, and continue to cook for 1 minute. Remove from the heat and add the butter, whisking until emulsified. Taste and adjust seasoning, then dress the fish with the sauce and garnish with sliced lemons.

Mushroom Catsup

MAKES ABOUT ½ CUP

1 pound cremini mushrooms

¼ teaspoon grated fresh ginger

¼ teaspoon freshly ground black pepper

¼ teaspoon ground mace

1 whole clove

Kosher salt to taste

IN a food processor fitted with the metal blade, pulse the mushrooms until finely chopped. You want at least 2 cups chopped mushrooms, but more is fine. Combine the mushrooms, spices, and 2 cups water in a small saucepan and cook over medium heat until reduced to one-quarter or less of the initial volume, about 30 minutes. Press through a fine-mesh sieve into a bowl, being careful to extract all the liquid. Season with salt.

I'LL BET YOU DIDN'T EVEN KNOW YOU WERE EATING LIKE A RUSSIAN

ODDLY, IN A TIME when the fancy menus were all printed in French, virtually all restaurants had also finally transitioned to the modern and familiar style of dining we know today: *service à la Russe*. Before then, and dating back at least to the Middle Ages, tables were set all at once, groaning platters of food that was hot, cold, savory, and sweet all intermingled. This was refined into a few courses, each still consisting of a mix of large dishes to be shared, still hot, cold, and otherwise. The final evolution is the one we know today, where each diner is served a single dish in a carefully orchestrated series, the entire meal progressing from starting soups to small delicacies, roasts, and finally desserts (still a fairly new and exciting concept), a progression that inspired the phrase "from soup to nuts."

Canapés:
Anchovy, Windsor, Caviar, and Smoked Salmon

MAKES 12 *The remaining recipes from this chapter come from Charles Ranhofer's epic tome,* The Epicurean, *a book whose encyclopedic complexity floored me when I first opened it and still amazes me to this day. These assorted canapés are a perfect place to start and are considerably larger than the one-bite hors d'oeuvres we are used to today, which allows for considerably more decoration (which is half of the point). All of these canapés make use of the anchovy butter, so prepare it first. You will need three shapes of bread—3 round, 3 oval, and 6 rectangular. All should be approximately 3 inches at the widest point. The easiest way to make them is to cut slices a little over ¼ inch thick and use a cutter, then toast them. This recipe makes enough anchovy butter for all 12 canapés. The amount you use for each may vary slightly.*

1 loaf unsliced white bread, sliced and cut as described above

FOR THE ANCHOVY BUTTER:

2 sticks (16 tablespoons) unsalted butter

2 teaspoons anchovy paste

½ teaspoon kosher salt

¼ teaspoon mustard powder

Pinch of finely ground black pepper

Pinch of ground cayenne pepper

ALLOW the butter to soften completely and whisk in all ingredients until thoroughly amalgamated.

Anchovy Canapés

3 round toasts

About 3 tablespoons anchovy butter

9 anchovy fillets

2 large eggs, hard-boiled

Finely chopped fresh parsley

SPREAD the surface of each toast with a thin layer of anchovy butter and arrange the fillets in a spiral pattern, trimming to fit if necessary. Separate the egg white and yolk. Press the yolk through a sieve into a bowl and finely chop the white. Fill the spaces between the fillets separately with egg yolk, egg white, and parsley. Pipe a thin line of anchovy butter around the perimeter of each toast.

Windsor Canapés

4 ounces cooked white meat chicken

4 ounces baked ham

4 ounces cooked beef tongue

1 stick (8 tablespoons) unsalted butter

3 ounces aged cheddar cheese

2 teaspoons Dijon mustard

¼ teaspoon ground cayenne pepper

3 oval toasts

A few cornichons

½ cooked beet

Finely chopped capers

About 3 tablespoons anchovy butter

Aspic (page 335; optional)

ADD the chicken, ham, tongue, butter, cheese, mustard, and cayenne pepper to the bowl of a food processor fitted with the metal blade and pulse until smooth, scraping down the sides several times. Cover the top of each toast with this mixture, leaving a small margin around the edge. Cut the cornichons and beet into extremely fine strips and place in a crosshatch pattern over the spread and trim to match the edges, pressing them in slightly. Place a small piece of caper in each of the diamonds created by the crosshatch. Pipe a thin line of anchovy butter around the perimeter. These can be chilled and finished with a bit of aspic. To do this, let the aspic cool to a jelly stage and apply very carefully with a brush. Chill and set. Any leftover filling can stored in the refrigerator and enjoyed as a pâté.

Caviar Canapés

3 rectangular toasts

About 3 tablespoons anchovy butter

2 ounces Osetra or your favorite caviar

½ medium or large white onion, very thinly sliced

SPREAD the surface of each toast with a very thin layer of anchovy butter and then spread the top with a generous layer of caviar, leaving a small margin around the edge. Use the flat edge of a knife or a small offset spatula to make sure the edges of the caviar are sharp. Selecting the longest and straightest pieces of white onion, make a border around the caviar and trim to fit.

Smoked Salmon Canapés

1 large egg, hard-boiled

3 rectangular toasts

About 3 tablespoons anchovy butter

3 ounces smoked salmon cut into thin strips

Finely chopped fresh parsley

SEPARATE the egg white and yolk. Press the yolk through a sieve into a bowl and finely chop the whites. Spread the surface of each toast with a very thin layer of anchovy butter and then arrange strips of smoked salmon in a simple bar pattern, alternating smoked salmon, parsley, egg white, and yolk. Pipe a thin line of anchovy butter around the edge.

Attereaux of Fat Livers

MAKES 4 *This type of presentation, where different delicacies were layered, was common in this age of extravagance. Such dishes go by a slew of names, mostly French, that usually indicate their shape or style. Here, rich foie gras is interspersed with beef tongue and sauced before being breaded and fried.*

1 (4-ounce) lobe foie gras

4 ounces cooked beef tongue

2 cups low-sodium beef stock

Kosher salt

Sweet paprika

About ¼ cup Villeroi Sauce (recipe follows)

Grated truffle

2 cups breadcrumbs

3 large eggs, beaten thoroughly

Vegetable oil for frying

Lemon slices, for garnish

CUT the foie gras into slices a little less than ¼ inch thick and cut these into 1-inch squares; you will need 16 squares. Do the same with the beef tongue, again making 16 squares. Cook the foie gras squares in a very hot nonstick pan for 30 seconds per side and let cool. Put the beef stock in a wide saucepan over medium heat and let cook until reduced by about 90 percent and the consistency is glaze-like, about 20 minutes. Season with salt. Sprinkle the foie and beef tongue with paprika, and brush the tongue with the reduced beef stock and the foie gras with enough Villeroi sauce to coat. Assemble 4 attereaux, each with 4 pieces of tongue alternating with 4 pieces of foie gras; secure each with a skewer. Carefully smooth or trim the sides until flat and consistent and dust with truffle. Heat the frying oil to 375°F in a medium saucepan. Dredge the skewered towers in breadcrumbs, then dredge in the eggs and dredge in the breadcrumbs a second time. Fry until golden brown, working in batches, if necessary, to avoid crowding. Remove the skewers, cool slightly, and serve.

Villeroi Sauce

MAKES ABOUT 3 CUPS *This rich, classical sauce pairs well with chicken, pork, and vegetables.*

FOR THE VELOUTÉ:

1⅓ quarts low-sodium chicken stock

1 stick (8 tablespoons) unsalted butter

1 cup all-purpose flour

FOR THE SAUCE:

2 tablespoons unsalted butter

2 ounces ham, cut into very small dice

¼ cup white wine

2 cups velouté (see left)

1 pinch freshly grated nutmeg

1 tablespoon champagne vinegar

4 egg yolks

¼ cup heavy cream

Kosher salt

1 tablespoon finely chopped cooked cremini or button mushrooms

1 teaspoon minced fresh parsley

TO make the velouté, heat the chicken stock in a medium saucepan over low heat. Melt the butter in a separate medium saucepan over medium-low heat, add the flour, whisking to combine thoroughly, and cook until blond, about 2 minutes. Add the chicken stock about ¼ cup at a time, whisking until completely mixed and bringing to a boil between additions. Continue to cook until all stock is incorporated and the mixture is velvety smooth. (Any leftover velouté can be used to make the Chaudfroid Sauce, see page 335.)

TO prepare the sauce, melt the butter in a small saucepan over medium heat and add the ham. Cook until colored and then pour off the excess butter. Add the white wine and reduce until almost dry. Reduce the heat to low, add the velouté, nutmeg, and vinegar and simmer for 5 minutes. Whisk together the egg yolks and cream in a heatproof bowl and add the ham mixture in a thin stream, whisking constantly. Return this mixture to the saucepan and cook, whisking constantly, until it has thickened, 5 to 7 minutes. Taste and adjust seasoning, strain through a fine-mesh sieve into a bowl, and fold in the mushrooms and parsley. This sauce will keep refrigerated for up to 1 week. Gently reheat to use.

Ballotines of Squab or Quail à la Madison

MAKES 4 SQUAB OR 6 QUAIL *Put away your phone. Clear your schedule. And then . . . I have a confession to make. I have, in fact, only completed half of this recipe, although I have done that many times. The second half involves taking mutton fat mixed with wax and carving an elaborate stand of griffins holding scallop shells, upon which you place an armature that holds the actual ballotines. Then, of course, there are vegetables cut as flowers, tomatoes stuffed with jelly, whole truffles, glazed larks, foie gras, crescents of beef tongue, and it just goes on and on from there. Really. But trust me, creating a stuffed bird that resembles an elaborate pastry bombe is more than enough. A modern silicone dome mold makes the process much easier, and you should choose between squab and quail based both on personal preference and the size of your mold, which should be at least ¼ inch or so larger than your stuffed and cooked bird, to allow for the layers of sauce, truffle, and aspic.*

FOR THE POULTRY:

4 semi-boneless squab or 6 semi-boneless quail

Kosher salt

Freshly ground black pepper

FOR THE FILLING:

2 tablespoons ¼-inch-dice black truffle

2 tablespoons ¼-inch-dice cured ham

2 tablespoons ¼-inch-dice fat from cured ham

2 tablespoons ¼-inch-dice foie gras

2 tablespoons shelled whole pistachios

1 tablespoon Madeira wine

FOR THE FORCEMEAT:

4 ounces chicken breast, cut into ½-inch dice

8 ounces ground pork

8 ounces liver pâté

1 teaspoon kosher salt

¼ teaspoon freshly ground black pepper

1 teaspoon shaved truffle

FOR THE ASPIC:

3 envelopes (2 tablespoons plus 1½ teaspoons) powdered gelatin

2½ cups clarified chicken or veal stock

¾ cup Madeira wine

½ teaspoon kosher salt

FOR THE CHAUDFROID SAUCE:

2 cups velouté (see page 333)

2 cups aspic (see above)

FOR THE GARNISH:

1 large black truffle

PREHEAT the oven to 325°F.

SEMI-BONELESS game birds usually retain the bones of the wings and the legs. Run the tip of a sharp knife down the leg, just touching the bones, to open the leg and then gently detach the meat from the bones with a scraping motion. For the wing bones it is often easier simply to remove the wing entirely, especially on smaller birds like quail. Season with salt and pepper and refrigerate. For the filling, combine the truffle, ham, fat, foie gras, and pistachios in a bowl and sprinkle with the Madeira. Refrigerate for at least 30 minutes and up to 2 hours. For the forcemeat, combine the chicken, pork, pâté, salt, pepper, and truffle shavings in the bowl of a food processor fitted with the metal blade and pulse to form a smooth paste, scraping down the sides several times. Fold this mixture together with the filling. Lay out the game birds and spread them thickly with this preparation and fit them into round or oblong molds, making sure they fill the molds completely and squaring the open area with a spatula. Place the molds on a sheet pan, cover them with a sheet of parchment paper and another sheet pan, and bake until they are thoroughly cooked and reach at least 165°F on an instant-read thermometer, 40 to 50 minutes. Allow to cool completely. Unmold carefully and clean the molds.

TO prepare the aspic, first bloom the gelatin for a few minutes in ¼ cup cold water, then combine the clarified stock, Madeira, salt, and bloomed gelatin in a small saucepan on low heat and simmer until the gelatin is completely melted. Strain through a fine-mesh strainer into another small saucepan. For the chaudfroid sauce, combine 2 cups of the the velouté sauce (page 333) with 2 cups of

the aspic and whisk to combine thoroughly. Taste and adjust seasoning. Allow the sauce to cool almost completely and partially fill the molds. Return the cooled stuffed birds to the molds and allow to cool completely. It is vitally important with every step to cool completely or they will be damaged when unmolding. Unmold and clean the molds. Cut the truffle into thin slices and then use a cutter to cut those slices into fanciful geometric designs. The only rule is that the smaller the individual pieces are, the more difficult it will be to get them to stay in their proper positions in the final ballotine. Allow the unmolded and sauced ballotines to warm slightly so that the truffles can be pressed gently into place. You can apply a little bit more chaudfroid sauce around the edges to help with this. Again, chill and allow to set completely. Remelt the remaining aspic over very low heat. You can add a drop or two of food coloring at this stage to add to the confection-like unreality of the final product. Allow the aspic to cool to a thick, jellied consistency and fill the molds partway with it. Return the stuffed, sauced, and truffle-topped birds to the molds, pray to the aspic gods, and allow to set completely. Unmold, trim the edges, and serve at room temperature.

COCKTAILS: POUSSE L'AMOUR
AND PINEAPPLE PUNCH

THE RECIPES ON THE FOLLOWING PAGE, Pousse l'Amour and Pineapple Punch, highlight cocktails at two ends of the spectrum, both of which have fallen somewhat by the wayside and both of which come from the greatest bartender of the period, Jerry Thomas. Thomas's 1862 *How to Mix Drinks: Or, the Bon Vivant's Companion* and his later 1876 *Bartender's Guide* are considered the first classics of the genre. The pousse l'amour is the first in a long line of layered cocktails that steadily increased in complexity and number of layers until falling out of favor in the 1930s, although they have had several resurgences when bartenders wanted to display their technical skills. Punches, on the other hand, were an absolute mainstay of dining beginning in the colonial era, often stimulatingly tea-based and large enough to refresh, or demolish, a small party.

THE BITTERED SLING
COMES OF AGE

ALTHOUGH THE origin of the word "cocktail" is hotly debated, the evolution of this particularly American innovation is not. Straight spirits, often being too harsh for casual drinking, lent themselves to combination with other ingredients, setting off a never-ending quest for perfection. The British in India popularized the punch, a name that probably derives from the Hindi word for five, for the five ingredients: spirits, sugar, lemon or lime juice, water, and spices. This combination was, not surprisingly, tremendously popular and spread rapidly. A large bowl of punch was also, equally unsurprisingly, too much for a single drinker, so a smaller, simplified version was invented, the sling, with only the spirit, water, sugar, and sometimes nutmeg. The final innovations came with the addition of bitters, originally medicinal extracts of herbs and aromatics, and the commercial availability of ice, which raised the drink to another level. The result, the bittered sling, soon came to be called the cocktail. People may continue to debate the origin of the term, some arguing for the "cocked tails" of non-thoroughbred racehorses as a metaphor for the adulterated pure spirits, others insisting on a tale of a stolen rooster, while others will fight to the death for a mispronunciation of a French word for "egg-cup." Of course, it doesn't end there and, like all of these debates, probably never will. These will remain, however, discussions that can only be improved upon by the company of the drink in question.

Pousse l'Amour

SERVES 1 *This drink is described as one of a group of "fancy cocktails," and I recall it being described as "very popular with the ladies," egg yolk and all. The recipe does not include exact measurement, but the ingredients can be eyeballed satisfactorily.*

About 2 jiggers maraschino liqueur
1 egg yolk

About 2 jiggers vanilla cordial
About 1 ounce cognac

FILL a glass roughly halfway with the maraschino. Using a long-handled bar spoon, carefully slip in the egg yolk without breaking it. Invert the bar spoon and very slowly pour the vanilla cordial (about the same amount as the maraschino) into the bowl of the spoon and down the side of the glass, so that it forms a layer on top of the maraschino. Do the same with the cognac, but add just enough to cover the surface of the vanilla. Serve.

Pineapple Punch

SERVES 1 WILD PARTY OF 20

4 pineapples, peeled and sliced
2 cups sugar
Juice of 4 lemons (about 1 cup)
2 cups dark rum

2 cups brandy
½ cup Curaçao
4 bottles Champagne, chilled
Orange slices, for garnish

PLACE the pineapples in a bowl and toss with the sugar. Cover and refrigerate for at least 30 minutes. Add the lemon juice, rum, brandy, and Curaçao, stir, and chill in the freezer until very cold but not frozen, about 40 minutes. Place a large block of ice in a punch bowl and add this mixture and the Champagne, stirring gently to mix. Garnish with the orange slices and serve immediately.

APPETITES OF GOTHAM

IN NINETEENTH-CENTURY NEW YORK, the only dish that could rival a juicy steak or a dozen oysters was turtle soup. Green snapping turtles were abundant along the East Coast, and turtle soup quickly became a staple of early American cuisine, reigning as one of the premiere national dishes from the colonial period well into the early years of the twentieth century. However, as turtles were overfished, they became increasingly expensive, and the soup became more of a delicacy. And so, in the invention of mock turtle soup, we find the perfect representation of the democratization of haute cuisine.

If mock turtle soup brought elite cuisine to the masses, then the boardinghouse represented a kind of egalitarian nineteenth-century housing. And it was this form of housing that would produce a population of hungry boarders looking for a place to eat.

When Walt Whitman was asked about the nature of the American Yankee he responded, "They are a boarding people." Particularly in New York, where space has always been expensive, there were thousands of boardinghouses. They were where an individual could rent out a room— no private kitchen or bathroom was included (perhaps making them akin to the college dorm room of today). Though boardinghouses had common living areas as well as daily scheduled meals, provided by the proprietor of the home, who was more often than not a woman.

Fitting the needs of every kind of individual looking for a roof over his head, boardinghouses were diverse in style and price. Thomas Butler Gunn, a British journalist and cartoonist in 1857 noted "Cheap Boarding-Houses on a Large Scale," "Fashionable Boarding-Houses Where You Don't Get Enough to Eat," "The Dirty Boarding-House," "The Theatrical Boarding-House," "Boarding-Houses Where There Are Marriageable Daughters," "The Boarding-House Where the Landlady Drinks," as well as vegetarian boardinghouses, French boardinghouses, and Southern boardinghouses. But one thing these all seemed to share was terrible food. Gunn wrote of the universality of dreadful boardinghouse food: "Like death, no class is exempt from it." Of the food he encountered during his sojourns at various boardinghouses, he wrote,

It was a singular and beautiful study to observe the many transformations a single dish endured. In the breakfast steak of to-day you might recognize the corned beef of yesterday's dinner, and reasonably anticipate encountering it in to-morrow's meatpie, and the next day's hash. We got to dating from the advent of certain portions of animal food, reckoning upon our fingers the lapse of days by them.

That food situation created a sizable group of people looking for more appetizing meals outside the boardinghouse—generating the need for even more eateries to emerge.

The boardinghouse population also impacted the evolution of the restaurant in other, perhaps unforeseen, ways. Waves of young single immigrants moving to America, alone, without family and of marriageable age, suddenly found themselves free of dating restrictions that might have been imposed on them back at home. In fact, one could argue that this period was the beginning of modern "dating" as we know it. A young man or woman didn't necessarily need approval from their family or community regarding whom they might court. And where were all these young couples supposed to date? Enter the restaurant.

Taylor's was the place to take a fashionable young woman on a date by the mid-nineteenth century. Opened in 1852, in the ground floor and basement space of Taylor's International Hotel, this sprawling ice cream parlor was marketed toward young women, serving what was deemed to be a "feminine" menu of ice cream, sweets, and delicate little dishes. It became a prime courting space for young couples and one of the first restaurants in the city to cater a lunch exclusively for women.

Restaurants did not allow women to dine without the accompaniment of a man until 1868, when Delmonico's decided to part with the old ways. Soon eating establishments like Taylor's, Thompson's, and the Brevoort Hotel featured a ladies-only lunch, and attempted to balance the scales by not allowing men to dine unless they were accompanied by a female escort. Male-only eateries and bars became a relic of a bygone age, another social mores left in the dust as America bounded into the future.

One of the most popular restaurants of the period was at the corner of Broadway and Prince Street. In 1831, Irish immigrant William Niblo transformed his famous Bank Coffee House into Niblo's Garden, a park with a dining room at the very center. The dining room was massive, catering to hundreds of hungry diners at once. He hired hunters to scour the American hinterland for increasingly impressive items to serve. One of his staggering game menus included bald eagle, hawk, owl, raccoon, and a six-foot wild swan. Niblo was known to serve whole bear, smoking hot and standing in the middle of the dining room, a sort of nod to medieval subtleties and an outrageous showpiece. Niblo was one of New York's first restaurateurs specializing in the spectacular—trying to figure out the formula of what would not only attract diners, but convince them to come back again and again.

However, the origin story of the American restaurant (as we think of it today) really belongs to Delmonico's. What started as a pastry shop in 1827 and became a full-service French restaurant in 1830 was truly the first restaurant the city had ever seen. Delmonico's offered food à la carte from a menu. Meals were served *à la russe*. The large-format menus changed daily and were written in French. These early Delmonico's menus introduced New Yorkers to an entirely novel concept of dining; it was leisurely and luxurious, the food complex and foreign yet mingling with notes of familiarity.

Realizing they needed more help to run the thriving business, the Delmonico brothers sent for family reinforcement from Switzerland. Lorenzo Delmonico, their nephew, arrived in New York in 1831 at the age of nineteen. He would become the face and future of the Delmonico's empire—a larger-than-life mythic Medici of the nineteenth century. When John died in 1842 and Peter quit, having had enough of restaurant life, the business was left to Lorenzo. Under his lead the restaurant became iconic. Famous patrons included business tycoons like J. P. Morgan, Andrew Carnegie, and John D. Rockefeller as well as the Prince of Wales, Napoleon III, Charles Dickens, Mark Twain, Theodore Roosevelt, Oscar Wilde, and all other manner of rich and famous in between.

Between 1830 and 1923 there were eleven iterations of Delmonico's; some locations only lasted a few years and three were destroyed by fire, while others were open for decades—though never more than four at once. After the first two locations on William Street burned down in a fire in 1835, a third restaurant known as the Citadel (which still exists today at South William Street) was built. Though eight more locations followed, the Citadel remained the heart of the Delmonico's empire. The growth of Delmonico's was rather extraordinary in the ways it paralleled the growth of New York. As Manhattan expanded northward, Delmonico's moved with it; from the financial district it crept up Broadway to Fourteenth Street, to Twenty-Sixth Street and finally to Forty-Forth Street.

What made Delmonico's such an innovative establishment in the landscape of New York City history, and specifically the history of the New York City restaurant, is that Delmonico's anticipated the movements, cultural leanings, and trends of New York before the city itself did. When Lorenzo decided to move the restaurant north to Fourteenth Street in 1862, many doubted the new location would survive, believing it to be too far uptown from the city's center. Instead, New Yorkers found the epicenter of Gilded Age fine dining at this location. Delmonico's served as a cultural institution that drove trends, the way restaurants do today—but arguably, Delmonico's was the first. The food and drink served at Delmonico's was imitated in restaurants across the country.

Such a restaurant needed a powerhouse chef at its helm, and Lorenzo found this person in Charles Ranhofer, America's first celebrity chef. Born in France in 1836 to a family of professional cooks, by the age of fifteen he had completed a pastry apprenticeship and was the head baker of a restaurant in Paris. At twenty he came to America, intrigued by stories of opportunity, and after a brief stint at nearby competitor Maison Dorée, he became the head chef of Delmonico's in 1862.

Ranhofer ran the kitchens of Delmonico's for thirty-four years, gaining a reputation as a world-class chef in command of one of America's greatest kitchens. His fame is attributed to the dishes he invented, such as lobster Newburg and baked Alaska, which incorporated classical French techniques yet embodied the essence of nineteenth-century American cuisine. Many of the legendary dishes he served are immortalized in his seminal thousand-page cookbook, *The Epicurean*. This work does not just contain recipes and menus, but instructions about how to serve meals, how to time them appropriately, how to set the table, what wines to serve with each course, and how this model varies depending on the guests at the table.

The food served at restaurants like Delmonico's, the Fifth Avenue Hotel, and the Hoffman House in the later half of the nineteenth century represented the new American haute cuisine. French sauces and preparations still gave their menus a distinctly French air, but many of the choicest meats, fish, and poultry were uniquely American ingredients. A chicken might be served *à la Lyonnaise*, but diamondback terrapins, little neck clams, and canvasback ducks from the Chesapeake Bay, fed on a diet of wild celery and served with hominy or samp, were specifically American specialties. America's distinct regional cuisines had been determined by the natural resources available, as well as the culinary traditions of the people who had settled in that area. With increasing access to the food-ways of the United States made possible by the Erie Canal and railway lines with refrigerated cars, all of these regional cuisines became available in New York. This culminated in a high-end gastronomic fusion of North American fare that was filtered through the cooking techniques of count-less immigrant groups, presented in a format determined by Parisian *restaurers*, but adapted to the social and cultural specifications of Gotham.

Chocolate Soufflé

MAKES 6 INDIVIDUAL SOUFFLÉS *We have seen chocolate's roots as an unsweetened sacred beverage and how it lent its complex bitterness to savory chile-infused stews. But here chocolate has finally, finally reached its familiar apogee as the star of the dessert stage, in light and airy technical elegance.*

5 tablespoons unsalted butter, plus more for ramekins

¼ cup sugar, plus more for ramekins

5 ounces bittersweet chocolate

1 tablespoon all-purpose flour

¼ teaspoon kosher salt

¼ teaspoon arrowroot

2 tablespoons whole milk

1 teaspoon vanilla paste

4 large eggs, separated

4 egg yolks

3 tablespoons lightly sweetened whipped cream

PREHEAT the oven to 375°F.

PREPARE six 6-ounce ramekins by coating the insides lightly with butter and sprinkling the insides with sugar. Rotate the ramekins to coat evenly and discard excess sugar.

MELT the chocolate, 4 tablespoons butter, and ¼ cup sugar together in the top of a double boiler over low heat. In a small bowl, whisk together the flour, salt, and arrowroot. Combine the milk, remaining 1 tablespoon butter, and vanilla paste in a very small saucepan and bring to a boil over medium heat. Add the flour mixture and stir, whisking vigorously and continuously until a thick paste forms and pulls away from the sides of the saucepan. Transfer this mixture to a large bowl and allow to cool until warm, and then very vigorously whisk in the 8 egg yolks, a few at a time, until thoroughly combined. Stream in the melted chocolate mixture and whisk to mix completely. In a clean bowl, whip the 4 egg whites to soft peaks and fold them into the chocolate mixture in three additions, including the whipped cream with the final addition. Do not overmix—it is okay if it remains slightly streaky. Distribute the mixture evenly among the ramekins, leveling off the top with a small spatula, and then run the tip of your knife around the top inside edge of each to create a separation between the batter and the ramekin. Bake in the preheated oven until just set, about 15 minutes. Allow to cool and serve.

Alaska Florida

MAKES 6 INDIVIDUAL SERVINGS *This is the original baked Alaska recipe that conceals two kinds of ice cream in a Savoy biscuit (essentially a sponge cake) topped with meringue, so that when the dish was briefly returned to a very hot oven or broiler, the meringue would brown while leaving the ice cream unmelted. Today, with blast chillers and kitchen torches to easily brûlée the meringue, this is relatively simple. In Delmonico's chef Charles Ranhofer's day, this was the height of culinary wizardry and akin to the liquid nitrogen and spherification showpieces of today's modernist spectacles. Use silicone molds like those used for the Ballotines of Squab or Quail à la Madison on page 335; they should be about 3 inches in diameter.*

FOR THE SAVOY BISCUITS:

½ cup plus 2 tablespoons all-purpose flour

½ cup plus 2 tablespoons potato starch

7 large eggs, separated

1 cup plus 2 tablespoons sugar

1 vanilla bean, split and scraped

FOR THE BANANA ICE CREAM:

4 ripe bananas, peeled

2 cups heavy cream

1 cup sugar

¼ teaspoon kosher salt

FOR THE VANILLA ICE CREAM:

2½ cups heavy cream

1½ cups whole milk

1 vanilla bean, split and scraped

1 cup plus 2 tablespoons sugar

¼ teaspoon kosher salt

FOR THE MERINGUE:

4 egg whites

½ cup sugar

¼ teaspoon cream of tartar

Pinch of kosher salt

FOR ASSEMBLY:

About ½ cup apricot jam

PREHEAT the oven to 375°F.

TO make the Savoy biscuit, whisk together the flour and potato starch. In a stand mixer fitted with the whisk attachment, whip the egg whites to soft peaks, slowly adding the salt and 2 tablespoons of the sugar. In the clean bowl of a stand mixer fitted with the whisk attachment, whip the remaining 1 cup sugar, the egg yolks, and the vanilla bean seeds until the mixture is pale and thickened and forms a thick ribbon when you lift the whisk. Fold one-third of the whites into the yolk mixture. Gently fold in the remaining whites in two further additions. Sift the

dry ingredients over the mixture in three additions, carefully folding them in between additions until just barely incorporated with no lumps. Divide evenly among 6 silicone molds and bake in the oven until they are firm, spring back from a touch, and a toothpick comes out clean when inserted, 18 to 20 minutes. Allow to cool completely, then freeze until firm. Trim the bottom of each flat about ¼ inch above where it has risen out of the top of the mold, cutting off the bottom disk in one piece. Set these disks aside and, using a small ice-cream scoop, hollow out the center of each cake. Using the back of a spoon, coat the insides of these cakes with 1 to 2 tablespoons of apricot jam each and return them to the freezer.

TO make the banana ice cream, combine the bananas, cream, sugar, and salt in a blender and blend smooth. Fill the hollowed out centers of the cakes halfway with this mixture and freeze until firm. For the vanilla ice cream, whisk together the cream, milk, vanilla bean seeds, sugar, and salt until the sugar is completely dissolved and process in an ice cream maker, following the manufacturer's directions. While the ice cream is still soft, fill the hollowed out cakes to the top and cover with the reserved disks. Freeze until completely firm. For the meringue, whip the egg whites, salt, and cream of tartar in an electric mixer fitted with the whisk attachment and slowly add the sugar until stiff peaks form. Transfer the meringue to a piping bag fitted with a star tip. Unmold the ice cream filled sponge cakes from the molds and pipe meringue to cover them completely. Brown the meringue under a broiler or with a kitchen torch. Serve immediately.

THE RESTAURANT:
A HISTORY OF THE WORLD

THE FRENCH GASTRONOME JEAN-ANTHELME Brillat-Savarin wrote in 1825, "Few among the crowds which patronize our restaurants every day pause to think that the man who founded the first restaurant must have been a genius endowed with profound insight into human nature." Decades before restaurants would appear in every major metropolis across the globe, Brillat-Savarin understood how powerful this new space was.

Today there are over ten thousand restaurants in New York City. An enormous number, though more than halved from its pre-pandemic number of twenty-four thousand—the latter phenomenon proving the restaurant really is a mirror for wider trends that the city experiences. The sheer scale of eateries in New York tells us how critical this institution is to the life of this city and its people.

Walk the streets of Manhattan today and you will find remains of the nineteenth-century restaurant. Pockets in Midtown contain the vestiges of the English chophouse in twenty-first century steakhouse form. The Financial District still contains a host of quick lunch spots—though now they are more of the make-your-own-salad variety. Along the shores of Brooklyn, oysters are being replanted in an effort to restore the waters of New York to their former glory. Happy hour with cheap oysters has made a return, as have new chic interpretations of oyster cellars.

In fact, the memorabilia of thousands of years of food history is strewn all over the city. The trompe l'oeil style of Roman cuisine found its rebirth in molecular gastronomy, and persists even in the Michelin-starred farm-to-table restaurants that serve fantastically beautiful and unusual little presentations of delicately arranged ingredients invoking a spirit or a story.

We find remnants of the Great Circulation nearly everywhere across the city: in Italian red sauce joints, on slices of pizza; in the spicy and luscious curries of Indian restaurants; in the mouth-numbing dishes of Sichuanese cuisine; in the salsa verdes spooned over rare skirt steaks in corner bistros; in french fries everywhere; in the tangy citrus dressing of a ceviche; in chocolate ice cream perched atop a waffle cone sold from a jingle-playing truck in the summertime.

The spices of the Silk Road pop up in bakeries selling cinnamon babka, fall pumpkin pies, or apple cider doughnuts. Shadows of Queen

Taytu linger over injera topped with shiro wet served in one of the city's Ethiopian restaurants. Henry VIII's love for the spectacular lives with us in cakes topped with sparklers carried out to the dining room by waiters singing "Happy Birthday." Thick hand-pulled noodles topped with meat that melts in your mouth offers faint glimmers of Harun al-Rashid and his companions Jafar and Abu Nuwas.

The legendary late chef and TV personality Anthony Bourdain wrote in the preface to his book *Kitchen Confidential* that the best part about working in restaurants is "To be part of a historical continuum, a secret society with its own language and customs." Bourdain understood the historical nature of working in a New York City restaurant; it's not just about the laborious hours of preparing, cooking, and serving food, the rush of a busy dinner service, or the philosophy of a new menu—working in a restaurant, and indeed eating in a restaurant, places you in a much larger story. It situates you in the grand narrative of history, ready to be consumed by the future.

Acknowledgments

FIRSTLY, THANK YOU TO our incredible agent, Andrianna deLone, for all her support and guidance—and for finding this book a home. Our editors, Elizabeth Smith and Natalie Danford. Elizabeth, you helped find a way to translate an ephemeral oral history event into the written word. Your thoughtful ideas, suggestions, and humor helped to make this book what it is. Natalie, you had the patience and precision to demonstrate how to transform the idea for a recipe, the ingredients and techniques, into a genuine and usable recipe. Also, for the endless discussions of techniques and textures: Is it thin like milk? water? pea soup? Thick like oatmeal? peanut butter? We are eternally grateful to both of you. Thank you to Dr. Jessica B. Harris for writing the foreword—you are an icon of American culinary history and we are so grateful you were willing to be a part of this project.

Jim Muschett at Rizzoli, for believing in this project from the very first day it came across his desk. You have steered the helm of this big unyielding ship with grace, and found the right person for each aspect of its construction. Thank you to Sarah Scheffel and Tricia Levi for their meticulous edits. A huge thank you to our designer Alison Lee Bloomer, who took a mess of ideas and made them into a beautiful book. And to David Lindroth for his lovely maps and illustrations.

Thank you to the most epic photo team we could have ever dreamed of working with: photographer Lucy Schaeffer and food stylist Victoria Granoff. The week we shot for this book was one of the hottest in New York City history, there was no working AC, and Jay was roasting whole pigs, turkeys, chickens, ducks, and fish at full flame. But you two came in with high spirits and big smiles, every day. You are both so very very good at what you do, it was an honor to watch you work. We will always think back fondly to the stories shared at our lunchtime nook, high up in the Brooklyn sky, and of course, the frequent trips to the walk-in to stay cool. Additional thank you to Dressler Parsons who lent her artistic prowess to the puff pastry. And to Edward Columbia and Julian Allen-Barfield for all their production help on everything from sharp canapes to perfectly melted wax. Extra thanks to Fai Ho Kwok for a bit of retouching magic.

Our deepest gratitude to all the scholars who helped to translate centuries-old recipe titles into modern English. Charles Perry and Nawal Nasrallah for their medieval Arabic translations. James C. McCann for all his generous help with research on Ethiopian food. Colleen Taylor Sen for her work on Indian cuisine. Richard Tan for assistance translating recipes from classical Chinese. Michael Cooperson for so generously allowing us to use his translation of Caliph al-Ma-mun's poetry. And to Ken Albala for an approving nod that we were in fact on the right track with this thing.

In 2018, Edible History was fortunate enough to do a residency at the Museum of Food and Drink here in New York City. The support and collaborative energy we received from the whole team helped propel our little supper club to the next level. We are grateful to all the friends we made during our time at MOFAD: Anna Orchard for bringing us on. John Hutt for being a total badass in the kitchen, and a real scholar. Also to Colin Walker, Camila Rinaldi, Debbie Holloway, Dressler Parsons, Nicole Lebsenson Angulo, and Peter J. Kim. Thank you to Izabella Wojcik at The James Beard House for her continued support throughout the years. To Brooke Costello—your belief in what we were and are doing has made this all possible. You provided us with the infrastructure to make Edible History real. And, finally, to Rosemary McGuinnes and Matt Duong for setting in motion all the many steps it would ultimately take to make this book come to fruition. Thank you.

VICTORIA'S PERSONAL THANKS:

I'd like to start by thanking my teachers. Celeste Tramontin for teaching me how to interact with a book and encouraging me to fill the margins with my thoughts and ideas. George Snook for making European history come alive in the classroom every single day. Mark Weinsier for telling me I was smart. That was powerful beyond belief. Gina Luria Walker, who introduced me to the art of recovering the dead—and the importance of rewriting history that no longer serves us. To Oz Frankel for helping me to carve out my own space in the history world and fully embrace it. To Jeremy Varon for allowing me to take a risk, to experiment, and have some fun with the past. And to Linda Gold, who is greatly missed. For six months we sat every Thursday afternoon in my high school cafeteria over peanut butter and jelly sandwiches and coffee, and you taught me about feminism, Jungian symbolism, and pagan mythology. I understand how lucky I am to have found myself in each of your classrooms.

To my friends and family who have spent years listening to me talk about this whole food history thing. I am deeply grateful for all the support I have received. I'm not quite sure how I got so lucky to have so many wonderful humans in my life. Thank you to Katie Mullen, Lucy Lydon, Laura Oladeji DeAngelis, and Heather Darwent for their advice every step of the way. And to Stephanie Knight, William Knight, Joe Lovett, Jim Cottrell, Bianca Chu, Liv Proctor, Sonia Jackett, Emily Duke, Laura Estreich, Krista Muirhead, and Barry Grossman for their love and encouragement. And to Jonny. You came in late on this journey but you helped me end it on the highest note.

Lastly, I'd like to thank my parents Sue Williams and Roland Flexner. I've spent my entire life watching you two bring your art into this world with intention, determination, and style. I hope I can make you both proud.

JAY'S PERSONAL THANKS:

So many people help and inspire a project, in so many different ways. Some of you taught me to cook, some of you worked alongside, with Edible History or not, some of you lent me support, advice, or ovens. Some just made life a little easier; some read poetry. Abigail Frankfurt, John Hutt, Brooke Costello, Blake Abene, Malcolm Livingston III, Colby Spikes, Jeff Srole, Mario Manzano, Nicholas Porcelli, David Penna, Evan Fouche, Lukas Zienko, Devin Schneider, Tim Chin, Samantha Cohen, Jesse Breneman, Jack Saari, Nora Helen, Monica Ozog, Dylan Going, Abe De La Houssaye, Sean Scotese.

About the Authors

EDIBLE HISTORY is a New York City–based supper club founded in 2014 with the goal of bringing people into the conversation of history through food. Over the years they have hosted historical dinners across the city; in pottery studios, at urban farms, in warehouses, neighborhood bistros, defunct bars, museums, and private homes. In 2018 Edible History held a residency at the Museum of Food and Drink. In 2019 and 2020 they were invited to cook at the legendary James Beard House. This is the founders' first book.

VICTORIA FLEXNER is a food historian and the founder of Edible History. She writes, lectures and hosts historical dinners around New York City.

JAY REIFEL has a background in fine dining, classical pastry, and has a deep love of history, especially as it relates to food and culture. He has baked bread with schizophrenics, and written everything from one-liners to questionable science fiction. In his culinary career, he has worked with food scientists, historians, and translators, eaten everything from pigs' brains to live insects, learned from all of them (and thinks you should too).

JESSICA B. HARRIS is a culinary historian, college professor, cookbook author, and journalist. She is the author of twelve critically acclaimed books documenting the foods and foodways of the African Diaspora including *High on the Hog: A Culinary Journey from Africa to America*, which was adapted into a four-part Netflix series of the same name. She is professor emerita at Queens College, City University of New York, and has lectured across the globe. In 2020 she received the James Beard Lifetime Achievement Award.

Recipe Sources

CHAPTER ONE: ANCIENT ROME

ALL FROM *Apicius* by Marcus Gavius Apicius, 1st century CE

Fine Spiced Wine, Pearled, ALSO REFERENCED IN *Natural History*, Pliny, 77 CE

Croquettes of Lobster or Scallops with Cumin Sauce

Varro's Beets and Squash Stewed with Chicken (The Black Dish), ALSO REFERENCED IN *History of Rome*, Cassius Dio, 2nd century CE

Trimalchio's Pig with Lucanian Sausage, ALSO REFERENCED IN *Satyricon*, Petronius, 1st century CE

Peas Supreme Style

Ham in Pastry

Poached Pear Custard

Honey Nut Sweets

CHAPTER TWO: BAGHDAD

ALL FROM *The Annals of the Caliphs' Kitchens*, Ibn Sayyar al-Warraq, 10th century

Rolled Sandwiches, Baghdadi Style

Murri

Cold Dish of Carrots

Fried Eggplant

Slippery Pasta with Meat and Dipping Sauce

Whole Fish Three Ways

Stuffed Whole Fish Cooked Three Ways

Vinegared Stew

Pastry for the Elite

Latticed Fritters

CHAPTER THREE: THE SILK ROAD

Stuffed Eggplant, *Soopa Shastra*, Mangarasa III, 1508

Jackfruit, Mango, and Bitter Melon Salad, *Manasolasa*, Someshvara III, 12th century

Walnut-Stuffed Fish, *The Book of Dishes*, Muhammad b. al-Hasan b. Muhammad b. al-Karim, 13th century

Walnut-Lamb Patties, Muhammad b. al-Hasan b. Muhammad b. al-Karim

Lamb Spread, *Soup for the Qan*, Hu Sihui, 14th century

Turmeric-Colored Tendon, Hu Sihui

Bear Soup, Hu Sihui

Apple Fritters for Lent, *Libro di cucina / Libro per cuoco*, Anonimo Veneziano, 14th/15th century

Cooked Wine, Anonimo Veneziano

CHAPTER FOUR: RENAISSANCE ITALY

Ravioli, *The Neapolitan Recipe Collection*, 15th century

Squab Potage of Fresh Fava Beans, *The Neapolitan Recipe Collection*

Florentine-Style Meat in a Baking Dish, *The Neapolitan Recipe Collection*

Garnished (Armored) Turnips, *The Opera of Bartolomeo Scappi,* Bartolomeo Scappi, 1570

Oil-Braised Tuna Steaks, Bartolomeo Scappi

Stuffed Leg of Lamb, *An Anonymous Tuscan Cookery Book*, 14th/15th century

Lombard Sauce, Bartolomeo Scappi

Verjus Garlic Sauce, Bartolomeo Scappi

Black Grape Sauce, Bartolomeo Scappi

Cherry Torte with Rose Petals, *The Art of Cooking*, Maestro Martino, 1465

Zabaglione, Maestro Martino

CHAPTER FIVE: TUDOR ENGLAND

Spinach Fritters, *The Good Huswifes Jewell*, Thomas Dawson, 1595

Rich Cheese Tart, *Gentyll Manly Cokere*, 15th century

Mince Pie, *The Forme of Cury*, Samuel Pegge, 1490

Roasted Venison, Thomas Dawson, 1595

Sugared Salad with Flower Petals, Thomas Dawson, 1595

The Cockenthrice, *Harleian Manuscript*, 15th century

Cinnamon Sauce, Samuel Pegge

Spiced Digestive, Samuel Pegge

Decorated Marzipan, *The Good Huswifes Handmaide for the Kitchin*, Thomas Dawson, 1594

CHAPTER SIX: AL ANDALUS

ALL FROM *Anonymous Andalusian Cookbook,* 13th century

Small Birds or Meatballs Made of Sheep's Meat
Chicken Soup (That Regulates the Humors)
Artichoke Stewed with Chickpeas
Jewish "Buried" Casserole
Green Stew of Fish
Roasted Duck with Nuts and Garlic
Nut-Stuffed Breast of Lamb
Sugar Nougat Mousse
Almond Crepe Pudding

CHAPTER SEVEN: THE GREAT CIRCULATION

Indigenous and Peruvian Ceviches, traditional
Mole Mestizo with Turkey and Chorizo, traditional
Tomato Sauce in the Spanish Style with Rack of Lamb, *The Modern Steward,* Antonio Latini, 1692
Salt Cod Stew, *The Opera of Bartolomeo Scappi,* Bartolomeo Scappi, 1570
Fish in Banana Leaves with Indonesian Peanut Sauce, traditional
Sweet Potato Pudding, Grenville Family Recipe Collection, 1640–1750
Frothed Chocolate, *The Indian Nectar,* Henry Stubbe, 1662
Goan Layered Custard, Bartolomeo Scappi

CHAPTER EIGHT: ETHIOPIA

All traditional, WITH REFERENCES FROM *Some Records of Ethiopia 1593–1646,* Manoel de Almeida and *Impressions of Ethiopia: Abyssinia under Menelik II,* Docteur E. Merab, 1921

Berbere Spice Mix
Spiced Clarified Butter
Beef Jerky
Pea and Lentil Stew
Spiced Raw Beef with Dipping Sauce
Turmeric Stewed Chicken
Whip-Cut Lamb Leg
Ethiopian Flatbreads

CHAPTER NINE: VERSAILLES

ALL FROM *The French Cook,* Francois Pierre La Varenne, 1651 and *The French Pastry Chef,* Francois Pierre La Varenne, 1653

Pottage of Green Peas or Frogs' Legs
Braised Partridge
Oyster-Stuffed Capon
Larded Saddle of Hare with Pepper Sauce
Squab Torte
Stuffed Carp in Puff Pastry
Glazed Whore's Farts
Frangipane Tourte

CHAPTER TEN: NEW YORK CITY

"Silver Shell" Oysters, *Handbook of Practical Cookery,* Pierre Blot, 1884
Stewed Cucumbers, Hannah Glasse AND ALSO IN *A New System of Domestic Cookery,* Maria Rundell, 1806
Mock Turtle Soup, *The Art of Cookery Made Plain and Easy,* Hannah Glasse, 1775
Stewed and Fried Rump Steaks, Hannah Glasse
Baked Turbot, Hannah Glasse AND ALSO IN Maria Rundell
Canapés: Anchovy, Windsor, Caviar, and Smoked Salmon, *The Epicurean,* Charles Ranhofer, 1894
Attereaux of Fat Livers, Charles Ranhofer
Ballotines of Squab or Quail à la Madison, Charles Ranhofer
Pousse L'Amour and Pineapple Punch, *The Bar-Tender's Guide; or How to Mix All Kinds of Plain and Fancy Drinks* by Jerry Thomas, 1876
Chocolate Soufflé, Charles Ranhofer
Alaska Florida, Charles Ranhofer

Bibliography

GENERAL FOOD SOURCES

Apicius, Marcus Gavius. *Apicius: Cookery and Dining in Imperial Rome.* Edited & translated by Joseph Dommers Vehling. New York: Dover Publications, 1977.

Black, Maggie. *The Medieval Cookbook.* London: The British Museum Press, 2007.

The Book of Sent Soví: Medieval Recipes from Catalonia. Translated by Robin M. Vogelzang. Edited by Joan Santanach. Barcelona: Tamesis, 2008.

Brears, Peter. *All the King's Cooks: The Tudor Kitchens of King Henry VIII at Hampton Court Palace.* London: Souvenir Press, 2011.

Dalby, Andrew, and Sally Grainger. *The Classical Cookbook.* Los Angeles: Getty Publications, 2012.

Faas, Patrick. *Around the Roman Table: Food and Feasting in Ancient Rome.* Chicago: University of Chicago Press, 1994.

Giacosa, Ilaria Gozzini. *A Taste of Ancient Rome.* Translated by Anna Herklotz. Chicago: University of Chicago Press, 1992.

Henisch, Bridget Ann. *The Medieval Cook.* Great Britain: The Boydell Press, 2009.

Klemettilä, Hannele. *The Medieval Kitchen: A Social History with Recipes.* London: Reaktion Books, 2012.

McCann, James C. *Stirring the Pot: A History of African Cuisine.* Athens: Ohio University Press, 2009.

Montanari, Massimo. *Italian Identity in the Kitchen, or Food and the Nation.* Translated by Beth Archer Brombert. New York: Columbia University Press, 2013.

Muhammad b. al-Hasan b. Muhammad b. al-Karim. *A Baghdad Cookery Book: The Book of Dishes (Kitab al-Tabikh).* Translated by Charles Perry. London: Prospect Books, 2005.

Ranhofer, Charles. *The Epicurean: A Complete Treatise of Analytical and Practical Studies on the Culinary Art.* Chicago: The Hotel Monthly Press, 1893.

Redon, Odile, Francoise Sabban, and Silvano Serventi. *The Medieval Kitchen: Recipes from France and Italy.* Translated by Edward Schneider. Chicago: University of Chicago Press, 1993.

Scents and Flavors: A Syrian Cookbook. Translated by Charles Perry. New York: New York University Press, 2020.

Scully, Terence. *The Art of Cookery in the Middle Ages.* Great Britain: The Boydell Press, 1997.

Sitwell, William. *A History of Food in 100 Recipes.* New York: Little, Brown and Company, 2013.

Thomas, Jerry. *How to Mix Drinks or the Bon-Vivant's Companion.* New York: Dick & Fitzgerald, 1862.

BIBLIOGRAPHY BY CHAPTER

CHAPTER ONE: ROME

Beard, Mary. *SPQR: A History of Ancient Rome.* New York: W. W. Norton, 2015.

Carcopino, Jérôme. *Daily Life in Ancient Rome.* Translated by E. O. Lorimer. New Haven: Yale University Press, 2003.

Cary, Earnest, and Herbert B. Foster. *Roman History Dio Cassius.* Cambridge: Harvard University Press, 2014.

Edwards, John. *The Roman Cookery of Apicius: A Treasury of Gourmet Recipes & Herbal Cookery.* Point Roberts, Wash: Hartley & Marks, 1984.

Everitt, Anthony. *Cicero: The Life and Times of Rome's Greatest Politician.* New York: Random House, 2003.

Gwynn, David M. *The Roman Republic: A Very Short Introduction.* Oxford: Oxford University Press, 2012.

Harper, Kyle. *The Fate of Rome: Climate, Disease & the End of an Empire.* Princeton: Princeton University Press, 2017.

Holland, Tom. *Rubicon: The Last Years of the Roman Republic.* New York: Anchor Books, 2003.

Kelly, Christopher. *The Roman Empire: A Very Short Introduction.* Oxford: Oxford University Press, 2006.

Murphy, Cullen. *Are We Rome? The Fall of an Empire and the Fate of America.* New York: Houghton Mifflin Harcourt, 2007.

Petronius. *The Satyricon*. New York: New American Library, 1960.

Pliny the Elder. *Natural History: A Selection*. Translated by John F. Healey. London: Penguin, 1991.

Southon, Emma. *Agrippina: The Most Extraordinary Woman of the Roman World*. New York: Pegasus Books, 2019.

CHAPTER TWO: BAGHDAD

Al-Khalili, Jim. *The House of Wisdom: How Arabic Science Saved Ancient Knowledge and Gave Us the Renaissance*. London: Penguin Books, 2010.

Annals of the Caliphs' Kitchens: Ibn Sayyar al-Warraq's Tenth-Century Baghdadi Cookbook. Translated by Nawal Nasrullah. Leiden: Brill, 2010.

Bennison, Amira K. *The Great Caliphs: The Golden Age of the Abbasid Empire*. New Haven: Yale University Press, 2009.

Cooperson, Michael. *Al-Ma'mun: The Revival of Islam*. London: One World Academic, 2005.

Islam: From the Prophet Muhammad to the Capture of Constantinople. Translated and edited by Bernard Lewis. New York: Oxford University Press, 1987.

Kennedy, Hugh. *When Baghdad Ruled the Muslim World: The Rise and Fall of Islam's Greatest Dynasty*. Cambridge: Da Capo Press, 2004.

Lassner, Jacob. *The Topography of Baghdad in the Early Middle Ages: Texts and Studies*. Detroit: Wayne State University Press, 1970.

Le Strange, Guy. *Baghdad During the Abbasid Caliphate*. New York: Cosimo Classics, 2011.

Marozzi, Justin. *Baghdad City of Peace, City of Blood: A History in Thirteen Centuries*. Boston: Da Capo Press, 2014.

Moller, Violet. *The Map of Knowledge: A Thousand-Year History of How Classical Ideas Were Lost and Found*. New York: Doubleday, 2019.

Selove, Emily, ed. *Baghdad at the Center of the World, 8th–13th Century: An Introductory Textbook*. Fargo, North Dakota: Theran Press, 2019.

Sinbad: And Other Stories from the Arabian Nights. Translated by Husain Haddawy. New York: W. W. Norton, 2008.

CHAPTER THREE: THE SILK ROAD

Corn, Charles. *The Scents of Eden: A History of the Spice Trade*. New York: Kodansha America, Inc., 1998.

Dunn, Ross E. *The Adventures of Ibn Battuta: A Muslim Traveler of the Fourteenth Century*. Berkeley: University of California Press, 2012.

Frankopan, Peter. *The Silk Roads: A New History of the World*. New York: Vintage Books, 2017.

Freedman, Paul. *Out of the East: Spices and the Medieval Imagination*. New Haven: Yale University Press, 2008.

Hansen, Valerie. *The Silk Road: A New History with Documents*. New York: Oxford University Press, 2017.

Krondl, Michael. *The Taste of Conquest: The Rise and Fall of the Three Great Cities of Spice*. New York: Ballantine Books, 2007.

Libro di cucina / Libro per cuoco (Anonimo Veneziano). Translated by Thomas Gloning and Ludovico Frati. Universitat Giessen, 2000.

Milward, James A. *The Silk Road: A Very Short Introduction*. New York: Oxford University Press, 2013.

Muhammad b. al-Hasan b. Muhammad b. al-Karim. *A Baghdad Cookery Book: The Book of Dishes (Kitab al-Tabikh)*. Translated by Charles Perry. London: Prospect Books, 2005.

Nabhan, Gary Paul. *Cumin, Camels, and Caravans: A Spice Odyssey*. Berkeley: The University of California Press, 2014.

Narayan, R. K. *The Ramayana*. New York: Penguin Books, 1977.

Sen, Colleen Taylor. *Feasts and Fasts: A History of Food in India*. London: Reaktion Books, 2015.

The Travels of Marco Polo. Translated by Manuel Komroff. New York: W. W. Norton, 2003.

CHAPTER FOUR: RENAISSANCE ITALY

An Anonymous Tuscan Cookery Book: Anonimo Toscano. Translated by Ariane Helou in 2013 on arianehelou.com.

Bellonci, Maria. *The Life and Times of Lucrezia Borgia*. Translated by Bernard and Barbara Wall. New York: Harcourt Brace and Company, 1953.

Boccacio, Giovanni. *The Decameron*. Translated by G. H. McWilliam. London: Penguin Books, 1995.

Burke, Peter. *The Italian Renaissance: Culture & Society in Italy*. Princeton: Princeton University Press, 2014.

Burkhardt, Jacob. *The Civilization of the Renaissance in Italy*. New York: Penguin Books, 1990.

Cantor, Norman F. *In the Wake of the Plague: The Black Death and the World It Made*. New York: Simon & Schuster, 2001.

De Grazia, Margreta. "The Finite Renaissance." *Journal for Early Modern Cultural Studies*, vol. 14, no. 2 (Spring 2014): 88–93.

Findlen, Paula. "The 2012 Josephine Waters Bennett Lecture: The Eighteenth-Century Invention of the Renaissance: Lessons from the Uffizi." *Renaissance Quarterly*, vol. 66, no. 1 (Spring 2013): 1–34.

Findlen, Paula, and Kenneth Gouwens, "Introduction: The Persistence of the Renaissance." *The American Historical Review*, vol. 103, no. 1 (February 1998): 51–54.

Gregorovius, Ferdinand. *Lucrezia Borgia: According to Original Documents and Correspondence of Her Day*. Translated by John Leslie Garner. New York: Benjamin Blom, 1968.

Hibbert, Christopher. *The House of Medici: Its Rise and Fall*. New York: William Morrow, 1974.

Huizinga, John. *The Autumn of the Middle Ages*. Translated by Rodney J. Payton and Ulrich Mammitzsch. Chicago: University of Chicago Press, 1996.

Kelly, John. *The Great Mortality: An Intimate History of the Black Death and the Most Devastating Plague of All Time*. New York: HarperCollins, 2005.

Maestro Martino. *The Art of Cooking: The First Modern Cookery Book*. Translated by Jeremy Parzen. Berkeley: University of California Press, 2005.

McIver, Katherine A. *Cooking and Eating in Renaissance Italy*. Lanham, Maryland: Rowman & Littlefield, 2015.

Monfassani, John. "The Rise and Fall of Renaissance Italy." *Aevum* (September–December 2015): 465–481.

Origo, Iris. *The Merchant of Prato*. New York: The New York Review of Books, 2018.

Scappi, Bartolomeo. *Opera dell'arte del Cucinare*. Translated by Terence Scully. Toronto: University of Toronto Press, 2008.

Scully, Terence. *The Neapolitan Recipe Collection*. Ann Arbor: University of Michigan Press, 2000.

Starn, Randolph. "Renaissance Redux." *The American Historical Review*, vol. 103, no. 1 (February 1998): 122–124.

Strathern, Paul. *The Artist, the Philosopher and the Warrior: Da Vinci, Machiavelli and Borgia and the World They Shaped*. New York: Bantam Books, 2009.

Tollebeek, Jo. "'Renaissance' and 'fossilization': Michelet, Burckhardt, and Huizinga." *Renaissance Studies*, vol. 15, no. 3 (September 2001): 354–366.

Trivellatom, Francesca. "Renaissance Italy and the Muslim Mediterranean in Recent Historical Work." *The Journal of Modern History*, vol. 82, no. 1 (March 2010): 127–155.

Willard, Charity Cannon, ed. *The Writings of Christine de Pizan*. New York: Persea Books, 1982.

CHAPTER FIVE: TUDOR FEAST

Breverton, Terry. *The Tudor Kitchen: What the Tudors Ate & Drank*. Stroud: Amberley Publishing, 2015.

Dawson, Thomas. *The Good Huswifes Handmaide for the Kitchin*. London: Richard Jones, 1594.

Dawson, Thomas. *The Good Huswifes Jewell*. London: Edward White, 1595.

Gentyll Manly Cokere. Translated by James L. Matterer, 2009. godecookery.com/pepys/pepys.htm

The Harleian Collection, *Harleian MS.279.xxviij*.

Licence, Amy. *Living Like a Tudor: Woodsmoke & Sage: A Sensory Journey through Tudor England*. New York: Pegasus Books, 2021.

Pegge, Samuel. *The Forme of Cury*. Translated by Glyn Hughes. Winster: Foods of England, 2016.

Picard, Liza. *Elizabeth's London: Everyday Life in Elizabethan London*. New York: St. Martin's Press, 2003.

Porter, Stephen. *Shakespeare's London: Everyday Life in London 1580–1616*. Stroud, England: Amberley Publishing, 2011.

Sim, Alison. *Food & Feast in Tudor England*. Stroud, England: Sutton Publishing, 1997.

Sim, Alison. *Pleasures & Pastimes in Tudor England*. Cheltenham, England: The History Press, 1999.

CHAPTER SIX: AL-ANDALUS

Candida, Martinelli, ed. *The Anonymous Andalusian Cookbook*. Translated by Charles Perry. Italophiles.com, 2012.

Catlos, Brian A. *Kingdoms of Faith: A New History of Islamic Spain*. New York: Basic Books, 2018.

Constable, Olivia Remie, ed. *Medieval Iberia: Readings from Christian, Muslim, and Jewish Sources*. Philadelphia: University of Pennsylvania Press, 2012.

Harvey, L. P. *Islamic Spain 1250–1500*. Chicago: University of Chicago Press, 1992.

Lewis, David Levering, *God's Crucible: Islam and the Making of Europe 570–1215*. New York: Liveright Publishing, 2018.

Menocal, María Rosa. *The Ornament of the World: How Muslims, Jews, and Christians Created a Culture of Tolerance in Medieval Spain*. New York: Little, Brown and Company, 2002.

CHAPTER SEVEN:
THE GREAT CIRCULATION

Cliff, Nigel. *The Last Crusade: The Epic Voyages of Vasco da Gama.* New York: Harper Perennial, 2012.

Crosby, Alfred W. *The Columbian Exchange: Biological and Cultural Consequences of 1492.* Westport, CT: Praeger Publishers, 2003.

Diamond, Jared. *Guns, Germs, Steel: The Fates of Human Societies.* New York: W. W. Norton, 1999.

Díaz, Gisele, and Alan Rodgers. *The Codex Borgia: A Full Color Restoration of the Ancient Mexican Manuscript.* New York: Dover Publications, 1993.

Fray Bernardino de Sahagún. *Florentine Codex: General History of the Things of New Spain.* Translated by Arthur J. O. Anderson & Charles E. Dibble. Sante Fe, New Mexico: The School of American Research, and The University of Utah, 1975.

Gerbi, Antonello. *Nature in the New World: From Christopher Columbus to Gonzalo Fernández De Oviedo.* Translated by Jeremy Moyle. Pittsburgh: University of Pittsburgh Press, 2010.

Graeber, David, and David Wengrow, *The Dawn of Everything: A New History of Humanity.* New York: Farrar, Straus and Giroux, 2021.

Grenville Family Recipe Collection 1640–1750, Folger manuscript V.a.430.

Hobhouse, Henry. *Seeds of Change: Six Plants that Transformed Humanity.* New York: Harper & Row, 1986.

Latini, Antonio. *The Modern Steward or the Art of Preparing Banquets Well.* Translated by Tommaso Astarita. York: Arc Humanities Press, 2019.

MacQuarrie, Kim. *The Last Days of the Incas.* New York: Simon & Schuster, 2007.

Mann, Charles C. *1491: New Revelations of the Americas Before Columbus.* New York: Vintage Books, 2011.

Mann, Charles C. *1493: Uncovering the New World Columbus Created.* New York: Vintage Books, 2011.

McNeill, William H. *Plagues and Peoples.* New York: Anchor Books, 1998.

O'Brian, Patrick. *A Book of Voyages.* London: HarperCollins, 2014.

Parker, Charles H. *Global Interactions in the Early Modern Age, 1400–1800.* New York: Cambridge University Press, 2010.

Restall, Matthew. *When Montezuma Met Cortes: The True Story of the Meeting that Changed History.* New York: HarperCollins, 2018.

Stubbe, Henry. *The Indian Nectar.* London: Andrew Crook, 1662.

Subrahmanyam, Sanjay. *The Career and Legend of Vasco da Gama.* Cambridge: Cambridge University Press, 1997.

Townsend, Camilla. *Fifth Sun: A New History of the Aztecs.* New York: Oxford University Press, 2019.

CHAPTER EIGHT: ETHIOPIA

French, Howard W. *Born in Blackness: Africa, Africans, and the Making of the Modern World, 1471 to the Second World War.* New York: Liveright Publishing Company, 2021.

Gnisci, Jacopo, ed. *Treasures of Ethiopia and Eritrea in the Bodleian Library, Oxford.* Oxford: University of Oxford Press, 2019.

Hassen, Mohammed. *The Oromo & The Christian Kingdom of Ethiopia 1300–1700.* Woodbridge, England: Boydell & Brewer, 2017.

The Kebra Nagast: King Solomon, The Queen of Sheba & Her Only Son Menyelek—Ethiopian Legends and Bible Folklore. Translated by E. A. Wallis Budge. Pantianos Classics, 1932.

Marcus, Harold G. *A History of Ethiopia.* Berkeley: University of California Press, 2002.

McCann, James C. *Stirring the Pot: A History of African Cuisine.* Columbus: Ohio University Press, 2009.

Nersessian, V. and Richard Parkhurst, *Journal of Ethiopian Studies,* vol. 15 (August 1982): 79–104.

Pankhurst, Richard. *The Ethiopians: A History.* Malden: Blackwell Publishing, 2001.

Prutky's Travels to Ethiopia and Other Countries. Translated and edited by J. H. Arrowsmith-Brown. London: Hakluyt Society, 1991.

Salvadore, Matteo. *The African Prester John and the Birth of Ethiopian-European Relations, 1402–1555.* New York: Routledge, 2018.

Tamrat, Taddesse. *Church and State in Ethiopia 1270–1527.* Los Angeles: Tsehai Publishers, 2009.

Zewde, Bahru. *A History of Modern Ethiopia 1855–1991.* Athens: Ohio University Press, 2001.

CHAPTER NINE: VERSAILLES

Drazin, Charles. *The Man Who Outshone the Sun King: A Life of Gleaming Opulence & Wretched Reversal in the Reign of Louis XIV.* Boston: Da Capo Press, 2008.

La Varenne, Francois Pierre. *La Varenne's Cookery: The French Cook; The French Pastry Chef; The French Confectioner.* Translated by Terence Scully. London: Prospect Books, 2005.

Mansel, Philip. *King of the World: The Life of Louis XIV.* Chicago: University of Chicago Press, 2019.

Schama, Simon. *Citizens: A Chronicle of the French Revolution*. New York: Vintage Books, 1989.

Spawforth, Tony. *Versailles: A Biography of a Palace*. New York: St. Martin's Press, 2008.

Van Goeth, Aurora, and Jules Harper. *Louis XIV: The Real Sun King*. Barnsley, England: Pen and Sword Publishing, 2018.

Wilkinson, Josephine. *Louis XIV: The Power & the Glory*. New York: Pegasus Books, 2020.

CHAPTER TEN: NEW YORK CITY

"Account of the Ball Given in Honor of Charles Dickens in New York City." *New York Aurora–Extra*, February 14, 1842.

Andrieu, Pierre. *Fine Bouche: A History of the Restaurant in France*. London: Cassel, 1956.

Batteryberry, Michael, and Ariane Batteryberry. *On the Town in New York: The Landmark History of Eating, Drinking, and Entertainment from the American Revolution to the Food Revolution*. New York: Routledge, 1999.

Blot, Pierre. *Handbook of Practical Cookery*. New York: D. Appleton and Company, 1884.

Bourdain, Anthony, *Kitchen Confidential*. New York: HarperCollins, 2000.

Brillat-Savarin, Jean-Anthelme. *The Physiology of Taste*. Translated by Anne Drayton. London: Penguin Books, 1994.

Burford, Robert. *Description of a View of the City of New York*. London: T. Brettel, 1834.

Burgess, W. F. *New York in Slices*. New York: 1849.

Burrows, Edwin G., and Mike Wallace. *Gotham: A History of New York City to 1898*. New York: Oxford University Press, 1999.

Deutsch, Jonathan, and Hauck-Lawson, Annie, eds. *Gastropolish: Food & New York City*. New York: Columbia University Press, 2009.

Diamond, Becky. *The Thousand Dollar Dinner: America's First Great Cookery Challenge*. Yardley, Pennsylvania: Westholme, 2015.

Dickens, Charles. *American Notes*. London: Penguin Books, 2000.

Goodwin, A. T. *The Picture of New York*. New York: 1828.

Elias, Megan J. *Food on the Page: Cookbooks and American Culture*. Philadelphia: University of Pennsylvania Press, 2017.

Evans, Meryle R. "Knickerbocker Hotels and Restaurants, 1800–1850." *New York Historical Society Quarterly*, 36 (October 1952): 377–409.

Freedman, Paul. *Ten Restaurants That Changed America*. New York: W. W. Norton & Company, 2016.

Glasse, Hannah. *The Art of Cookery Made Plain and Easy*. London: L. Wangford, 1775.

Greene, Asa. *The Perils of Pearl Street: Including a Taste of the Dangers of Wall Street*. New York: Betts & Anstice, and Peter Hill, 1834.

Grimes, William. *Appetite City: A Culinary History of New York*. New York: North Point Press, 2009.

Gunn, Thomas Butler. *The Physiology of New York Boarding-Houses*. New York: Mason Brothers, 1857.

Hewitt, John H. "Mr. Downing and His Oyster House: The Life and Good Works of an African American Entrepreneur." *New York History*, vol. 74, no. 3 (July 1993): 229–252.

Hone, Philip. *The Diary of Philip Hone: 1828–1851*. Edited by Bayard Tuckerman. New York: Dodd, Mead & Company, 1910.

Hooker, Richard J. *A History of Food and Drink in America*. New York: The Bobbs-Merrill Company, Inc, 1981.

Irving, Washington. *Knickerbocker's History of New York*. 1890.

Kadinsky, Sergey. *Hidden Waters of New York City: A History and Guide to 101 Forgotten Lakes, Ponds, Creeks, and Streams in the Five Boroughs*. New York: The Countryman Press, 2016.

Kaufman, Cathy. "Structuring the Meal: The Revolution of *Service à la Russe*." *Academia*, 2001.

Kurlansky, Mark. *The Big Oyster: History on the Half Shell*. New York: Random House, 2006.

Lobel, Cindy. *Urban Appetites: Food & Culture in Nineteenth-Century New York*. Chicago: University of Chicago Press, 2014.

Lobel, Cindy. "'Out to Eat': The Emergence and Evolution of the Restaurant in Nineteenth-Century New York City." *Winterthur Portfolio*, 44, nos. 2/3 (Summer–Autumn 2010): 193–220.

Prentice, Archibald. *A Tour in The United States*. London: Charles Gilpin, 1848.

Ranhofer, Charles. *The Epicurean*. New York: Charles Ranhofer, 1894.

Rundell, Maria. *A New System of Domestic Cookery*. London: John Murray, 1806.

Salter, Gail. "New York City Restaurants: Vernaculars of Global Dining." *Journal of Architectural Education*, vol. 56, no. 3 (February 2003): 27–39.

Shaplan, Robert. "Delmonico: The Rich New Gravy Faith." *The New Yorker*, November 10, 1956.

Smith, Andrew F. *New York City: A Food History*. Lanham, Maryland: Rowman & Littlefield, 2014.

Smith, Andrew F., ed. *Savoring Gotham: A Food Lover's Companion to New York City*. Oxford University Press, 2015.

Spann, Edward K. *The New Metropolis: New York City, 1840–1857*. New York: Columbia University Press, 1981.

Sprang, Jessica. *The Invention of the Restaurant: Paris and Modern Gastronomic Culture*. Cambridge, Massachusetts: Harvard University Press, 2001.

Thomas, Jerry. *The Bar-Tender's Guide; or How to Mix All Kinds of Plain and Fancy Drinks*. New York: Dick & Fitzgerald, 1876.

Thomas, Lately. *Delmonico's: A Century of Splendor*. Boston: Houghton Mifflin Company, 1967.

Wall, Diana Dizerega. "Examining Gender, Class, and Ethnicity in 19th-Century New York City." *Historical Archeology*, vol. 33, no. 1, Confronting Class (1999): 102–117.

Ward, Samuel. *History of Delmonico's*. New York Public Library, Manuscripts, *Samuel Ward Papers*, Box 5.

Whitman, Walt. "Life in a New York Market," in *Walt Whitman: The Journalism*. Edited by Herbert Bergman (New York: P. Lang, 1998), p. 57. Originally printed in the *Aurora,* March 16, 1842. whitmanarchive.org/published/periodical/editing/aurora.html.

Wilson, James Grant, ed. *The Memorial History of the City of New York: From Its First Settlement to the Year 1892, Volume III*. New York: New York History Company, 1893.

Edible History was launched in 2014 with the goal of bringing people into the
conversation of history through a universally accessible medium: food.
For more information, please visit: ediblehistorynyc.com

First published in the United States of America in 2023 by
Rizzoli International Publications, Inc.
300 Park Avenue South New York, NY 10010
www.rizzoliusa.com

Publisher: Charles Miers   Proofreader: Tricia Levi
Associate Publisher: James Muschett   Managing Editor: Lynn Scrabis
Editors: Natalie Danford and Elizabeth Smith   Editorial Review: Sarah Scheffel
Design: Alison Lew Bloomer   Food Styling: Victoria Granof
Production Manager: Colin Hough Trapp   Maps and Illustrations: David Lindroth

Reproduced with permission of the translator, Michael Cooperson, translation of "Ma'mum"
in *Al-Ma'mun: The Revival of Islam* (London: Oneworld Academic, 2005), 88–89.

Printed in China

2023 2024 2025 2026 / 10 9 8 7 6 5 4 3 2 1

ISBN: 978-0-8478-7345-6
Library of Congress Control Number: 2023931818

Visit us online:
Facebook.com/RizzoliNewYork
Twitter: @Rizzoli_Books
Instagram.com/RizzoliBooks
Pinterest.com/RizzoliBooks
Youtube.com/user/RizzoliNY
Issuu.com/Rizzoli